Cheryl,

It really true you bought this.

talked about, my grandfather spent many hours on the phone with the author of this book contributing his story of Choiseul before his passing. His name was

Benjamin Franklin Caperton III
aka "Cape"

He was a true American hero as well as my personal hero. I feel lucky to say he was my "Papa".

Love,
Charlya

MW01030924

MISSION
RAISE HELL

MISSION RAISE HELL

The U.S. Marines on Choiseul

October–November 1943

JAMES F. CHRIST

Naval Institute Press
Annapolis, Maryland

Naval Institute Press
291 Wood Road
Annapolis, MD 21402

Library of Congress Cataloging-in-Publication Data

Christ, James F.
Mission Raise Hell : the U.S. Marines on Choiseul, October-November 1943 / James F. Christ.
p. cm.
Includes bibliographical references.
ISBN 1-59114-113-3 (alk. paper)
1. World War, 1939-1945—Campaigns—Solomon Islands—Choiseul. 2. World War,
1939–1945—Campaigns—Solomon Islands—Choiseul—Personal narratives, American. 3.
United States. Marine Corps. Parachute Battalion, 2nd. I. Title.
D767.98.C47 2006
940.54'265931—dc22
2005037419

All drawings by Howard "Barney" Baxter are copyrighted by the artist and used
with his permission.

Printed in the United States of America on acid-free paper ∞

12 11 10 09 08 07 06   9 8 7 6 5 4 3 2
First printing

CONTENTS

PREFACE

This is a narrative history of the Second Marine Parachute Battalion's diversionary raid on the island of Choiseul as remembered by seventy-one U.S. Marine paratroopers, each of whom was present in that action in 1943, from October 28 to November 4.

To write this story, I collected every piece of written information that I could locate, and I contacted every living member of the battalion—each was listed by the Association of Survivors—to make this recollection as accurate as possible. I have used the official *War Diary* written by Pfc. Eugene Gesch as a template. Gesch typed this when he was on Choiseul more than sixty years ago, and I included other recollections to add flesh to the skeleton. Although my goal was complete historical accuracy, men present at several of the same actions or incidents shared completely different memories from one another. I did my best to faithfully represent the events that occurred that week in 1943.

One interview I found particularly fascinating was that of the commanding officer of the Second Marine Parachute Battalion, Lt. Gen. Victor H. Krulak. I have never heard so many men speak of another man with such high regard. Men that I have grown to admire and respect like Robert Brutinel, Norman Dibbens, Bruce "Red" McClure, and others describe General Krulak as "fine," "tough," "brave," "smart," "fair," and "good," among many other adjectives. That is one reason why I chose to start my chapters with their quotations.

The one question everyone asks me is, "Why did you write this book?" I first got the idea to write about this forgotten part of history after reading *Black Hawk Down*, *Band of Brothers*, and *A Bridge Too Far*, among others. These are narrative histories of U.S. military actions written like novels. I decided to echo that style for this story. This book began accidentally. I was writing about the experiences on Iwo Jima of these same Marines. Because Choiseul was only a seven-day operation, the men were able to remember it more clearly than their time on Iwo Jima. Everyone remembered the day they arrived, their combat actions (which were easy to determine because each company fought independently), and the day they left. Once I obtained the official *War Diary*, it all fell into place.

I felt privileged to be so trusted by the seventy-one men who opened up and told me about their very personal and private memories. Many of them had never spoken openly about their wartime experiences before they talked to me on tape. A few of the men agreed to talk only after their wives and families prodded them into it with the rebuke that they were the sole survivors with whom I had not yet spoken. Several times I received phone calls from a wife who turned from the receiver and ordered, "Come here," or "Talk to him," and soon afterward a Marine would come on the line.

I fear some of the Marines will be disappointed because the story they read will be different from their memories. This was because of the many conflicting recollections of the same incident or firefight. I even ran into differences in opinion concerning the weather. Half the men said it never rained once while they were on Choiseul. The other half all talked about the miserable, incessant downpour. Some said they never saw any female natives on Choiseul, while the rest claim they did. I tried to get my manuscript to all seventy-one men for their corrections, but that proved to be impossible; most of the men were adamant that what they had told me was the way it had happened and that the other guys were remembering it incorrectly. "You gotta stop talking to so-and-so," or "Uh-uh. I'm telling you, it didn't happen like that." The funny thing is, I am convinced each man is telling me the truth as he remembers it.

It was also difficult to narrow down the time of day of events that happened so long ago. For example, Pfc. Eugene Gesch said the incident where he heard Maj. Tolson Smoak say, "My ass is pointing up into the mountains and we don't want to go that way," happened in the evening. But the only time that the *War Diary* had Major Smoak going on a patrol was during the morning and early afternoon of October 29. Also according to the *War Diary*, that was the only patrol where both Smoak and Sgt. Paul Mullins (the man Gesch remembers him talking to) were on the same patrol.

Pfc. Bruce "Red" McClure said his entire platoon scouted down to Sangigai on October 29, yet the *War Diary* said it was Colonel Krulak's seventeen-man patrol. When asked, Colonel, now General, Krulak said it was his nineteen-man patrol. Also, Red did not remember the unit separating at any time. Pfc. Orrin Hall remembers going with Colonel Krulak's patrol, but he was in Red's squad. Red went to Sangigai (the author can only assume with Sergeant Mullins's small patrol) and Hall went with the colonel and the small firefight along the coast. Cpl. Benjamin F. "Cape" Caperton III was Red and Hall's assistant squad leader and he said the rest of the squad did not go on that patrol, nor to Sangigai. He said Red and Hall had to have been selected independently.

There were so many discrepancies that I went in frustration to ask Robert Brutinel for his opinion on how to handle them. He was not home when I called, so I vented to Mrs. Brutinel. She said she was not at all surprised at the inconsistent memories and likened them to a car accident where multiple witnesses see the same thing entirely differently. That I understood.

In this book I wrote down men's memories and thoughts, but I could not possibly have known exactly what a man was thinking or the time of day he was thinking it. These recollections were written because I feel they add to the story and are important in relating the personality of the battalion in the months prior to the operation. However, *every* time and date written in this book is taken from the official *War Diary* that was written on Choiseul during the operation.

Like a detective, I tried to put pieces of the puzzle together. Pfc. Rudolph Engstrom said he went to mass at the battalion hideout while on Choiseul, but he did not remember what day or even what time—only that it was during daylight. I wrote that it happened on October 31, and I will use this as an example of how I organized noteworthy events that were not listed in the *War Diary*.

The battalion chaplain was with E Company from dawn to dusk on October 30 while they attacked Sangigai, away from the mountain hideout. Therefore, the mass service could not have been on October 30. He was with G Company in the Warrior River area from the dawn of November 1 to dusk on November 2, so it could not have been either of those days. It seems unlikely that they would have had the time on the day they arrived. There was too much work to be done carrying supplies and equipment, chopping firing lanes, setting defenses, and conducting combat patrols. The same goes for the last day, November 3, because they had to carry everything back down and set up their defenses at Voza. To me, that leaves October 31 as the most probable day that a mass service would have been held. At that time, the battalion had dead and critically wounded men that would need the power of prayer. This is the reasoning I used for similar events throughout the book.

It was difficult to write about the many separated G Company patrols that were scattered around on November 1 and 2, and to write about who was on which landing craft personnel ramp (LCPR) when they were saved by Lt. John F. Kennedy's *PT 59*. I found Pfc. George P. Adams's memory to be amazing, and he said that his patrol went out on November 1, not

November 2. Yet the *War Diary* said that Sgt. Rahland Wilson's five-man patrol (with Pfc. Roy J. Gallagher and Private Adams) was sent back on November 2. PM1 John Holland and Pfc. Howard "Barney" Baxter remembered men splitting from the party on November 2, although they didn't remember who was in the group that split. Also, Adams said he helped haul the wounded Cpl. Edward "Jimmy" Schnell on board *PT 59*, but said he was not on Lt. Rae Duncan's boat. Cpl. Mike Vinich *was* on Duncan's boat and he did not remember picking up Adams and the rest of Sergeant Wilson's men. With conflicting accounts such as these, it is clear how difficult it was to try to sort through the memories and come out with the truth.

I found several other troubling differences in memories. For example, in Robert Donovan's *PT 109*, he interviewed Lt. John S. Stevens, a doctor attached to Hq Company. Although all the men remember Stevens fondly, not one of them remembers him being there. Holland insists that he was not. PM3 Paul Salfrank says he only saw Holland treating Jimmy. Pfc. William O'Gieglo says a corpsman treated Schnell. It is very confusing.

In *John F. Kennedy, War Hero*, Richard Tregaskis has Kennedy's PT finding three LCPRs, not two. He says that two of the LCPRs were sinking, but Kennedy only rescued eight men. Every G Company Marine interviewed for this book said there were only two boats and that all the Marines from both boats were packed on the 59.

Despite such obstacles, I would like the Marines to know that I have done my very best to get the story right.

ACKNOWLEDGMENTS

A special thanks to:

Robert Brutinel, whose contact with my father led, eventually, to my researching and writing this book. He deserves additional thanks for lending me his copy of *History of the 5th Marine Division* and books he used at the parachute school.

Norman Dibbens, for giving me a copy of his personal notes from 1943. They were immeasurably helpful with names, dates, casualties, and the organization inside F Company.

Charles Allman, for sending me the official Second Marine Parachute Battalion *War Diary*, which was typed by Eugene Gesch in a foxhole on Choiseul.

Howard "Barney" Baxter, for allowing me to illustrate this book with his drawings from 1943.

Lt. Gen. Victor H. Krulak, for inspiring the title of this book. I had agonized over an appropriate title, but nothing describes the actual operation like General Krulak's "Mission: To Raise Hell," which I altered slightly to *Mission Raise Hell*.

James Ward, for sending me issues of the Association of Survivors magazine, *The Opening Shock*, and other literature about the Second Marine Parachute Battalion.

Robert Adams, for his copy of the Association of Survivors *Master Roster of Marine Paratroopers* and Richard Keresey's *Gunga-Dick and the Marine Paratroopers*.

Robert Brutinel, Norman Dibbens, Bruce "Red" McClure, Ned Russell, J. N. Clark, Billy Joe Cagle, Victor Kurlak, and James Ward, who invited me into their homes for hours of interviews. In some cases, these men even picked me up at the airport, fed me, and offered me a place to sleep for the night when the interviews ran late.

William O'Gieglo, James Ward, J. N. Clark, Robert Brutinel, Robert Adams, Bruce "Red" McClure, John Holland, Victor Krulak, and Norman Dibbens for providing photographs from 1943 when they were young paratroopers.

Ned Russell, Robert Brutinel, Benjamin F. "Cape" Caperton III, John Holland, Bruce "Red" McClure, Norman Dibbens, J. N. Clark, Paul Salfrank, Robert Adams, George Adams, Eugene Gesch, Howard "Barney"

Baxter, Orrin Hall, Richard Reneau, Victor Krulak, and the other men who allowed me to pester them with phone calls when I had questions.

The seventy-one U.S. Marine paratroopers who took the time to speak to me and let me record their fascinating experiences.

My brother John Joseph Christ and my friend Jenny Fillipello, for being honest about my first rough drafts—which forced me to write better. I would also like to thank Sue Stein for her help.

My brother Joseph Christ, my sister Mary Ellen Anderson, my mother Peggy Ann Christ, and my friends Tore Anton, Andrew Robles, Ann Foster and Katharine Taylor.

Dave Severance and his wife, Barbara, for their kindness. Dave helped me obtain a map and advised me on Marine terminology.

To my good friends Jay Templeton, Marty Boetel, and Michael Figueroa, thanks for always being there for me.

My father, John Christ, for pushing me to do this and for editing my writing.

A grateful thank you to Athena Garrett, who endured three years of interviews, travel, phone calls, and hours of my typing on a computer. Without your patient support, this book would never have been written. Thank you for being a wonderful mother to our two boys, Nolan and Trace.

And finally, I would like to honor all of the U.S. citizens who served in the U.S. Marine Paratroops in World War II, with special recognition of these fourteen Marine paratroopers who gave their lives on the island of Choiseul in 1943:

> Pfc. Kenneth Andrews (missing in action)
> Pfc. Frank Augustine
> Pfc. Kemper Biggs
> Pfc. Frank Finnie (missing in action)
> Pfc. Robert Gallaher
> Pfc. Leo Gruidl
> Pfc. Gerald Harbert
> Lt. Samuel Johnston
> Pfc. Chris Kosma
> Sgt. Frank Muller
> Pfc. Milton O'Neal
> Pfc. William J. Provost
> Cpl. Edward "Jimmy" Schnell
> Pfc. John Slivkoff

It is not too late for a grateful nation to say "Thank you."

INTRODUCTION

This book is a story about the fighting early in World War II when the forces of the United States in the Pacific were primarily defensive, trying to halt Japanese expansion and to engage in limited offensive actions. It was before the Allies enjoyed complete air superiority; before the industrial might of the United States produced the weapons and machines that enabled American forces to overwhelm the Japanese forces and invade their home island defenses; before strategic bombing crippled Japanese industry and enormous carrier task forces descended on their islands with tens of thousands of amphibious assault troops. It was a time when Americans were still outnumbered on the battlefield, when the Marines and Japanese fought on equal footing in the jungles of the South Pacific with rifles, grenades, and knives.

How did the Second Marine Parachute Battalion come to be on the island of Choiseul for seven days in 1943? When the Japanese sphere of influence was at its height in 1942, they had sweeping successes that over-ran Allied forces throughout the western Pacific, and they were poised to strike Australia and New Zealand. Having taken the British Solomon Islands, they were building an airfield on Guadalcanal, one of the south-ernmost islands in the Solomon chain. From that airfield, they would be able to use their bombers to strike the sea-lane that was the lifeline between the United States and Australia. They would also be able to provide land-based fighter support to their invasion forces.

To counter this threat, in August 1942, the United States took its first offensive action of the war. The First Marine Division made a surprise land-ing on Guadalcanal and overran the airfield while the First Marine Raider Battalion took neighboring Tulagi and the First Marine Parachute Battalion took Gavutu-Tanambogo. The battle for the Solomons had begun, and it would be a taxing, bloody affair for both sides. One year later, with Guadalcanal firmly in American control, the Allies were battling for the other islands in the chain. One of those islands was Vella LaVella where the Second Marine Parachute Battalion of the First Marine Parachute Regiment had landed on October 1, 1943. The parachutists were chasing down the last of the Japanese soldiers scattered in its jungles.

The strategic planners set their sights on the next island in the Solomons—Choiseul—but they did not need to take it. It had no airfield, and to wrest it from the five to six thousand Japanese soldiers stationed there at any given time would be just another jungle bloodletting. Besides, Choiseul was exactly where the enemy expected the attack to come.

Unbeknownst to the Japanese, the Allies had developed a new strategy they were preparing to put to the test. They would begin an island-hopping campaign and simply bypass Choiseul altogether, invading Bougainville instead. They had practiced this strategy only once before when they bypassed the island of Kolombangara. If the Japanese knew Bougainville was where the next attack would come, they would send troops garrisoned on Choiseul up The Slot to reinforce Bougainville by barge. It was important to make the enemy think Choiseul was where the next attack would come.

That is where the Second Marine Parachute Battalion came in. The strategic planners knew they needed an elite group of men for such a daring and ambitious raid. Gen. Alexander A. Vandegrift knew that the Second Marine Parachute Battalion was a highly motivated, untapped resource. They were trained specifically for fighting behind enemy lines and using guerrilla tactics and amphibious operations. Up to that point, they had been an ignored asset, relegated to mop-up duty on Guadalcanal and Vella LaVella, pursuing the remnants of Japan's defeated battalions. Then, after more than a year, they finally had a real objective. Their commanding officer, Lt. Col. Victor H. Krulak, was summoned to Guadalcanal for a briefing and given their mission; it would be called Operation Blissful.

Krulak's 650-man battalion was to invade Choiseul and raise hell. The battalion was to make the noise of an entire division. A successful diversion would pull enemy troops off Bougainville, drawing them away to bolster Choiseul's defenses. After two weeks of this ruse, with the real invasion firmly established at Bougainville and the Japanese swarming on Krulak's battalion, the enemy would collapse on a paper bag as the Marine parachutists adroitly vanished—withdrawn by sea in the dark of night.

Because of the island's dense tropical jungles, the Marines would be unable to parachute in; they would make an amphibious landing instead. The site of the invasion was Voza, a village friendly to the Australian Coastwatchers and the only Allies on the island. Intelligence reports indicated a break in the huge coral reef that ran the length of the island, enabling them to sneak ashore along a relatively deserted strip of the island between the two largest concentrations of Japanese soldiers at Sangigai and Choiseul Bay.

The time and date for the diversion was set for 0100 on October 28, with an attack on the enemy barge station of Sangigai on October 30, followed by a second attack to the northwest on November 1. This was two days prior to the real invasion at Empress Augusta Bay on Bougainville, also scheduled for November 1. If the diversion were successful, two days would be just enough time for the enemy to transfer troops from Bougainville to reinforce Choiseul.

Help would come from two Australian Coastwatchers already familiar with the island, Sub-Lt. Carden W. Seton and Lt. Nick Waddell. Allied with the Australians was a large contingent of Choiseulian natives who agreed to assist the paratroopers when they disembarked. They would guide and aid the Marines while on the island.

In case of emergencies, aside from promised air support from the land-based aircraft on Vella LaVella, the patrol torpedo (PT) boat base at Lambu Lambu on that island would be the only supporting naval unit the battalion would have to call on.

Krulak was given specific orders—make contact with the enemy, but do not engage in pitched battles. Told only to hit and run, the Second Marine Parachute Battalion was warned not to get bogged down. There were not enough resources, neither troops nor ships, to bail them out. There would be no rescue. First Marine Amphibious Corps (IMAC) could send no reinforcements. Krulak's Marines would be on their own.

Chapter 1

AN INTRODUCTION TO WAR

He had outstanding leadership qualities and exceptional intelligence.

Pfc. Howard "Barney" Baxter, G Company,
of Lt. Col. Victor H. Krulak

"You guys better get your butts off this beach," warned a Seabee in a white hat. "The Nips are gonna hit this place with dive-bombers any minute." Pfc. J. N. Clark of Springfield, Illinois, had just stepped off a Higgins boat onto a gorgeous South Pacific beach. Clark's Marine battalion was landing on an enemy island, expecting Japanese machine-gun fire to riddle their platoon as the men ran up the sand toward the jungle. Clark was greatly surprised, instead, to be met by this middle-aged American working with the U.S. Navy's construction battalion. Clark did not have time to ask questions, though. The ominous roar of approaching aircraft sent him scrambling for cover just as six Japanese dive-bombers came swooping down on the Allied landing forces.

It was October 1, 1943, and U.S. Marine paratroopers of the First Marine Parachute Regiment were landing on the island of Vella LaVella. They came ashore to a most unforgettable welcome, courtesy of the Japanese. The Second Marine Parachute Battalion was part of that regiment and it had almost 650 men pouring on shore by landing craft, vehicle and personnel (LCVP) and landing ship tank (LST). Some of the Marines were already working their way inland, but others were still on the ships.

Pfc. Ned Russell, a G Company paratrooper, was an eighteen-year-old Apache from Clarkdale, Arizona. He was moving with his platoon through the jungle along a well-worn trail when a whistle blew, signaling everyone to take cover. The Marines dove for the deck just as the jungle trail they had been on a second before was chewed up by a torrent of bullets. Two spitting streams of fire from the sky passed with elemental force, ripping up dirt as they went. Branches and leaves fell around them in lazy contrast to the enemy plane just clearing the treetops. The plane was heading for the beach where the landing ships were unloading the rest of the battalion with its huge stocks of supplies and munitions.

Lt. Col. Victor H. Krulak, the commanding officer of the Second Battalion, took cover behind a log at the jungle's edge. A terrified corpsman took

1

the prone position beside him as the roar of airplane engines came closer and closer.

"Sir, aren't you scared?"

"Sure, I'm scared," replied Krulak. "Aren't you?"

Before the corpsman could answer, a bullet went through his head, exiting his upper back. It killed him instantly. The enemy planes roared overhead.

Pfc. Robert Brutinel and Pfc. Billy Joe Cagle were two Easy Company Marines moving off an LST onto the beach. Billy Joe was just stepping onto the sand and Brutinel was working his way down the ramp. They looked up to see a big red rising sun on the bottom of an airplane coming at them incredibly fast. Neither Marine had been in combat before, and neither had seen a Japanese plane, so it took a second for it to register. The New Zealand crewmen on the LST were manning their antiaircraft guns and blasting point-blank at the approaching aircraft, but the enemy plane flew right through their ack-ack fire. A metal cylinder dropped from the belly of the plane and fell lazily toward the disembarking Marines. The paratroopers were powerless to move as the 500-pound bomb dropped, seemingly in slow motion. Their eyes followed the bomb's descent as it passed over them, disappearing down the ship's elevator shaft. Brutinel had one leg on the ramp and one on the beach when the bomb exploded. The concussion was so powerful it threw him into the air. He staggered, trying to keep his balance as he ran up the beach for the safety of the jungle.

Sgt. Oscar Frith, from Abbeville, Louisiana, was in charge of a .30-caliber machine-gun section. He and Pvt. Richard Reneau, also of Easy Company, had already disembarked from the LST and were at the jungle's edge when the plane shot overhead so fast their necks whipped around as their eyes tried to follow it. Two more planes, right behind the first, screamed overhead and the paratroopers saw two U.S. Marine Corsairs right behind the Japanese dive-bomber, blasting away with their machine guns. Tracers shot through the air and seemed to eat up the enemy plane, but it kept on flying. "Flame 'is ass!" roared Frith in his thick Cajun accent.

Frith and Reneau watched the Corsairs chase the enemy dive-bomber away from the LST, but not before it had dropped its bomb and obliterated the landing ship. A huge plume of smoke and flame shot up from the LST, and men along the beach dove for cover or sprinted for the safety of the jungle. The steel ship seemed to blow apart. It was small consolation to the two Marines when the enemy plane, smoking, flaming, and riddled by .50-caliber bullets, crashed into the ocean.

PM1 John Holland of Texas was a twenty-two-year-old U.S. Navy corpsman assigned to G Company. He was standing on the beach and saw the LST blown to pieces. He watched in horror, paralyzed, as the explosion hurled men—and parts of men—fifty feet into the air in all directions. The bodies, pieces of wreckage, and torn steel landed in the surf all around the burning carcass of the ship. Before the smoke even cleared, Holland was running to help. He could see wounded and dead men in the water, bobbing or floating in their life jackets, but because Holland could not swim, he had to let others help those men. Instead, he went over to board the ship, because if there were any survivors they would need immediate medical help.

As Holland neared the LST, black smoke poured out of the wreckage with angry flames stabbing out of the dark clouds. Holland could not see a single living man as he ran up the ramp into the smoking bowels of the ship. The carnage surrounding him at that moment was unlike anything he had ever seen or imagined. Everything was just gone, eradicated by the blast. All that remained was twisted, burning metal.

Suddenly, Holland saw a right shoulder with the arm still attached. It was hanging over the water from a piece of twisted metal about two feet off the side of the deck. Probably in a state of shock himself, Holland inexplicably reached for the shoulder to pull it in but as he leaned out, another explosion rocked the ship and he was thrown overboard. He landed on his head and back in the water, hitting so hard he lost his equilibrium. He could not swim and started to panic, flailing and thrashing to reach the surface. Holland struggled and fought, knowing he was drowning and going to die. How had this happened? A hand grabbed him by the back of his shirt and his head cleared the surface. He soon realized a landing craft personnel ramp (LCPR) was practically on top of him and a coxswain held him firmly, looking down at him.

"I got you," said the man. "You're okay." The coxswain pulled the half-drowned corpsman on board and leaned him against the hull of the landing craft so he could catch his breath.

"What's your name?"

"John," answered the coughing, gasping corpsman. "John Holland."

"Nice to meet you," said the coxswain, "My name is..." Holland could not even hear him. He was exhausted and in shock. He was unable to regain his senses right away, and did not snap out of it until they reached the beach. When he finally came to, he realized someone was talking to him. It was the guy who had saved him from drowning.

"I can't thank you enough," said Holland. "You saved my life."

"Don't worry about it. But if I ever see you again you can thank me properly by buying me a drink."

"Hell, yes," agreed Holland, "a bunch of them. I'm from San Diego. You look me up and I'll take you out for the night of your life."

"You're on," said the coxswain.[1]

Holland stepped onto the beach and hurried over to where Marines were setting the wounded men down along the shore. The first man he came upon was a navy chief boatswain's mate who had lost a leg just below the knee. Holland quickly put a hemostat on the femoral artery to keep the man from bleeding to death and dumped Sulfa liberally on the severed stump. He noticed with relief that Dr. Richard Lawrence, the battalion doctor, and a few corpsmen were already on the scene prioritizing and administering to the steady stream of wounded that rescuers were dragging out of the surf.

"Holland," shouted Dr. Lawrence from the edge of the jungle, "get your stuff and get to the airfield. The Nips hit it hard and the Seabees have casualties. They need corpsmen. Get going."

Since Holland's landing maybe one hour before, all he had known was confusion. An airfield? Like most of the Marine paratroopers, he thought Vella LaVella was an enemy island. What were Seabees doing here before the combat troops? Holland finished treating his wounded patient, grabbed his medical pouch, and ran to a waiting truck. As he ran, he realized that the air attack was not over yet; he could see planes dogfighting overhead as he climbed up the tailgate of the truck. The truck headed inland, speeding along a jungle road. Holland looked out the back—and all he could see was chaos.

Back on the beach, a huge portion of the paratroopers' supplies and munitions had been destroyed on the LST. It was critical to get what remained safely hidden before it, too, was destroyed. The paratroopers rushed to hide their remaining crates of bullets, grenades, and food in the jungle. Even while they worked, though, many were mesmerized by the battle that raged in the skies overhead. High above, eight Army Air Corps P-38s were engaged in a wild, swirling dogfight with ten Japanese Zeroes, while below them Marine Corsairs chased the five remaining enemy dive-bombers that were attacking the invasion fleet and the airfield. The Corsairs blew three dive-bombers out of the air, but to the horror of the Marines watching on the ground, some of the P-38s were sent flaming into the sea before the fighting in the skies above them abruptly ended. The enemy planes suddenly peeled off, disappearing to the northwest with the Corsairs and remaining P-38s in hot pursuit.

With the skies above finally clear of danger, Colonel Krulak began to organize his battalion as his first casualty reports began to come in. Fourteen of his paratroopers had been killed and a number of others had been wounded. Krulak directed his officers and noncommissioned officers (NCOs) to get things moving again before a second wave of bombers hit them. The Marines continued moving their supplies and equipment inland.

"Hey, Billy," called Pfc. Hardy Brown from the jungle edge along the beach. "That Jap dive-bomber tried to give ya' a birthday present." Billy Joe Cagle was Brown's childhood friend from a Texas orphanage Cagle had been placed in when his parents died of typhoid fever in the late 1920s. He and Hardy had known each other for as long as Cagle could remember; they were practically brothers. That day, October 1, was Cagle's nineteenth birthday and that "present" Hardy was referring to was a 500-pound bomb. Cagle knew that if he had waited even thirty seconds before stepping off that LST, he would be dead. (At nineteen, Cagle was actually one of the oldest enlisted Marines in his company. Most of the others were only eighteen years old, with a handful of seventeen-year-olds who had either lied about their age or entered the corps via early-in slips from their parents. Only the officers were "old men" in their twenties.)

For his first guard duty shift, Private Clark rode shotgun on a bulldozer for one of the Seabees working to extend the airfield. Both men were sweating profusely in the tropical heat. Not twenty minutes into his shift, the Seabee turned and said, "It's too hot and there's not enough room for both our big asses. Why don't you go somewhere else?"

Clark found some shade and sat out his shift. When it was over, he headed back to the Second Battalion bivouac. On the way, he passed a long row of fighter planes. Clark saw mechanics working on a Marine Corsair that looked like Swiss cheese. "Look at that plane," said Clark with disapproval to his buddy Pfc. Raymond Hoskins. "That thing's shot full of holes." Clark was thinking how unfair life was. He had wanted to be a Marine aviator but had been turned down because he had dropped out of high school to enlist in the Marines at age seventeen. He looked at this damaged plane and decided the pilot had been lousy. Clark knew he could do at least as good as that guy. The name on the side of the plane read "Boyington."[2]

The Marines settled into life on Vella LaVella. Most of their postings were to guard duty at the various military installations there. A few of those installations were the airfield, the PT boat base, and the Seabee construction units that worked deeper into the jungle extending the airfield and building bigger camps.

Cpl. Mike Vinich of Landers, Wyoming, was assigned guard duty at the PT boat base at Lambu Lambu cove. He stood nonchalantly watching the crews load up fuel and ammunition for their nightly runs, and spied two officers standing together talking. One of them looked like Lt. Byron White, the famous All-American halfback from the University of Colorado. "Excuse me, lieutenant?" said Vinich to the navy officer. "Are you Byron White?"

"Yes," White replied.

"Sir, I knew Irvin Cheney, your blocking back at CU from Landers, Wyoming," said Vinich.

"You knew Irvin?" laughed White.

"Sure," said Vinich. "I lived just nine miles from him. He was my closest neighbor."

Vinich and White began to talk about their mutual friend and Vinich learned that Lieutenant White was the intelligence officer for Squadron 9 at Lambu Lambu cove. After a moment, White introduced Vinich to the lieutenant standing beside him. "Mike, this is Jack Kennedy," said White, adding with a crooked smile, "but you can call him 'the ambassador's son.'" Vinich shook hands with the slender, sandy-blond lieutenant and noted he had a good grip.

"So you're from Wyoming?" asked Kennedy casually in his thick New England drawl.

"Yes, it's beautiful country," answered Vinich.

"I was fortunate enough to travel there once," said Kennedy. "I loved Wyoming's mountains and its clean air."

They talked and Vinich was impressed that this lieutenant seemed to know so much about Wyoming's geography—Yellowstone, the Grand Tetons, and so on. Kennedy showed a great deal of respect and appreciation for the outdoors, too, something Vinich found uncommon in most city folk and flatlanders. That, more than anything, won Vinich over. White invited him back for a barbeque the following afternoon and from then on Vinich returned to the PT base as often as he could.

For the greater part of October on Vella LaVella, the Second Marine Parachute Battalion was subjected to continuous guard duty and found that once again they had missed out on the fighting. The paratroopers had landed expecting to wrest the island from the Japanese. The average private, corporal, or sergeant had no idea of the bigger strategic picture and was surprised to find Americans and New Zealanders already on Vella. It was true that the island still held Japanese—the Allies had recently landed and controlled only a small area of jungle around the airfield and the PT base. The Marine paratroopers were here to protect these footholds and push the enemy off the island, but they found the Japanese already in the advanced stages of withdrawing their troops to neighboring Choiseul and Bougainville. There were only a few stragglers, so the Marine patrols kicked up very few firefights in the jungle. Instead of frequent company- and battalion-sized actions, as the men had anticipated, they got into rare squad- and patrol-sized firefights that usually resulted in the Japanese withdrawing into the thick jungle without returning fire. Most of the eager young paratroopers felt they were missing out on the war.

What the green Marines could not know was that these jungle patrols and small-unit actions would help them immeasurably in the days to come. In less than a month, they would be on another enemy island, but this time the Japanese would have no intention of retreating. They had pulled troops off Vella LaVella specifically to reinforce the other two neighboring islands that they would not retreat from—Choiseul and Bougainville.

After eighteen days of the Marine paratroopers' aggressive combat patrols deeper and deeper into Vella La Vella, Colonel Krulak was summoned to Guadalcanal for a briefing at First Marine Amphibious Corps (IMAC) headquarters on October 19. There he learned that his battalion had been given a very important mission: to invade Choiseul and raise hell. Months before, the strategic planners had formulated a plan for the invasion of Choiseul, the next island in the Solomons chain. Up to that point—with the exception of Kolombangara—the Allies had advanced island by island, but IMAC wanted to bypass Choiseul altogether. It was too heavily defended and lacked the strategic importance of Bougainville. Bougainville was where the next major Allied invasion would come. A diversion on Choiseul would weaken the Bougainville defenses because the enemy was sure to rush troops to bolster the invaded island.

Krulak knew why his battalion had been chosen for the diversion. A few months before, Col. Gerald Thomas came to inspect them while they trained on New Caledonia. There had not been any warning—he just showed up. Thomas said he wanted to see what type of training the battalion was conducting. The paratroopers had been doing a live-fire exercise, one that Krulak had his men doing all the time. Krulak always tried to use live ammunition whenever he could. Colonel Thomas was keenly impressed by the teamwork he saw and the mutual trust and affection among the men. He went back to Guadalcanal and told Gen. Alexander A. Vandegrift that the Second Marine Parachute Battalion was ready to go and that he had better get them going.

The original plans would be used only insofar as the Second Marine Parachute Battalion would land at the original invasion site. Because the jungles of the South Pacific negated the use of airborne assault, the paratroopers would make an amphibious attack. Krulak's battalion would land on October 28, conduct offensive operations for two weeks, and then slip out under cover of darkness after the real Bougainville invasion was secure. The battalion was told not to get bogged down; they would receive no reinforcements. They were promised air support and would have the PT boat base at Lambu Lambu to call on in case of emergencies, but other than that, the paratroopers were on their own. The operation would be code-named Blissful.

As Krulak prepared to return to Vella LaVella, Colonel Thomas gave him one last word of warning. "When you go on this raid, don't expect us to bail you out. We don't have the resources to do it. Do not get involved in a wrestling match. Hit and run! Raise hell! But don't let yourself get drawn into a battle. You're completely on your own."

Krulak returned to Vella LaVella with his mission, and on October 24 he assembled his entire battalion. He knew they were an extraordinary group of men. They were all double volunteers; that is, they had volunteered to be Marines and again to be paratroopers, accepting the hazards that both brought. They had been well trained when Krulak took them over, albeit a little disorganized. General Vandegrift and his operations officer, Colonel Thomas, had cautioned Krulak when he first took command more than six months earlier. "These are lively people and they need to be shaken down." That was certainly true, but Krulak found them eager to respond. They were willing to train hard and to live hard and they were prepared for battle. Krulak addressed his men in front of a large map of the Solomon Islands. Almost 650 Marine paratroopers sat, squatted, or stood before him.

"I have some good news for you," began Krulak loudly. "We've been selected for a special mission. Our battalion is going to make a raid on the island of Choiseul." Cheers erupted. Finally, they were going to see some real action. The colonel motioned for silence and continued. "General Vandegrift chose the Second Battalion because of our extensive training in guerrilla warfare and operations behind enemy lines. In fact, his exact words were, 'Victor, your command is probably the best-trained outfit in the South Pacific that meets all the criteria required for this operation.'"

More cheers from the young warriors. It was about time. The original members of the Second Marine Parachute Battalion had been anticipating action since the day they left San Diego, October 9, 1942, more than a year before. Instead of going to Guadalcanal where the battle was already raging, though, they were sent to New Zealand, where they continued to train. On January 10, 1943, they were sent to New Caledonia, where they stayed for nine months. Still wondering when they would go into combat, the paratroopers figured they had to be the most overtrained battalion in the Pacific. They constantly held tactical problems in the field and continued nonstop amphibious and jungle warfare, as well as parachute training—a half dozen night jumps included. This well-oiled machine lacked only combat experience. That would soon no longer be true. Krulak continued with the briefing.

"Our raid is set for October 28th and is designed to make the Japanese believe that Choiseul is the target for the next Allied invasion. If our diversion on Choiseul is successful, it will draw Japanese troops off Bougainville and change the strategic picture in the Solomons. The Third Marine Division will be making that landing. If we succeed, we will prevent Marine casualties on Bougainville; so, you can see how important this mission is—and how great an honor it is. Our landing will coincide with a New Zealand invasion of the nearby Treasury Islands on October 27th in hopes that this will further confuse the Japanese high command."

As their commanding officer spoke, the men of his battalion hung on every word. Colonel Krulak was a charismatic speaker with a magnetic personality. He had outstanding communication skills, and it was a good thing he did, because at five feet, four inches tall, 130 pounds, and with a boyish face, he was not a very imposing figure. When he first arrived to take command of the battalion it would have been hard to find a Marine that was not skeptical about him. They sized him up immediately and based their opinions on his stature—until the colonel set them straight. He had taken over command in New Caledonia some months previously but had put an indelible mark on his battalion immediately. Within days, his men were calling him "the Brute."

Victor Krulak was born in 1913. He grew up in Coronado, California, and graduated from the U.S. Naval Academy in 1934. He was an athletic man—he rowed and boxed all four years at Annapolis—so the Marine Corps was a natural choice. To the young officer the Marines appeared to be a more attractive, exciting life. They were in places like Haiti and Nicaragua and were typically the first U.S. troops to fight. After graduation from Annapolis, Krulak went immediately to the nine-month Marine officer-training course at Quantico. After that course, he went to the Sixth Marines to command a rifle platoon. After December 7, 1941, Krulak joined the Marine paratroops because he knew it would be a good way to get into the battle. Just like everyone else, Krulak wanted to do his part. He did not crave war. It was just what Marines did.

Corpsman Holland listened to the colonel with great respect. He remembered on New Caledonia when Krulak had just arrived and they made a practice jump followed by a twenty-mile forced march. Krulak had landed on a farmer's fence post, hurting his back.[3] He was black and blue, his bruising immediate. As the closest corpsman, Holland was called over to attend his injured commander. Holland had grown up bronco and bull riding in Texas. He was used to his fair share of pain. Holland knew as he tended him that Krulak was badly hurt, but the gruff cowboy had not been won over yet by the little colonel. He expected Krulak to bow out of the march and board the trucks with the rest of the injured Marines. Instead, Krulak surprised him by leading the battalion on their twenty-mile march. Holland stayed close, expecting the colonel to fall out after the first mile. Although Krulak was obviously in considerable pain, the corpsman was forced to admit he was a tough little guy as one mile turned into five, ten, and finally twenty. Not until after the march was completed did the colonel allow Holland and PM3 Paul Salfrank to reexamine him. Holland had observed him closely during the entire march and concluded that the battalion finally had a commanding officer.

Pfc. James Ward listened to Krulak and he, too, had a great deal of respect for his commander. On the way from New Caledonia they had stopped unexpectedly for fuel at the island of Espíritu Santo in the New Hebrides. Ward's father was in the Seabees and Ward knew his dad was stationed there. Since they had just about twelve hours for the refueling, most of the Marines, including Ward, were ordered to stay on board ship. Even though his experience with officers told him he was going to be refused, he went to Krulak and asked permission to go ashore to see his father. Krulak's response surprised him. The colonel made a call to see if the story was true (the Brute knew only too well how the irresistible lure of liberty could turn his most honest Marine to the dark side), and when he found out it was, he gave Ward permission to go in. Ward would never forget the six hours he was able to spend with his father at Espíritu Santo. He had not seen his father since shortly after Pearl Harbor and would not see him again for another year and a half, after Iwo Jima. Many officers would not have gone to the trouble for their men, but Krulak did.

Private Clark watched Colonel Krulak and thought the Brute was quite a Marine. Krulak had first impressed him on New Caledonia within days of taking over command of the battalion. Clark was walking back to his barracks after a night guard shift and passed the colonel in the early morning. He gave Krulak a sharp salute and was astounded when the colonel said, "Good morning, Clark." Clark had seen Krulak only once before, and that was when the entire battalion was at formation. They had not even spoken, but the colonel knew his name. He must have studied the files of his men with the picture inside. How else could he possibly know?

Clark heard that when Krulak reported to Annapolis for his plebe year at the Naval Academy, he was going to be denied admittance because he was too short—an inch from the required height. The rumor was that Krulak made a buddy hit him on the head with a baseball bat so the swelling would give him the extra inch to pass his physical. Clark doubted the story was true, but it would not surprise him. That was how determined the colonel was. Krulak was definitely a gung ho Marine. As the colonel continued, Clark listened with anticipation to the briefing about what would be his first combat of the war.

"The Coastwatchers tell us that there are roughly five thousand Japanese troops on Choiseul: a regiment of fifteen hundred Imperial Marines midway in the island at the enemy barge station of Sangigai, and another large concentration around Choiseul Bay to the northwest. We will land at an unguarded beach between these two concentrations of enemy troops where there is a break in the huge coral reef that runs the length of the island. Once ashore, we will begin aggressive offensive operations against the enemy. The United States media had been truthful in our news releases and the Japanese spy network has found they can rely on what our media reports. That is why we believe this operation has an excellent chance for success. On October 30, IMAC will announce to the media that twenty thousand Marines have landed on Choiseul. To lend credibility to the news reports, we will attack the enemy barge station at Sangigai on October 30 and the Choiseul Bay area on November 1. Even though we are only a battalion, I feel confident we can pull it off."

Colonel Krulak motioned for someone to stand and said, "I'd like to introduce Sub-Lt. Carden W. Seton of the Royal Australian Navy." A man seated in the front row near Krulak stood up. Not many Marines in the battalion had seen a man as large as Seton. At six feet, four inches tall, 240

pounds, he was enormous. Standing beside the diminutive Krulak probably helped increase the illusion of his size. Seton's beard was brownish red,
and he wore black clothing and a black Australian bush hat.

"Lieutenant Seton will now brief you, "continued Krulak. "He and his
associate Nick Waddell know more about Choiseul than any white men and
have been performing as Coastwatchers there for the past fifteen months."

"G'day," began Seton with a deep, booming voice and a strong Australian
accent. "I'm well acquainted with the island, 'avin' served as superintend-
ent of a coconut plantation theya for the past ten years. Choiseul has been
mainly used as an interim stoppin' place for the 'evvy Japanese barge traffic up 'n' down The Slot. Now that the front 'as caught up to the island,
there are about six thousand Japanese troops, maybe more, defendin' it. Me
patna' Nick Waddell an' I 'ave organized about two 'undred local nytives on
the island to assist us durin' the landing an' in the gatherin' of informytion."
While Seton talked, the men listened intently to the giant and formed their
own opinions of the man.[4]

Pfc. Howard "Barney" Baxter of Santa Monica, California, was a G
Company replacement who had recently joined the battalion. As he
watched Seton, he could not help but think the huge Australian looked like
a trapped animal. Seton's eyes constantly shifted, darting from left to right
and back as he spoke, always scanning the trees around him. Barney noted
that Seton had the most intense eyes he had ever seen. He seemed to take
in everything; nothing escaped him. "I guess if you live by yourself in the
jungle, surrounded by the Japanese, you learn to stay vigilant, or you die,"
thought Barney.

Private Clark listened intently to the big Coastwatcher and sized him
up instantly as a fighter. Seton had a fierce look about him, and Clark wondered if there were many Marines as tough, mentally or physically, as the
giant Australian.

Pfc. Bruce "Red" McClure of Lawrence, Kansas, was a quiet, stoic man
by nature and not many men impressed him. Carden Seton was one of the
few who did. Red could not help but notice how the Australian dwarfed
the Marine officers—Maj. Warner T. Bigger and Maj. Tolson Smoak, both
six feet, two inches tall—beside him. It was not just the man's size that
impressed Red, though. Seton had a presence about him and you could
hear it in his voice. He knew what he was doing and instilled confidence
in those around him. The big Australian was a lot like Colonel Krulak in
this regard.

Although he had heard it before, Colonel Krulak listened and noted Seton was a very able man. The Brute felt confident in the Aussie's ability to do his job. Krulak could not help but notice, however, that the Australian suffered from recurrent bouts of malarial shakes as he spoke, and that he had never seen him not shaking since the day they had met. Seton seemed to be in great discomfort all the time; he was either shaking uncontrollably or burning with fever.

Seton continued to brief the paratroopers. "Most uv the island people are not friendly to either Ameriker or Japan an' are likely to kill both if given the opportunity. Ow'eva, our little band uv two 'undred are friendly ta the United States an' 'ave killed many Japanese." Seton motioned and two natives stood up. They were dark skinned and shorter than most of the Americans, but they were powerfully built.

"This is Peta Kiri," motioned Seton to one of the men, "an' this is Peta Nu, each uv 'oom 'ave saved me life many times so there is no doubt about their loyalty. Nick Waddell an' our nytive Allies will prepare a false beach landing site a couple a miles from Voza—ta confuse the Nips. Afta' we've landed at Voza, they'll drag the beach with palm fronds ta smooth out the footprints an' cover up any evidence uv our landing. Peta Kiri, Peta Nu, an' I will be with you until we land on Choiseul three days from now, so feel free ta ask any questions you like."

Colonel Krulak concluded the briefing by saying, "While we're on Choiseul, I don't want anyone addressing an officer using rank. Enemy snipers will naturally target leadership. If anyone calls me colonel, I'm going to respond, 'Yes, general.'" Krulak sent his men off to further company and platoon briefings with a final word. Motioning toward Peta Kiri and Peta Nu he said, "If either of these two ask you for anything, I suggest you give it to them."

In the days before the diversion, the Marine camp was busy with preparations. Supporting units at both the airfield and the PT boat base at Lambu Lambu were notified by Marine officers carrying sealed documents. The contents were top-secret messages informing the unit commanders of the diversion. The next few days passed in a blur of briefings for the paratroopers preparing for the attack. The Marines pored over maps of the island and learned as much as they could from Peta Kiri, Peta Nu, and Lieutenant Seton. On October 27, the battalion departed from Juno River by landing craft, mechanized (LCM) to rendezvous with four armored personnel destroyers (APDs) and one destroyer for the dangerous journey across The Slot to Choiseul. The Marines were ready and waiting, but the destroyers were not. When they finally showed up, the battalion transferred over to APDs *Ward*, *McKean*, *Crosby*, and *Kilty*, and under escort from the destroyer USS *Conway* and the squadron's nine PT boats, they disappeared into the darkness of The Slot for the island of Choiseul.[5]

Packed inside the APDs, the paratroopers went over last-minute briefings from their platoon leaders. Pfc. Carl Desanto was six-feet tall and weighed 170 pounds. He was an Italian from Essexville, Michigan, with a crooked nose that was the result of a Michigan Golden Gloves tournament. Desanto was a cook for Headquarters (Hq) Company who was basically out of a job because all that the Marines ate on Choiseul were K-rations and D-bars. For this operation Desanto would simply be an extra runner for Colonel Krulak. Although most of the Marines were silent and reflective, a rare few talked aloud with bravado as if the coming combat were a football game. They could not wait to get off the ships to close with the enemy.

Desanto was eager to leave the APD, but not because he was anticipating combat. On the contrary, he wanted off because he was sitting next to a bloodstained dead New Zealand soldier. Earlier that day the Kiwis had assaulted the Treasury Islands with these same ships. This soldier had been killed in action (KIA) and was laid out for return to New Zealand and a proper burial. The fallen soldiers lay in the same crowded troop compartments where the paratroopers sat. Seeing the Kiwi's bullet-riddled body did not make Desanto want to race eagerly into battle.

Private Baxter had just recently crossed the Pacific from California and noticed how strangely silent this troop compartment was by comparison. Barney sat and listened to Sgt. Thomas Siefke, of Toledo, Ohio, who was talking quietly to his buddies. The men looked concerned about going into battle for the first time. Sergeant Siefke was older than everyone else, in his twenties, dark haired, with blue eyes. He was five feet, seven inches tall and weighed 150 pounds. A married man, Siefke had a calming influence on those around him. He seemed educated, too. On Vella, Barney had heard him quoting poetry. Usually men howled with laughter when Siefke spouted off his verses, but not this time. The sergeant spoke without humor to his buddies beside him, reciting some lines Barney did not recognize. "Cowards die many times before their deaths; The valiant never taste of death but once."[6]

Chapter 2

INSERTION: OCTOBER 28

Of all the islands in the Solomons, Choiseul was the darkest.

Pfc. Harold N. "Hal" Block, E Company

APD *Ward*, 5,000 yards off Voza Village

Pfc. Howard "Barney" Baxter, G Company, was waiting to go down the nets to a bobbing Higgins boat. It was not yet midnight, still the twenty-seventh, and the Second Marine Parachute Battalion was poised to make its diversionary assault on Choiseul along a few hundred-yard spit of sand called Voza Beach. Lt. Rae Duncan had thoroughly checked Barney and the others to make sure they did not have anything that would make noise or would shine and that they were ready to go over the side. They removed all their watches and rings to cut down on possible metallic sounds and the lieutenant's last words before they went down the nets were, "Keep it quiet."

Duncan's Third Platoon was going in ahead of the rest of the battalion to establish a beachhead. They assumed that the beach was safe, but Choiseul was an enemy island—they had to expect anything. When Barney asked a veteran about it earlier, Cpl. William R. Zuegel put it simply: "We're going in to draw fire. It's better to sacrifice a platoon to a Japanese ambush than the entire battalion."

"Over the side." The order sent the paratroopers down the nets to the waiting Higgins boat. Barney dropped carefully into the bobbing craft and moved to get out of the way for the next man. The entire platoon was going in on one boat. Barney was a new guy, a replacement who had recently joined the battalion. He was wide eyed, nervous, and green as could be, and was standing next to a tanned, streetwise veteran. Barney was from Santa Monica, California, the veteran from Burgenfield, New Jersey. Although the two were different, they got along extremely well. Barney admired and wanted to emulate the tough Marine; the Easterner could not help but like this clean-cut young kid who never cursed, never drank, wrote faithfully to his mother, and always seemed happy. Baxter had been nicknamed "Barney" by the veteran the day he arrived because he looked like the comic strip character Barney Baxter. The cartoon kid had the same sandy brown hair, blue eyes, and all-American look. The nickname stuck.[1]

Veteran Corporal Zuegel was, in Barney's opinion, one of the finest Marines in the corps. He was also an excellent boxer. At the South Pacific Championships, Barney watched Zuegel destroy the New Zealand champion he was fighting in the first round. Zuegel was also an amazing shot. He had scored higher than anyone else had in the battalion at sniper school on New Caledonia. Zuegel was not in their platoon, but because he was a battalion scout he was going in with them anyway. Lieutenant Duncan had specifically requested him.

Duncan had issued orders on the destroyer and he repeated them once more. "Move quickly up the beach to the edge of the jungle. Spread out and set up a beachhead perimeter to protect the rest of the battalion's landing. Somewhere on this beach is the Australian Coastwatcher Nick Waddell and the native guides. Once we're in position, we'll make contact with them and begin our reconnaissance of the Voza area. Keep it quiet. Fix bayonets."

Duncan told them to keep quiet, but they all knew if there were any Japanese within half a mile, they would hear the boat's engine. Because there was constant enemy barge traffic on Choiseul, they hoped that the enemy lookouts would think the LCPR was a Diahatsu barge. Their boat moved to shore and all eyes scanned the beach, but it was almost too dark to see anything. There was a new moon that night and the wispy clouds made the darkness almost absolute. The boat came to a sliding stop in the sand and everyone scrambled over the sides or out the small front ramp. Barney jumped out and followed his Johnson light machine gun (JLMG) man Pfc. Frank Fagoni. As he ran, Barney looked around in the darkness. They had come ashore near a village of maybe half a dozen huts. To Barney it looked like something out of a Dorothy Lamour jungle movie, with soft white sand under beautiful thatched-roofed huts on stilts.

A seemingly impenetrable wall of darkness beyond the village formed a semicircle ahead of them maybe 150 yards off the beach. That was where the jungle started. With hearts pounding from adrenaline more than from the hundred-yard run, Barney and the others ran for the jungle edge.

It was so dark as they entered the rainforest that when they had taken one step off the beach it was as if they had closed their eyes. Even without moonlight, on the beach they could at least see around them. In the jungle, they could not see one foot in front of their faces.

Lieutenant Duncan positioned his men in a defensive perimeter inside the jungle, sent Zuegel to check the surrounding area, and waited for the Australian Coastwatcher. If the Japanese attacked, he had automatic weapons and was sure his platoon would give a good account of itself. Duncan placed a .30-caliber machine gun on each flank, with three Johnson guns interspersed per squad along his platoon line; then the paratroopers waited for friend or foe.

After fifteen minutes passed, and then thirty, they began to get nervous. There was no sign of the Australian Coastwatcher or the natives. Where were they? The invasion ships were sitting ducks waiting out there in The Slot. The Marines waited tensely and tried to decide what to do. Suddenly, they heard the sound of approaching boat engines.

"Load and lock. Commence firing at my command," whispered Duncan to his machine gunners as he moved along his platoon line. The rest of the battalion was not supposed to come ashore until they were given the signal. Duncan held the flashlight and knew he had not given the signal. Who was in these approaching boats? Duncan decided to chance a signal into the darkness. If the boats were the rest of the battalion, they would signal back. If they were Japanese, he would probably find out in a hail of machine-gun fire. Moving onto the beach Duncan signaled with his flashlight into the night. The countersign flashed out of the blackness after a few tense moments. The rest of the battalion was landing. The colonel must have decided they could not wait all night for a Coastwatcher that might be lost, late, or dead.

The first LCPR reached the shore, and Duncan's platoon saw the enormous figure of Sub-Lt. Carden Seton step off the ramp and onto the beach. The paratroopers watched Duncan move over to Seton, and no sooner had they begun to talk when at least a dozen natives stepped out of the jungle and moved over to them. Seton began to talk to them in their own language, giving them instructions.

LCPR off Voza

Fox Company paratrooper Pfc. Bruce "Red" McClure was standing next to his buddy Pfc. Carl J. Kuehne of Milwaukee, Wisconsin, as their boat neared the beach. Both men were former parachute school instructors at Camp Gillespie until the school closed and they were shipped overseas to join the Second Marine Parachute Battalion. They had arrived only days before, barely making this raid. Red, whose name came from his bright red hair, looked out over the side of his boat and was shocked at how beautiful this South Pacific island was. He was expecting combat and possibly violent death, and the unexpected contrast of peace and serenity really made an impression on him. Even in the darkness, Red could see palm trees blowing gently in the wind and wide untouched white sandy beaches.

Behind the silhouette of the trees was the darkness of the jungle with mysterious, black mountains rising up against the night skyline.

Their Higgins boat ran up onto the beach and the Marines scrambled out the small front ramp or leaped over the sides. Red expected enemy machine-gun fire to open up on them at any moment, but the first thing he saw was not an enemy soldier at all but the Coastwatcher Lieutenant Seton. The Australian had landed in the LCPR just ahead of them to help control the confusion. The big lieutenant was standing casually on the beach waiting for them. Red watched as the Marine officers approached to confer with him. Seton's dark clothing and wide-brimmed Australian bush hat almost made him invisible in the darkness. His voice was deep and authoritative behind the thick accent as he instructed the Marines to follow a local guide off the beach into the jungle. Red, Kuehne, and the others did as they were told and followed the guide. Just as they had done countless times in training problems, the sergeants instructed their squads to hold on to each other's cartridge belts to stay together as they moved into the darkness.

As the battalion landed, so did the equipment and supplies needed to sustain them. The problems involved with conducting an operation of this size were not in getting the men on shore; they were the logistics of the operation that were vital to its success. For this independent mission, where they would get no outside help, the battalion needed enough food to last fourteen days. They needed enough ammunition, mortar rounds, bazooka ammunition, rockets, and grenades to supply 650 men for no fewer than fourteen days of combat. They needed the radios, generators, maps, phones, telephone wire, and field equipment to keep a modern fighting force at peak efficiency. Without the radios, Lt. Col. Victor H. Krulak would not be able to call for air support, for PT boat assistance, or keep contact with his own companies as they conducted raids up and down the coast. Without the generators to supply power, the radios were useless. It was logistics—not just bravery—that would make the diversion a success. That was why every man coming ashore was armed to the teeth and loaded with ammunition, supplies, and equipment.

While the first LCPRs were unloading on the beach, Pfc. Norman Dibbens, a blond eighteen-year-old from Garden City, Kansas, watched the vanguard of the Marines moving toward the jungle. Dibbens expected machine-gun fire to rake across them at any minute. He was surprised to see them move off the beach unhindered just as they had done countless times in training. Dibbens was standing behind the shortest Marine in the corps and knew the Brute was in his Higgins boat. Krulak was living proof of the adage "It's not the size of the dog in the fight but the size of the fight in the dog!" When Dibbens saw the others moving up the beach, he was torn between the relief of escaping violence and battle and the disappointment of still not experiencing the very thing every Marine trains for— combat. At the same time, he was taken aback by the beauty of the panorama before him. "Oh lord!" he gasped, "this is really something!" True, every island in the Solomons was beautiful, but Choiseul surpassed them all. There was something majestic and mysterious about this island. His boat shuddered to a halt and Dibbens and the rest of the First Platoon, F Company, scrambled out. Dibbens watched Colonel Krulak move over to the huge, burly Australian Coastwatcher who towered over the slender American. Dibbens's attention was suddenly broken. "Dibbens," snapped Sgt. Bill Foote, "get over here and help get this generator off the beach."

Dibbens saw three Marines struggling with Colonel Krulak's heavy, cumbersome generator. Luckily, the generator had wheels. Unluckily, Choiseul had only two types of ground—sand and mud. Dibbens hurried over to help drag the heavy generator off the beach.

Assisting the Marine landing were several natives. These men and women lived exactly as their ancestors had lived for ten thousand years. The paratroopers had even been warned that many of the natives were still cannibals and headhunters. Dibbens watched the natives with curiosity. To his amazement, the women were talking loudly and made quite a racket. He thought, "They're acting just like a bunch of gals back home at a department store!" Dibbens wondered, as he helped the others half-carry, half-drag the generator off the beach, why the big Coastwatcher or one of the officers did not go tell them to be quiet. He was convinced the battalion had squandered any element of surprise they might have had. If the Japanese had no prior knowledge of their invasion, they surely knew by that point. All Dibbens had heard since they had landed at Voza was roaring engines, clanging metal, and shouting. Surely someone would notice a destroyer, four APDs, the numerous LCPRs, and a battalion of men—not to mention the noise made by the women. How could the Japanese not know they were here?

Private Clark moved off his landing craft into the warm Pacific bathwater. A blond F Company paratrooper in Cpl. William D. Cole's squad, Clark had just stepped onto the beach when Sergeant Foote snapped at him.

"Clark," he ordered, pointing at three struggling Marines carrying Colonel Krulak's big radio, "help them get that off the beach and up into the hills."

Clark ran over to the struggling Marines and grabbed a side of the cumbersome radio. Watching men vanish into the jungle ahead, Clark cursed his bad luck at having been picked by Foote. They followed a line of paratroopers moving into the jungle and soon four cursing Marines were stumbling blindly along the trail up the mountain. In daylight they would have seen a long connected single file of Marines moving through the jungle behind their guides. By then it was too dark to see the man in front of them. The natives had given them phosphorescent vines that the Marines rubbed on each other's backs to make a visible sheen in the darkness. Each followed the barely perceptible phosphorescent bobbing line holding on to the shoulder of the man ahead.

"What a pain in the ass," muttered Clark as he slipped in the mud and fell to his knees in the dark. Everything was damp and slippery in the Solomons from the incessant rain. It was amazing they did not drop the big radio every time they moved. All four Marines were having trouble in the mud under the awkward burden of the radio and their own personal equipment, weapons, and extra ammo. Clark had grown up on a farm and knew how to work hard, but this was difficult even for him. Each man carried an additional fifty pounds besides his own pack. In addition to the weight, they could feel mosquitoes landing on their faces but were helpless to do anything about them.

They had not moved much farther than a hundred yards off the beach when they came upon Seton. The Australian must have noticed how much trouble they were having because he told four of the natives to assist the Marines. Four short, barefoot natives jogged over. Clark was astounded when they hefted up the radio and moved effortlessly into the darkness.

Pfc. Thomas Preston of Indianapolis, Indiana, was in Clark's squad but he was not much luckier than Clark. He was assigned to carry crates of K-rations off their landing craft, and it reminded him of a Chinese fire drill. It was pitch black and everyone kept bumping into each other carrying supplies up the beach. They were like the Keystone Cops trying to get everything into the jungle so that the following morning Japanese aerial reconnaissance would not be able to locate their insertion point.

Pfc. Robert Adams of Kenedy, Texas, was in squad leader Sgt. John Baker's squad in the First Platoon, F Company. They formed up on the beach and Adams was talking to his buddy Pfc. Bernard Best and their assistant squad leader, Cpl. Frederick Akerson. The landing had seemed like complete chaos to Adams. "What a fucking mess. I hope this ain't an omen of things to come," Adams said out loud.

"Adams," interrupted Baker, "keep it down. You've got a loud mouth. Your voice carries."

Their squad moved off the beach under the guidance of one of the natives. Adams's assistant JLMG man, Pfc. Glenn Barbee, was holding on to his shoulder and somewhere back there in the all-encompassing darkness was the rest of the squad.[2] Adams had no idea what was going on around him. Connected hand to shoulder, the F Company Marines had no choice but to completely trust this unknown man who was leading them through the darkness. All Adams knew was that they were moving uphill.

The first two companies to come ashore were Fox Company and George Company. One of those G Company leathernecks was Pfc. George P. Adams, the company's radioman. His company commander, Capt. William R. Day, told Adams he chose him as his radioman because he liked Adams's southern accent. Adams was from Leeds, Alabama, and a descendent of John Quincy Adams. He carried a TBX radio and an M1941 Johnson rifle. An outdoorsman, Adams was not going to go into possible combat without a rifle and the Johnson was the best he had ever fired. Unlike many of the others, Adams had already had his baptism of fire on Guadalcanal almost one month before.

His squad was on a routine combat patrol in the area of Mount Austen when it had come across a large glade that opened from the jungle. As they crossed the clearing they came upon the body of a lone U.S. Marine, dead from gunshot wounds. Instinctively they dropped, fearful of snipers. After a number of anxious minutes passed with no danger, they began to search the area and were surprised to find the Marine surrounded by dead Japanese. He had killed five of the enemy before his own death in a lonely Alamo. They saw tracks in the all-pervasive mud leading away from the glade. They followed the tracks a number of miles to a hilly area of tall grass. At the base of adjoining hills, the tracks led to an unsuccessfully camouflaged cave.

They were ordered to move on the cave, and had not gone far when they drew fire from the dark opening. They dove for cover and began a hailstorm of fire on the cave face. The fire was so intense that any lookout was either suppressed or dead. While this went on, Adams's sergeant ordered him up to the side of the cave to lob a grenade in. Carefully working his way in, while the others fired on the opening, George pulled the pin on his grenade, waited a moment, and threw it hard into the opening so it would not be easily caught and thrown back. The explosion blew smoke and dirt out of the cave. As he waited for the smoke to clear, another

Marine ran up next to him with six sticks of dynamite tied in a bundle. The man lit the dynamite, lobbed it in to the cave and dove for cover. A tremendous explosion sealed the cave forever, entombing the enemy troops. His rifle across his shoulder, he set up his radio in Captain Day's temporary command post (CP) inside the G Company perimeter and waited for orders.

Another Marine on Choiseul who had seen limited action on the Canal was Pfc. Ned Russell. Within one hour of his arrival on Guadalcanal, the paratroopers were sent on combat patrols with veteran Marines to give them needed experience and to give the exhausted veterans a breather. As his patrol moved deep into the jungle they came upon several dead Japanese. They stank from recent death and Private Russell thought that no smell in the world would ever be worse. He now understood firsthand why the Japanese called Guadalcanal "the island of death." Being a green trooper, Private Russell was placed second in line, just behind the point man, to give him experience. Russell was nervous. Every fighting man in America had heard about Guadalcanal, and he was about to make his first combat patrol there. In a flash, the point man went to ground and brought up his rifle. The Marine fired a number of shots and Russell saw a small band of Japanese leap up and vanish into the jungle. Russell emptied his magazine at them, but he did not hit any of the Japanese. Because the jungle was so dense, all they had seen was a flurry of movement. Then the enemy was gone.

On Choiseul more than a month later, Russell looked over the side of his approaching boat and saw the beach swarming with troops. While he watched from the surf, NCOs on the beach were organizing and directing disembarking Marines to their appropriate squads and platoons. Unlike many of the others, Russell did not come ashore on an LCVP; he had landed in a rubber boat with six other Marines. Russell was in the weapons platoon, and carried a big A-4 .30-caliber machine gun. When they landed, he hoisted his A-4 onto his shoulder and followed Sgt. Anthony J. Skotnicki up the beach toward the jungle. Suddenly, he heard the shouted urgent warning that a Japanese floatplane was overhead and everyone started yelling, "Get off the beach!"[3] Russell and the others in his section raced toward the cover of the jungle. They were safely on shore, but half the battalion was still out on the ships waiting to come in.

APD *Ward*

PM1 John Holland was a G Company navy corpsman on the *Ward* preparing to go ashore. With dark hair and a deep gravelly voice, Holland was a gruff no-nonsense Marine. Civilians might think he lacked a good bedside manner, but Holland was not tending civilians and he knew he would not get any complaints from a Marine. Holland stood next to his buddy Sgt. Frank Muller and waited to go down the nets into a Higgins boat. He was standing near the fantail when an explosion blew fifty yards away in the ocean. He dove for protection, but noticed his buddy had not even flinched. Muller just looked down at him. "John," he said mildly, "the next time you're taking cover, don't get under a depth charge."

Holland looked up and saw at least ten depth charges stacked above him. All the Marines in the vicinity cracked up laughing until Muller ordered everyone quiet, and they went back to peering into the darkness toward Choiseul. Nobody could see much because the night was so black. That ebony shadow ahead in the darkness told them where Choiseul was, and somewhere on that beach an Australian Coastwatcher with roughly two hundred natives was supposed to be waiting to help them get their equipment ashore. Word soon passed down the line for them to hurry because the floatplane had dropped the egg—meaning the invasion had been discovered.

Holland and the other G Company paratroopers were finally ordered over the side, and they scrambled down the nets. When Holland got down near the LCPR he could feel how rough the surf was. The little Higgins boat bobbed like an apple next to the bigger destroyer. The Marines had done this many times and trained going down the nets to avoid injury. Hands on vertical ropes, feet on horizontal ropes, so they did not step on the hands of the man descending below. Men were sometimes killed when they were not paying attention or lacked experience, crushed between the destroyer and the Higgins boat. Holland had just stepped down into the smaller LCPR when it slammed against the destroyer. At exactly that moment there was a barely audible groan of pain from some-one next to him in the darkness. He did not hear any other sound. The boat was full and headed for shore.

Holland's boat hit the beach and he began moving up toward the jun-gle, his .45 in hand. He heard a faint moan just off to his side. Looking over he could barely make out the shape of a man. It was one of the natives, Peta Nu, and he was holding his hand. Holland reached over and touched his shoulder and Peta Nu extended his wounded hand. It was so dark Holland could barely see; he felt more than he saw while examining the wound. The hand was badly mangled, broken in several places, but Peta Nu never flinched as he was examined. At that moment Holland remembered the noise he had heard on the LCPR. Peta Nu must have gotten his hand stuck between the destroyer and the landing craft. Unlike the experienced Marines, the Choiseulian obviously had never been transferred between a destroyer and a Higgins boat and did not know the dangers. Holland marveled at this man's self-control because he had likely broken every bone in his hand. Holland bandaged it using a piece of wood as a makeshift splint. Peta Nu was surely in considerable pain but he never let on. Holland simply set the hand in a position that would best promote healing, and when he finished, Peta Nu walked off into the night.

The last to come ashore were Easy Company and Hq Company. Pfc. Harold N. "Hal" Block of Hermiston, Oregon, was an E Company paratrooper who arrived carrying large bags of rice. The rice was for the natives in payment for the assistance they were supplying to the Marines. Hal returned to his Higgins boat dozens of times, carrying bag after bag of rice onto the beach. Dozens of natives were waiting to pick them up and carry them swiftly into the darkness.

Pfc. Hugh Greely of Minneapolis, Minnesota, was standing in a crowded Higgins boat moving toward the beach. Greely was an E Company Marine praying they would make it to shore quickly, but it was not the Japanese bombers he was worried about. Greely was worried about the amoebic dysentery that had plagued him for the last few days, making his life miserable. He had been told to report to sick bay on Vella LaVella, but he had refused. Unlike on Vella LaVella and Guadalcanal, Greely knew Choiseul was going to be the real thing. He was not going to let his buddies go into battle without him. He knew he would be in constant discomfort and have to fall out from time to time, but he did not see a problem. The four-stacker they went over on had a head, and once on the island he could always just move off into the jungle and drop his dungarees. What he had not thought about was the short ride to the beach on the crowded Higgins boat. No sooner had he climbed down the nets then he had to go. He was trying to hold himself until they got to the beach, but there was no stopping the dysentery. By the time the ramp dropped, Greely had soiled himself. Muttering in anger and frustration, he moved onto the beach and pulled down his trousers to clean himself, using sand as he had been taught to do in boot camp. His squad was moving off into the jungle and he did not want to get lost in the darkness and confusion, so, furious at his situation, he moved quickly to follow them.

Pvt. Richard Reneau of Boise, Idaho, was another E Company parachutist who was in a bad medical state. Suffering from jaundice, he had also been told to report to sick bay. Like Greely, though, he had refused because he did not want his buddies to go into combat while he stayed behind in safety. Once they were on Choiseul, though, and he realized how weak and exhausted he was, he began to think he might have made a mistake. He was assigned to help unload equipment, and he made for a large stack of supplies. Instead of carrying them off the beach into the jungle, though, he lay down behind them. It was so dark he knew nobody would see him, and there was so much confusion he probably would not even be missed. Reneau felt a little guilty and knew he should be working, doing his part, but he was too sick. He figured he would wait until most of the work was done before he came out. He was too sick to care about an enemy attack, so he lay down in the sand to sleep.

Reneau had not even been resting for a minute when he heard his platoon lieutenant ask, "Where's Reneau?" He knew he was goofing off, so he said to himself, "Rich, you gotta get up." Rising unsteadily, he hefted a crate of supplies onto his shoulder and carried it up the beach inside the jungle where the rest of the men were stacking them. He worked hard, determined to at least do his part, regardless of how sick he was. After they finished getting the crates of rations, grenades, and munitions hidden in the jungle, Reneau sat down to sleep, but was suddenly awakened. The work was not yet finished. They were told to grab as much equipment as they could carry and move up to the mountain camp. He was in absolute misery, but Reneau lifted a crate of grenades in addition to his own weapons, pack, and ammunition, and formed up in the line that would stumble blindly through the jungle up to the mountain hideout.

The last of the E Company Marines were making their way off the beach.[4] Brutinel formed up with his squad. He could see Seton directing men into the jungle. One of Seton's guides led them away, and Bob turned to look back at the natives behind them sweeping the sand with palm fronds. A battalion of men makes an enormous sign for any Japanese floatplane to see, but the natives made short work of it. Soon the beach looked just as it had before they had arrived.

0045—Voza

G Company had formed a perimeter, establishing and widening the beachhead at Voza. In the Third Platoon, Barney was sitting beside his JLMG man Fagoni when Lieutenant Duncan passed down the line. The lieutenant handed each man a vial of medicinal brandy.

"Drink this," whispered Duncan to Barney. "It's brandy. It'll help keep you awake." Barney was not a drinker, but he was tired and did not want to fall asleep on his shift so he downed the foul liquid in one gulp. "Ugh," he grimaced. It tasted awful but he felt an instant rush to his head and added, "This stuff really works."

"I thought you didn't drink."

"I didn't."

He and Fagoni waited in their hole and watched the natives unloading and moving equipment into the jungle around them. Their strength and endurance impressed him. They hoisted crates of supplies and ammunition as if they were empty boxes. In addition, they were agile, moving easily over the same trail the Marines slipped and fell on.

Just inside the G Company perimeter, Hq Company set up a temporary CP. This would be the battalion's headquarters until they could move up to the mountain camp. Pfc. Norman Wurzburger of the "Hell's Kitchen" neighborhood in New York City was an Hq Company radioman and one of the few Parris Island Marines in the Second Marine Parachute Battalion. Most of the other Marines on Choiseul had gone to boot camp in San Diego. Wurzburger was shivering from the malaria he had gotten on Vella LaVella, but he was working, setting up his TBX radio. They wanted the Japanese to know they were on Choiseul, but they did not want them to know where, unless it was the dummy beachhead that Coastwatcher Lt. Nick Waddell had prepared to the northwest. They knew that the enemy already had an idea where they had come ashore because they had twice bombed the landing force. Luckily, the Marines had taken no casualties. When a third enemy plane came over at 0100 and dropped two additional bombs, the Marines were already well into the safety of the jungle; once again, the bombs missed the ships.

Pfc. Eugene Gibbons of Lake Elmo, Minnesota, was attached to the Hq Company. He was in the experimental rocket platoon, a highly secret unit under the command of Lt. Bob Murphy. Their unit was assigned to the battalion to provide an extra combat punch. Gibbons, Pfc. Charlie Jones, Sgt. Nolan Burnett, and the other five members of the rocket "platoon" carried their 4.5-inch rockets deep into the jungle with help from the natives. Gibbons was the platoon radioman and did not have much to do. He knew it was highly unlikely that he would ever use his radio on this operation. Gibbons could also tell by looking at the jungle and its heavy canopy of trees that it was unlikely they would fire their rockets here because they could not fire through trees.

Private Block had long since finished carrying the last bags of rice off the beach, after which he joined a line of E Company Marines carrying supplies up to the mountain hideout. Hal was thinking about the uproar that had occurred when the natives found out they were being given white rice. They had been promised black rice and demanded that the Marines hold up their end of the bargain. Black rice, a delicacy in this part of the world, is nutritionally superior to white rice. The officers had assured Lieutenant Seton and the natives that the mistake would be corrected and they would have the "right" rice air-dropped the following day. Hal wondered if the natives would renege on their promises of assistance until they received their food.[5]

They were moving at a snail's pace up the hills and it was so dark Hal could not see a thing. He had his hand on the shoulder of the man in front of him when the column came to a halt. That often happened for some reason or other and the men stood, waiting for everyone to start moving again. They had thankfully moved into an area of low vegetation, and because there were thinner trees overhead, they had some natural light from the moonless sky. Hal was carrying his weapons, pack, and ammunition along with two mortar rounds and a cloverleaf (mortar stand). His supplies got heavier as he waited. He could just barely see a tree stump in the darkness near him and decided to sit down until the line began moving again. He placed his hand on the stump to help guide himself down, but the "stump" gave an angry grunt and jerked away. Hal nearly came unglued and yanked his hand back. The stump turned out to be one of the natives who had been squatting along the trail until a Marine tried to use him as a barstool. Hal almost lost his first pair of shorts that night and the native disappeared from sight after taking but a single step off the trail.

The column moved out again, slipping and tripping toward the mountain camp. Hal soon came to a big log on the steep trail that the men had to climb over. He almost bumped into two more natives positioned there to help the paratroopers find their way. These two seemed to find it amusing that Hal and the others were having so much trouble in the mud. All that the Marines could see were their white, smiling teeth whenever someone slipped or cursed. When it was Hal's turn, he went to lift the heavy equipment over, but he tripped and fell in the mud. He slid back, almost wiping out the line of men behind him. Frustrated and exhausted, Hal suddenly had an idea. Before they had left, everyone had loaded up on "pogey bait"—candy bars. Most of the guys had already eaten theirs, but Hal had two left. His experience on Vella LaVella told him that chocolate was the one commodity that the natives prized above all else. Hal fished out both his Hershey bars and waved them toward the men to get their attention.

"Help carry?" he asked. The natives' eyes got huge. They quickly grabbed the candy bars, Hal's pack with mortar stand, and easily climbed over the log, moving up toward the mountain camp.

Meanwhile, E Company paratrooper Private Reneau was almost at the end of his strength. The combination of his yellow jaundice, the weight of his weapons, ammo, equipment, and supplies, and the dark, muddy, steep trail almost finished him. It was all Reneau could do to reach the mountain bivouac.

Mountain Camp

The Marines made bivouac and immediately began setting up their perimeter. They dug holes, placed listening posts, and set guards. When dawn gave them enough light to work by, they would chop firing lanes. Until then, the Marines used phosphorescent vines from the jungle strung up as ropes to guide them to the guard and machine-gun outposts surrounding their perimeter. Without the vines to guide them, the possibility of getting lost and attracting friendly fire was high. After their defenses were set up, the men searched in the dark for the best, most comfortable spot they could to set up their hammocks. The hammocks were new and had never been used by any of the U.S. armed forces. The First Marine Parachute Regiment was entirely equipped with them and the Second Marine Parachute Battalion would be their field test. The men strung them up between trees in the dark and then climbed in to go to sleep.[6]

Having carried the colonel's generator up the mountain, Private Dibbens was dismissed to find his platoon. With difficulty, Dibbens found his squad and began setting up his hammock. He secured it between two trees and climbed in to try to get some badly needed sleep. Dibbens had been asleep for maybe half an hour when something brushed against him in the night. He did not wait for the Japanese soldier to stab him first, but lashed out with his Ka-Bar knife. The muffled curse of a very surprised Marine told him he had narrowly missed someone moving past on his way to guard duty. Lucky for the other Marine, Dibbens only managed to slice a gaping hole in the netting of his own hammock.

Captain Manchester's CP

Pfc. Billy Joe Cagle had just arrived at the section of jungle designated as the Easy Company CP. Following behind Capt. Robert R. "Chesty" Manchester, Billy Joe was Chesty's runner and had to stay close should the captain need him for something. Billy Joe was a burly blond who was also a company scout. Chesty spoke to Billy Joe in the darkness. "Find Seton," he said. "He's down on the beach with G Company. Tell him that we've made bivouac, and if he's ready, bring him up to meet with Colonel Krulak and me."

That was it. Billy Joe could tell Chesty was busy so he said, "Yessir," and left. He turned around and followed the hand-to-shoulder line of Marines trickling slowly into the area. It was not all that bad while there were Marines coming up, but when the last of the men passed him and he was walking alone in the dark, it became unnerving. The darkness was absolute, and Billy Joe could not see anything.

Pfc. Donald "Hink" Hinkle of Pierre, South Dakota, was a slender blond, blue-eyed Marine, and, like Billy Joe, he was a battalion scout for Captain Manchester. In fact, Hink and Billy Joe had gone through the same reconnaissance school together on New Caledonia. Hink was setting up his hammock in the darkness when he was told to report to Captain Manchester's temporary CP. He stumbled his way over in the blackest night he had ever known, whispering for directions. When he finally arrived, he could hear Colonel Krulak and Captain Manchester but he could not see them.

"Sir?" he whispered.

"Over here."

Hink was still unable to see them, but he walked toward the sound and tripped on something in the darkness, almost falling. "Watch out," said Chesty. Hink caught himself and realized he had almost tripped over Krulak and Chesty. They were both under a tent-half, looking at a map. They were careful not to have any visible light that might be spotted from the air; they had covered their map with a thick canvas tent-half and struck a Zippo lighter. Chesty ordered Hink to tell Maj. Warner T. Bigger to come up to the mountain camp for an officer's briefing with Colonel Krulak. Bigger was back down at Voza with G Company. Hink was dismissed and moved blindly down the long trail for the second time that night, back to Voza.

0130—Jungle Trail

Billy Joe was stumbling blindly down the mountain in the direction he hoped was Voza Beach. To anyone moving at night the stars and moonlight on a South Pacific beach provide natural illumination; night vision is usually pretty good, especially on a clear night with no cloud cover. Billy Joe had neither. It was a cloudy night, a new moon, and he was in the jungle, not on the beach. The dense banyan rainforests of the central Solomons are so thick that the brightest full moon cannot penetrate the thick canopy of trees overhead. Vision is zero. Billy Joe groped and felt his way like a blind man back down through the jungle and grumbled to himself about being made Chesty's runner. Although he liked his captain, he hated being around so much brass because every once in a while he had duty like this.

Choiseul was an enemy island with five thousand Japanese soldiers, any one of whom could be waiting in ambush inches from him. To add to Billy Joe's uneasiness, this part of the world is full of poisonous snakes, scorpions, plants, and spiders so he hated using his unprotected hands to feel his way in front of him. To add to his predicament, he was in completely unfamiliar terrain. The only thing he knew was that if he kept moving downhill, following the sound of the small river or large stream that paralleled the path down from the mountains, he had eventually hit the ocean. Once on the beach, he would be able to see again. Thankfully, men and natives were still moving supplies up in the darkness so Billy Joe could hear them and orient himself by their sound. He had probably already wandered off the trail. The natives had hewed it earlier that day and it still was not worn in. It was difficult to know if he was on or off the trail because of all the overhanging branches and tree limbs across it. Just when it seemed he had to be lost, Billy Joe arrived at Voza Beach and, as if he had flipped a light switch, he was able to see again. Almost immediately, Billy Joe saw the big Australian. As he approached him he thought, "That Seton is somebody." Billy Joe walked over and noticed the Australian was still admiring the new carbine Colonel Krulak had given him as a gift from the Second Marine Parachute Battalion. Seton saw Billy Joe approaching and turned to him.

"This thing's a real beauty," he said, referring to the little weapon that looked ridiculously small in his big hand.

"Mr. Seton," began Billy Joe in his thick Texas drawl, "Cap'n Manchester tol me ta tell ya we're in position and I'm ready ta take ya up ta him and Colonel Krulak." Billy Joe felt stupid relaying the message, because Seton knew the island like the back of his hand. In fact, he wanted Seton to lead him back up so he would not get lost.

"Right," said Seton in his deep Australian accent. "Tell Captain Manchesta I'll meet him theya. You go on, Yank. I know tha way." Knowing Seton was concise, Billy Joe turned and left. He thought it was funny that the Australian had called him a Yankee, because he was a Texan, a Southerner, definitely not a Yank. With the same trepidation as before, Cagle moved off into the darkness back up toward the mountain bivouac.

Likewise, Hink had been walking blindly in the darkness to give Major Bigger his message. It was so dark the two might have passed each other without knowing it. Hink thought he should have reached the G Company bivouac by then, and he worried he had somehow wandered off the track and was lost in enemy territory. He had kept the sound of the flowing water on his right, so he should be okay. But, like Billy Joe had experienced, Hink's mind began to play tricks on him.

Suddenly, Hink smelled cologne. He had heard that the Japanese wore cologne or perfume, so he immediately brought up his Ka-Bar in the darkness. What Marine would wear cologne on an invasion? In fact, it smelled more like perfume. Hink waited but he could not hear anything. It was so dark he could not see the leaves that were touching him. He checked his compass with its phosphorescent direction indicators and knew he should be on track. He decided to chance one additional step, brought his foot forward, and promptly fell into a foxhole.

"Wha'? Who's there?" babbled two startled voices at once, their English saving them from Hink's Ka-Bar slash in the darkness.

"I'm looking for Major Bigger," said the terrified Hink in a barely controlled voice. "I accidentally fell in your hole, sorry."

"He ain't here," said a sleepy voice. "Now get off me."

Hink wanted to tell them not to sleep on an enemy island and to remind them that one of them should have been awake in the first place, but he felt lucky just to have gotten away without being stabbed. He continued down the trail, found Major Bigger on the beach, and gave him the message to report to Colonel Krulak. Once he had completed his task he did not bother to go back up the trail into the mountain. Captain Manchester had told him to wait on the beach for the rest of his platoon, Lt. John Richards's First Platoon, which was assigned to guard the Higgins boats all night. The boats were being taken out to a little island a couple thousand yards off Voza Beach that was supposed to be safe. Hink looked out into the surf trying to see any sign of land, but all he could see was complete darkness.

Zinoa Island, a tiny, lone islet just two thousand yards off Voza and directly across the channel, was a perfect place to hide the boats. Intelligence reported that overhanging mangrove and banyan trees shrouded the little island, which would be perfect for camouflaging the LCPRs. Equally important, it was supposed to be deserted. Richards and his platoon would check it out and spend the night guarding the boats on the little islet.

The LCPRs were essential for the battalion's raiding up and down the coast, and it was critical to keep them hidden from any Japanese overflights. Three enemy bombers had already made passes over the beach dropping bombs in the water. Luckily, they caused no damage. Despite their secrecy, it seemed that the enemy knew right where they were. Krulak wanted his boats hidden safely before more enemy planes showed up. If the diversion were to work, the boats more than anything would lend credibility to an invasion. Without them the battalion would have to attack everywhere on foot. Moving ten miles through the jungle could take infantry more than four hours, whereas the boats could do it in less than thirty minutes.

It was about 0130 when the LCVPs moved over to Zinoa Island. Because Japanese machine-gun barges ranged up and down The Slot and enemy planes patrolled overhead, it was essential to camouflage the boats well. When they reached the little island, though, it was hard to see a good landing site in the darkness. One of the four boats found what seemed to be a cove in the moonless night, and the coxswain moved in. It was difficult to navigate the boat in daylight let alone the darkness of night and the Higgins boat soon became stuck about forty yards from shore. The coxswain gunned the engine to try to force the boat in, but all he did was lodge them solidly onto an underwater obstacle. He tried to back up, but the craft would not budge. The engine was roaring and the already agitated navy lieutenant lost his temper. He shouted obscenities at the coxswain for making so much noise and getting them stuck.

Pfc. Frank Dudek of North Ridgeville, Ohio, was on that boat. He wanted to tell the navy lieutenant to shut up, but he did not dare say anything to an officer. Dudek quickly found out that Sgt. Philip Romero was not as concerned about military protocol as he was.

"You son of a bitch, you say another word I'm going to shoot you," threatened Romero. "This motor can be mistaken for any engine, your swearing can't. Shut up." Dudek exchanged a quick glance with his best friend Pfc. Ralph Beneke. The lieutenant was clearly furious but did not say a word. Sergeant Romero just glared at him, and ordered his squad out of the boat.

The Marines were easily able to stand in the shallow surf and push while the coxswain put the boat in reverse. With the help of the Marines and possibly because it held less weight, the boat backed off and got under way again. The Marines waded in and the coxswain was able to maneuver the boat into the little cove. They pushed the landing craft under a mangrove tree that leaned out over the water and Romero ordered his men to cut branches with their Ka-Bars for additional camouflage. When they felt they had sufficiently concealed it from both sea and air, they dug in and set hourly guards. Everyone tried to get some sleep for the remaining few hours of darkness.

In a different squad, same platoon, company scout Hink also sat guard over an LCPR and waited for dawn. Once the sun rose, Lieutenant Richards wanted them to patrol the tiny island to make sure no enemy soldiers were there.

Voza

G Company had formed a small semicircular beachhead along the jungle with each of its platoons tying in to cover almost two hundred yards.

Deeper in the jungle, Baxter was sleeping with his Johnson Rifle across his lap. Frank Fagoni was asleep beside him. A light rain had begun to fall, dripping down from the thick canopy. The jungle popped with the sound of raindrops striking leaves and branches. It was Baxter's turn to stand watch while Fagoni slept, but the medicinal brandy had worn off; he was exhausted, and dozed off. Baxter had no idea how long he had been out when he felt a sharp kick. "Who's on watch here?" came an angry hiss Baxter recognized instantly. Although Baxter could not see him, he would know Lieutenant Duncan's voice anywhere.

"I was on watch, sir," said Baxter apologetically, but he was thinking, "Oh my god, I'm dead. I'm going to be court-martialed."

"Stay awake," whispered Duncan sternly. "We're depending on you."

His men had complete confidence in him, but Lieutenant Duncan was not the type to show emotion. He was big, with wide shoulders that tapered to a narrow waist. Duncan had been a former boxer, with the pug nose to prove it. His steel-gray eyes were intimidating and penetrating; those intense eyes told the men when he was angry. Baxter could not see those eyes in the darkness, but he knew they were boring holes in him. That was all Duncan said. He turned away, moving down the line checking other positions. Baxter was thoroughly ashamed at having let Duncan and his buddies down. More than fear of the Japanese, the thought that he had failed the others shook the last cobwebs of sleep from his brain.

On the same G Company line, Ned Russell sat behind his A-4 staring into the darkness. It seemed to the Arizonan that it had been raining nonstop since they had arrived on Guadalcanal. It was not enough to keep the bugs away, though—just enough to make it wet and uncomfortable. All through his guard duty a cloud of mosquitoes swarmed around him, siphoning off his blood. They were aggressive, too, but he did not bother to brush them away. If he killed one, two more took its place. Resigned to the fact that until he got to his hammock he would be living food for the ravenous insects, he just hoped he would not get malaria—that is, if he did not already have it. He had been taking Atabrine faithfully, but he knew a lot of guys that had been taking Atabrine faithfully still got malaria.[7]

0400—Zinoa Island

It was not yet dawn, and Dudek and the other men assigned to guard the Higgins boats on Zinoa woke to the "puttaputtaputta" of Washing Machine Charlie directly overhead. The small enemy bomber was flying down The Slot headed southeast, but when it was over their tiny island, it changed course and began to circle.

"Uh-oh," thought Dudek looking up at the silhouette against the dark sky, "he spotted us." Dudek was convinced that the Japanese plane had seen them because it was circling directly over them. Everyone got deep in their holes, waiting to hear the whistle of falling bombs, but the enemy plane just continued on. For the first time since Dudek could remember, a Japanese bomber had passed overhead and not dropped a bomb. He breathed a sigh of relief, closed his eyes, and went back to sleep.

0500—Voza

Dawn in the Solomon Islands is an impressive sight. Each morning was more beautiful than the previous one as the sun cast its hues of magenta, vermilion, and rust across the sky. If the saying "Red skies at night, sailors delight, red skies at morning, sailor take warning" had any truth, the Marines could expect a storm. However, most of the paratroopers were sound asleep and the ones standing guard were too dead tired to appreciate the magnificent sight. When Pharmacist's Mate Holland woke in the predawn light, he found the wounded native Peta Nu sleeping in the jungle next to him. He rechecked the splint on Peta Nu's hand and, while he re-bandaged it, Pfc. Robert Nelson of Ponca City, Oklahoma, walked over.

"How's his hand?"

"It's busted up good."

"I saw him put it between the Higgins boat and the destroyer," said Nelson, "I tried to pull it back but the boats slammed together before I could reach him. That had to hurt like hell." After Holland finished re-bandaging Peta Nu's hand, he fished in his pack and took out a K-ration.

Holland was famished; he had not eaten since morning chow on Vella LaVella the day before. Peta Nu seemed to take great interest in Holland's food, and Holland realized the native probably had not eaten for twenty-four hours either. He opened his ration and offered some to Peta Nu, who smiled and said, "Thank you." (Both Peta Nu and Peta Kiri spoke excellent English.) Peta Nu tasted the K-ration and the smile died on his face. Holland could tell the man was trying to be polite as he worked the unappetizing food around his mouth. Holland fought his own laughter to see what Peta Nu would do. Would he spit it out or would he swallow it? Peta Nu finished his forkful but declined a second bite.

Holland remembered he had something else. Everyone loved chocolate, and Holland also had a D-bar in his pack. He took out the cellophane-wrapped D-bar and offered it to Peta Nu. He eyed this new threat warily. It was not until Holland took one end of the wrapper off that the man was able to see the brown texture of chocolate and his face lit up. Peta Nu took the D-bar with another "Thank you" and took a bite. Again, the smile died on his face. A D-bar looked like chocolate but that was its great deception. If the U.S. government sent their sons high-calorie chocolate bars that tasted good, they would have to send more of them. Because the D-bar tasted so bad, men would eat it only when there was nothing else.

The sun was up and G Company was able to look around the island they were on. Choiseul was truly a tropical paradise. Voza looked like something out of a Hollywood set. Sergeant Siefke woke in the morning light near the wreckage of a Japanese dive-bomber. The plane was upside down, half in the water and half in the jungle. They had dug in the night before in total darkness and all they knew was that they were near the surf. Cpl. Mike Vinich, Siefke's friend and assistant squad leader, awoke near Siefke. As their squad moved over to examine the plane, Vinich could not help but remember his first morning on Vella LaVella after their LST had been bombed. The whole scene reminded him of it: the jungle, the beach, a new island, and the previous bombing.[8]

As Vinich and the others climbed on the wrecked plane, Siefke saw something that interested him. The plane had a big rising sun on both its wings and a smaller one along the fuselage. Pulling out his Ka-Bar, Siefke decided to get his first souvenir of the war. He used the knife to peel the smaller rising sun off the plane and put it in his pack to take home.[9]

As soon as it was light enough to work, Pfc. George Shively of Branson, Missouri, and the other men in Capt. Arthur L. Bryant's communication platoon went to work, laying telephone wire from the beach up to Colonel

Krulak's new CP in the mountains. Shively had worked for Western Union before the war and was recruited into the unit because of his experience. Shively's sole job on Choiseul was to keep the line open from the telephone on the beach to Krulak's CP. The lookouts monitored the sea traffic near Voza, and if they saw anything at all—ship, plane, or coconut—Krulak wanted to know about it immediately. The only telephones they used were powered by sound. The obvious advantage of a phone was that the colonel would know immediately about enemy movement without sending a radio message that the Japanese could intercept.

Shortly after 0500, Captain Day told his platoon leaders to strike the beachhead and move up to the battalion's new bivouac in the mountains. The G Company men carried as much equipment and supplies as they could, and started the hike up the muddy track that E and F Companies had tripped and fallen on the night before. The bivouac in the jungle plateau was only a thousand yards up the mountain, so they made much better time in the light of day than their brother companies had made in the dead of night. All morning a stream of paratroopers and natives carried ammunition and supplies up to the new camp, paralleling a small river that ran from the mountains down to the ocean. In war, logistics wins battles, so before doing anything else, the battalion needed to safeguard its food and ammunition.

The camp location was a natural fortress, selected because it was defensible. It was between two fast-flowing rivers, behind impenetrable jungle, and backed up against a mountain with steep rocky ridges on a slightly inclined jungle plateau. The trees were immense, the undergrowth impossibly dense, and daylight never reached the jungle floor. Had it not been for Seton, the battalion would never have found the campsite. There was even a small pool under a waterfall that the Marines could use for bathing. The jungle was already strung with camouflaged hammocks from the other companies, and G Company moved to the flank to set up their own bivouac, tying in with the rest of the battalion. They then began setting up outposts and cutting firing lanes.

Zinoa Island

With the sun rising in the sky it was soon light enough to see. Lieutenant Richards ordered Sergeant Foote's ten-man squad to make a complete circumference around tiny Zinoa to make sure its shores were devoid of human habitation. Private Hinkle was in Foote's squad and he walked just off the lapping water at the jungle edge ready to fire on any Japanese lookouts they stumbled on. They completed a full circle of the island's shores, found it deserted, and turned inland to reconnoiter the small interior. About a hundred yards in, they discovered a hut with a thatched roof. Unlike the huts at Voza, this one had walls. Sergeant Foote had his men deploy around the shack to take it under fire. Just as Hink and the others surrounded it, a rain-squall started pouring down on them. Sergeant Foote sent one man inside to check the hut and after he signaled it was safe, they continued searching the rest of the island. Once they were convinced that the islet held no enemy troops, Foote gave the okay to return to the hut for shelter. Everyone went in out of the rain except two men who stayed outside to stand guard. As soon as Hink entered the shack, he noticed a foul odor, and they could see a decayed body on the floor. The Marines stood over it trying to figure how it had died. Hink believed it was the remains of a young girl. He had heard that the Japanese kept Korean comfort girls and wondered if this poor thing had been one of them.

Mountain Camp

Private Brutinel was sitting by himself with his back to a tree cleaning his Johnson rifle. He had two pieces on his lap and the other in his hand when something fell out of the tree above him. It landed heavily on his shoulders and he glanced down to see a large snake. He shot one way and the snake went the other, vanishing into the thick bushes. They had been warned about the deadly brown snakes in this part of the world so when it landed on him, Brutinel did not wait to see whether or not it was poisonous.

Private Greely, who had been suffering from amoebic dysentery, had survived the misery of the night's trek up into the mountain camp to wake up in pain. He had been so distracted by his sickness that he never had time to worry about the Japanese. By the time he had reached the bivouac and set up his hammock, he had had an awful ordeal. Besides the aching pain in his bowels, he was raw from the march, and had had to spend the night in his own mess, which did nothing to help his deteriorating condition. "Get upwind of Greely," his buddies warned, aghast at the smell.

When Greely woke up after an hour or two of sleep, he still had a terrible pain in his abdomen and an angry rash. He looked around and saw the small jungle stream that ran along their camp and followed it just out of the battalion bivouac. There he set about cleaning himself and his dungarees. Afterwards he went looking for the battalion doctor. When he found Dr. Richard Lawrence, he told him about his miserable night, and the doctor gave him a handful of large tablets.

"Take these and go sit in the river," instructed Lawrence, "'cause they're going to make you go."

"Doc, I don't need to go."

"Just do as I say. They'll clean you out."

Greely took the pills and followed the stream down from camp so that nobody would be below him in the water, hung his dungarees out to dry on some branches, and sat in the flowing rivulet as instructed. The pills worked, that he found out for sure, but they did not get rid of his dysentery.

Jungle Trail

All morning long, certain men of Hq Company—Private Shively, Cpl. Jack Morgan, Pfc. Daniel Schlesinger, and Pfc. Robert Lemkhulm—strung combat wire to connect the phone at Voza to the one in the colonel's CP. Each reel of wire was five hundred yards long. They set up a phone at the lookout point concealed in the jungle at Voza, connected a wire to it, and unrolled the reel up the mountain. When they got to the end of the first five hundred–yard spool they tied a knot to the next reel before splicing the two ends together. This was so that someone tripping over the wire would not rip the splice apart. The knot, instead of the spliced ends, would absorb the pull. They carefully spliced the wires—copper to copper and steel to steel—and taped the splice securely to keep the ubiquitous moisture out. The wire was not heavily insulated because there was no voltage going through it—just a man's voice. The sound-powered phones had clips on the end that the men connected the wires to. Hq Company used three reels of wire in all to open communications between the beach and the colonel's mountain hideout. Two men hid by the Voza phone at all times to monitor any Japanese movement by sea or air.

Privates Schlesinger and Lemkhulm had almost permanent duty at Voza. They set booby traps on both flanks of the beach phone so that no enemy troops could approach them unseen in the thick jungle. From then on, twice a day, they would check the phones to make sure communications worked. Whenever the line was broken between the phones, Shively would be called in to locate and fix the break.

Near Voza

The Marine paratroopers moved supplies up into the mountain hideout throughout the first morning, but not everyone could work. Pfc. James P. Dugan's squad, F Company, was deployed as a listening post in the jungle to watch for the enemy. Unlike sandy Voza Beach a hundred or so yards away, the water lapped right at the trees where Dugan sat. A wrecked Japanese plane (the same one the G Company guys woke up next to) was lying upside down near them. Like Siefke's squad earlier, Dugan and the others had gone over and climbed on the wreckage to check it out. As they waited and killed time, they kept an eye on the sky for Japanese planes.

Sure enough, the Marines soon heard aircraft approaching and took cover in the jungle. Through the thinner canopy of trees along the shore they could make out two planes. They were U.S. Marine Corsairs and they flew overhead at about a thousand feet. Dugan watched the planes but did not think anything of it. Suddenly one of them turned to come back. "I wonder if he sees something," said Dugan to his squad members.

Maybe the Japanese were sending troops down to check on the invasion and this Corsair saw a column on the coastal trail and was going to strafe them. The Corsair was flying back, descending, but seemed to be heading for Dugan's area. "What the hell!" exclaimed Dugan. "He's coming right at us!"

As the Corsair got closer it started firing its six .50-caliber machine guns. The jungle around the Japanese plane was ripped apart. Trees a half-foot thick were chopped in two while shredded branches rained to the ground. The sound of bullets striking metal punctuated the sound of bullets ripping through the jungle. The Marines scrambled away from the wreck and fled into the jungle, cursing at the stupidity of the pilot.

Mountain Camp

One thousand yards up the mountain, Pfc. Carl Desanto was waiting in Colonel Krulak's CP. He could easily see the two Corsairs moving east along the shore from the higher altitude. He and Krulak watched one of them suddenly dive, start a strafing run, and blast away at somebody down near Voza. "Holy shit!" exclaimed Desanto. "They're shooting up our own guys."

Colonel Krulak must have had roughly the same thought, because quick as a fox, he reached into a wooden box and brought out an American flag. "Desanto," he snapped, "take this flag down and spread it out on the beach. Go!" In a flash Desanto was out of the CP and double-timing it down the mountain.

Dugan and his squad were hiding behind trees and aboveground roots about forty yards from the wreck, nervously watching for the Corsair to return. They still could not figure out how the pilot had mistaken them for enemy planes in the first place. The Corsair banked and came back for another pass over the same spot. It began firing again and its machine guns riddled the jungle shore around the wrecked plane. The pilot pulled up, climbing to rejoin his wingman. It was then that Dugan and the others realized the Corsair was on a joy ride, probably just clearing his guns and using the wrecked plane for target practice.

Desanto arrived on the beach to set out the flag but saw he did not need to because the Corsair had already rejoined his wingman.

1200—Mountain Camp

The battalion had moved all its stores of ammunition, rations, and equipment up to the mountain hideout. With its logistical survival temporarily ensured, it was time to begin the ruse. The first message broadcast to IMAC from Choiseul went out at 1212.

Pfc. Robert Perdzock was the radio operator, with Tech Sgt. James Duke more or less in charge of his group. Perdzock marveled at Duke's ability to fine-tune their radio. Duke was a miracle worker with that box of wires, capable of finding grid current dips that nobody else could.

As instructed, Perdzock began transmitting false messages to the other "regiments," telling them to proceed according to plan. He sent a message to inform IMAC that "the invasion was going by the numbers" and that "the entire division had landed." This misinformation was all part of the strategy intended for enemy radio intercepts.

Sgt. James Childs, a half-Sioux Indian from Tilden, Nebraska, was a Second Marine Parachute Battalion mess sergeant. Here on Choiseul he was out of a job, like Desanto, so he was assigned to Hq Company for them to use as needed. Basically, that meant he did what he wanted most of the time. He found the Hq Company fascinating because there were all kinds of special units attached that you never saw otherwise. There was even an experimental rocket platoon, and a heavy weapons platoon with new anti-tank launchers (bazookas). Navy officers were attached to the battalion to check the coast for possible PT boat bases and to manage the LCPRs, while army radar personnel were attached to check the mountain coast for the feasibility of setting up radar to track enemy air from Rabaul. There were generators, radios, and even typewriters.

Childs happened to be close to the CP when Perdzock sent the false message out about the division's landing, but Childs was not watching or listening to Perdzock. His attention was directed toward two Native American Marines sending messages on a different radio. They were regimental Navajo code talkers who were sending coded messages to IMAC informing them of the true operation. Childs, a Sioux, had no idea what they were saying because they were not speaking Lakota.[10]

Private Dibbens was not at the Hq Company bivouac but he heard them fire up the generator. The noise was so loud he swore under his breath. It seemed to echo off the mountain. The night before, Dibbens was worried that the Japanese had heard them land; by this point, they would know right where the camp was. It was so loud, how could they not? Dibbens wandered over to the Hq Company area and heard the broadcast sent by Perdzock. He immediately went back to tell his buddies. "It's begun," he said. "The radio operator said in an open uncoded message that 'The division has landed successfully. All twenty thousand men are moving toward their objectives.'"

Every Marine paratrooper knew that the whole reason for the Choiseul raid was to divert Japanese strength from Bougainville, the main Allied objective in the Solomons. Once the Marines arrived on Choiseul, the reality of that broadcast meant that soon the Japanese would be sending more and more troops here to stop their invasion. The Marines were outnumbered almost ten to one already. Dibbens looked around at their mountain bivouac and thought that at least they had picked a good spot if they had to defend it. He was grateful they had picked the mountains over the beach because not only was it easier to defend, the higher altitude was cooler—still hot, but not the man-killing heat of the humid jungle below.

At the command CP, Colonel Krulak called his officers in for a briefing. He repeated what he had already been over with them. "We need to make noise," he told them. "We need to make the Japanese believe that an Allied invasion has begun in earnest. To do that we need to hit them with a lot of small units over a broad front all at once. We need to look big. With that in mind, don't let your patrols get locked into a fight. Hit and run. Kill as many as you can and make a lot of noise, but get out."

Krulak knew that this meant he could not use his battalion as a whole. The largest operation they would conduct would be the next day's Sangigai raid, when they would be using two reinforced companies. After that, they would mostly conduct platoon-sized patrols because they would need everyone to defend their base with all its supplies. Even at Sangigai, their largest action, they would need to be careful not to get engaged.[11] At 1215 the first combat patrol was sent out by Krulak to reconnoiter the surrounding area.[12] A patrol of seventeen men led by Lt. William King, F Company, set out to search the area of Batua Point. Accompanying the patrol was Sgt. Wilbur Hills's squad, with two men from Hq Company's intelligence section (Bn-3), and three native guides.

They left the camp and took the well-worn trail down to Voza and turned right, taking the coastal trail northwest through the jungle toward Batua Point. They crossed a number of small rivulets and passed several abandoned Japanese lean-tos along the coast. The enemy camps were very small and primitive, with almost no equipment and certainly nothing of value. F Company reached the Baregosonga River at 1250 and began scouting the area.

Batua Point was a flat strip of beach approximately two hundred yards wide, backed by a steep mountain, a swamp, and the Baregosonga River, which was wide enough at the mouth to be navigable. It was immediately obvious to the Bn-3 men that this was a perfect place to set up a battalion lookout post. Any Japanese movement by sea would be seen from Batua Point. Any approach by land from the northwest would cross the exposed Baregosonga River. The steep mountain behind Batua prevented any flanking movement and forced approaching troops into the Baregosonga bottleneck. A squad of Marines hiding in ambush could surprise a much larger force and cut them to pieces from their protected positions in the jungle. Batua Point was a natural spot for the battalion's left-flank defenses. With this information, the patrol returned to the mountain camp and reported to the colonel.

1500—Mountain Camp

Colonel Krulak received his first post-landing intelligence from the Coastwatchers, who informed him of enemy positions in their area. The closest Japanese were still reported to be ten miles to the southeast at the enemy barge station at Sangigai and twenty miles to the northwest near Choiseul Bay.

At 1530, after receiving the information on Batua Point, Krulak ordered two listening posts set up on both the battalion's flanks: one to the northwest, at Batua Point, and the other to the southeast, not quite a mile from Voza. There, a small river cut the coastal trail and allowed a position from which to view barge traffic up the coast. Unlike Batua Point, however, it was not as easy to defend. The river was not nearly as wide or as deep there, and it had no natural terrain features to protect its flank. Unfortunately, however, because the closest Japanese troops were to the southeast, this spot would likely see action first.

Colonel Krulak then ordered George Company to keep a squad of Marines at each position and another down at Voza. The Japanese could always land by barge at Voza Beach although the listening posts should theoretically have seen them. The men were to monitor the outposts at all times.

1730—Zinoa Island

After spending an uneventful day on Zinoa, Lieutenant Richards ordered his platoon back to Voza. Sergeant Romero told his squad to board their LCPR while the coxswain fired up the engine. Dudek winced at the noise. Against the silence of the jungle, the engine sounded like an aircraft carrier whose planes were warming up on deck. If there were any Japanese nearby, they would know exactly where the Marines were situated. They made the quick trip over and ran ashore at Voza at 1800. Their relief was waiting for them. Romero and his men filed up the beach as a squad from the waiting weapons platoon left the cover of the trees to replace them. The navy lieutenant never said a word as Romero left and a native guide led Richards's platoon up to the mountain bivouac while the LCPRs took Lt. Douglas Morton's weapons platoon back out to Zinoa.

As Richards's platoon moved up to the mountain camp, many of the men scoured the jungle along the path for coconuts or other tropical fruit that grew there. Everyone was hungry and had only K-rations and D-bars to sustain them. Vella LaVella had been stripped clean, but Choiseul was ripe for the picking. Hink and his buddy Pfc. Doug Goulson were trudging along, hungrily eyeing coconuts high in a tree, when a native coming back down the hill saw them looking up. He had probably finished carrying supplies up to the camp and was returning for more. Hink and Goulson pointed at the coconuts and talked in a slow form of Pidgin English to try to get their point across. The man gestured for their machete, took it, and scampered up the tree faster than they thought possible. He lopped off two coconuts from the top of the tree and came back down quickly, proudly handing the fruit to the two men. Neither of the Marines could hide their disappointment.

"These aren't ripe," said Hink. "Why didn't you grab ripe ones?"

"Why did you grab the bad ones?" complained Goulson. He pointed up at the tree. "There are at least four ripe ones right there."

The native just looked confused, not understanding their displeasure. Lieutenant Seton happened to be moving along the trail at that point and he heard the Marines complaining.

"List'n ta these nytives," Seton advised in his deep voice. "They know what their about. Tha ripe ones'l give ya disentree. Graen coconuts a beda than ripe ones."

"Oh," said Hink, surprised. "Thanks, Mr. Seton." The last thing in the world either he or Goulson wanted was dysentery. Malaria was almost preferable to that.

1800—Zinoa Island

It was approaching dusk when the weapons platoon reached Zinoa. The Marines hurried to hide the boats and prepare their positions in the fading light. Cpl. Harry Milkert of Chicago, Illinois, was one of those Marines. Milkert was crew leader to a 60-mm mortar. He had expected to encounter the Japanese already, but just like on Guadalcanal and Vella, they hadn't yet. Milkert and the others hid their boat under mangrove trees and covered them with branches. Afterward they formed a perimeter, dug in, and rotated hourly guards.

In Sergeant Skotnicki's machine-gun section, Ned Russell was also sitting guard duty on Zinoa Island. He could hear the men nearby talking in hushed whispers. As usual, they were complaining. Russell wanted to tell them, "Shut the hell up," but he did not want to make any noise himself. Just because the E Company guys said Zinoa was deserted did not mean it was true. It was incredibly dark, and if any Japanese were hiding on their little island, Russell did not want to give away his position. The two men were complaining about the heat, the mosquitoes, sleeping in the mud, and everything else. Russell was used to hearing that kind of talk from the "white eyes" and it always made him mad.

Russell had grown up sleeping on the ground in the Arizona desert. The shack his parents raised him and his three brothers in had a dirt floor. He upgraded to a wood floor when he went to the Indian Boarding School when he was five years old, where he was beaten daily for minor infractions and for speaking Apache or Navajo. Young Ned hated the Indian school so much that he ran away when he was eight years old. He stole an apple and an orange from the school kitchen and crossed the Granite Mountains on foot. It took him two weeks to make it from Kingman back to Clarkdale where his parents lived. When he got home, he was promptly beaten and sent back to the Indian school.

Ned Russell was constantly in trouble and eventually sent to a reform school. After December 7, he ran away to enlist in the Marines, against the warnings of his older brother. "Ned, don't join the Marines. In the navy you'll always have somewhere to sleep and decent food. You don't own yourself in the Marines. It's too tough. Don't do it."

"Too tough?" thought Russell. Why, he wanted the toughest, but he was underage and getting in would not be easy. The first question the recruiter asked him convinced him he did not have a chance.

"Have you or any members of your family ever fought against the government of the United States?"

"Yes."

The recruiter was taken aback, "What do you mean?"

"My grandfather fought the Cavalry."

"Well, uh, I didn't mean that," said the recruiter. "That's okay, forget it." Then he asked, "Have you ever been convicted of a crime?"

"I just escaped reform school."

"You're just the type we want."

Russell was shipped immediately to San Diego for boot camp. He instantly saw the similarities between the Indian boarding schools and the Marine Corps. You wore a uniform, you marched constantly from one line to another, and someone was always yelling at you.

"This is not a wall," his drill instructor had shouted, pounding his fist against the side of their barracks. "It is a bulkhead. This isn't ground or street or floor," he roared stomping his feet down. "It's a deck. There are no longer stairs; there are only ladders." He lowered his voice, warning them in a tone more threatening than his shouts. "And God help you if you call this a gun." He was holding a Springfield .03. "It is a rifle. You're in the Marines, now, and you better start thinking and talking like a Marine."

Like most Native Americans, Russell was quiet, but if the men in his platoon had not known better, they would have thought he was mute. He never spoke first and always gave short answers. All anyone ever saw him do was sharpen his Ka-Bars. He always had three or four knives and he kept them all razor sharp. That was how he got his nickname, Ka-Bar Russell.

That night the men in Lieutenant Morton's weapons platoon sat an uneventful watch. At about 2230, they heard the sound of aircraft in the distance. They listened to the drone of approaching engines and got low in their holes. When the planes were almost directly overhead, they stopped flying on their line and began circling tiny Zinoa. In the darkness the Marines recognized the type of aircraft by their silhouettes: Japanese Zeroes. Suddenly, they went into a dive. The parachutists dropped deep in their holes as the planes came down and strafed the shoreline. Everyone sweated out the attack, but none of the enemy planes came within even fifty yards of the Marines. It was too dark to see where the Americans were hiding, so the Zeroes fired blindly along the jungle coast hoping to get lucky. Everyone just assumed the Zeroes were after their LCPRs. Why else would they strafe a deserted island? Thankfully, no damage was done to any of the boats, but how had the Japanese known they were there? The Marines would never have an answer to that question.

Chapter 3

FIRST CONTACT: OCTOBER 29

You haven't seen darkness until you've seen the jungle at night.

Pfc. Thomas Preston, F Company, of Choiseul

0500—Mountain Camp

The Second Marine Parachute Battalion had been on an enemy island for more than twenty-four hours, but aside from enemy aircraft, they had not seen any Japanese. It was time to find out just where the enemy was. At 0530 on October 29, two combat patrols simultaneously left the mountain camp in separate directions. Lt. Col. Victor H. Krulak led a party southeast toward Sangigai, while Lt. Gerald Averill took a patrol northwest to reconnoiter Moli Point.

Colonel Krulak's patrol left with nineteen Marines and five native guides.[1] The patrol consisted of Krulak, Maj. Tolson Smoak, Smoak's runner Pfc. Eugene Gesch, Sgt. Paul Mullins, and fifteen other Marines, including Pfc. Bruce "Red" McClure and Pfc. Orrin Hall. Colonel Krulak and the rest of the patrol moved southeast along the coast toward the battalion southeast flank listening post. From there they would continue on to Vagara Village and Sangigai.

This was the first combat patrol that Colonel Krulak had ever made. He had never made one on Vella LaVella because, as a battalion commander, he had no business making a platoon- or patrol-sized raid. On Choiseul, however, he led the patrol because he wanted to reconnoiter the area for the next day's attack. Krulak did not want to lead his men into battle without a sense of the terrain and route. He had decided on an envelopment attack that revolved on a timetable. The Brute needed to see for himself if it was realistic.

0545—G Company Listening Post

G Company was assigned guard duty on the battalion's two flanks. After setting up a squad on the southeast listening post, Lt. Samuel Johnston decided to send two of his battalion scouts—Cpl. William R. Zuegel and Cpl. Mike Vinich—to search the coastal trail. They moved cautiously along the jungle trail searching for Japanese troops or signs of their recent passage. They had not gone more than a quarter of a mile when Zuegel noticed a vine across the trail at ankle height. He signaled to Vinich and both men stopped and eyed the vine, which grew up a big banyan tree. Suspended from the tree was a bomb that looked almost like a small torpedo. "What the hell is that?" asked Vinich. "Is that a torpedo?"

It was a clever trap, designed for an airburst explosion that would maximize casualties. The two Marines were just wondering how they would defuse or safely detonate the booby trap when they heard movement behind them, and they dropped to the ground. Vinich looked back and could see it was a Marine patrol approaching, so he deliberately stood straight up and signaled them to stop. They did, and one man came forward. Both Vinich and Zuegel were surprised when Colonel Krulak, of all people, approached cautiously to find out what was going on. Vinich pointed to the trip wire and was mightily pleased when Krulak congratulated them on their vigilance. Like a student praised by his favorite teacher, Vinich could not help but feel proud. He and Zuegel had probably saved some of their comrades from certain death, and the colonel, whom Vinich greatly admired, was one of them. Krulak told them his patrol would take a wide berth around the trip wire. Once the patrol was safely past, Vinich and Zuegel were to get someone from demolitions to defuse the bomb. An explosion might alert the Japanese, so the colonel did not want it detonated.

0545—Lieutenant Averill's Patrol

At the same time that Krulak was leading his patrol to the southeast, Lieutenant Averill set out in the opposite direction; his orders were to reconnoiter Moli Point, almost fifteen miles up the coast to the northwest. The patrol was to search for enemy activity, check the terrain for troop movement possibilities, and locate any fresh water along the way. The Brute had also said, specifically, "If you come across a sick Jap, bring him in. Would love to have a prisoner for more intelligence of the area, but don't get into a wrestling match. Yours is a reconnaissance patrol, not a combat patrol . . . don't get into a wrestling match."[2] Averill understood. They simply didn't have the numbers to get into a fight.

Of the eleven Marines making that patrol, one was Pfc. Roy J. Gallagher of Larchwood, Iowa. Gallagher was five feet nine inches tall, weighed 150 pounds, and had brown hair and green eyes. His best buddy, Pfc. Andy Obrocta of Chicago, Illinois, was in his squad. It was not even 0600 but it was already blisteringly hot, and their clothes were stained with sweat. The two loaded up with ammunition before moving out.

Averill's patrol took the coastal trail past Batua Point to the Baregosonga River. Under the covering weapons of the G Company lookouts stationed there, and with considerable difficulty, Averill's patrol forded the river and vanished into the jungle on the northwest riverbank.

Colonel Krulak's Patrol

Red, Hall, and the rest of Colonel Krulak's patrol moved cautiously to the southeast, passing over sloping ridges and rocky shores along the coastal trail. Mindful of the booby trap Zuegel and Vinich had found, the point men were especially careful. In some places, the trail was well worn, but in others it was overgrown with foliage. They waded through a half dozen streams that fed into the ocean. There were gorgeous, pristine beaches with soft, white sand. Coconut trees sprinkled the shore and swayed in the breeze at the edge of the banyan and mangrove rainforest. Beautiful, mysterious, dark mountains went from one end of the island to the other, and countless streams bubbled down from waterfalls into gorgeous lagoons with impossibly blue, clear water. Had he not been on a combat patrol expecting Japanese machine-gun fire at any moment, and had it not been so unmercifully hot, Red thought to himself, "What a truly magnificent place this must be in time of peace. If you ever wanted a vacation spot, this is it."

A bit more than a mile from Voza they came to the first of many lean-tos the Japanese had constructed along the coast. They were abandoned lookout posts and coconut log bunkers with nothing but discarded blankets, helmets, and canteens. To both Hall and Red, just seeing the enemy positions was sobering even though the little camps looked like they had been abandoned for at least twenty-four hours. The fire pits held nothing but powdery ash.

Lieutenant Averill's Patrol

Gallagher and ten other Marines were moving northwest from the Barego-songa River toward Kuluni. The squad was stretched just inside the jungle moving parallel to the shoreline. Pfc. Jack Sapp was at point and Gallagher was walking between Pfc. Guy Brookshire, a Texan who was one of the best poker players in the Marine Corps, and Cpl. James Blasingame, a former parachute instructor at Camp Gillespie. The rest of the squad followed them. They had been told to pick up a guide southeast of Kuluni and were surprised to find the native right where Sub-Lt. Carden Seton said he would be. The guide greeted them in accented English and, with a motion for them to follow, led them to the northwest over some of the roughest terrain Gallagher had ever seen. The jungle was almost impenetrable, and the Marines had to hack their way through dense underbrush with machetes and bayonets. Climbing over and crawling under tree roots, using their blades to slice through kunai grass (also called sword grass), reeds, vines, and branches, they struggled through the thick vegetation. It was a stressful environment: they could be walking within five feet of a Japanese machine-gun nest and not even know it until fired on. The main reason they were making this patrol was to check the feasibility of infantry movement through this area. It was obvious that there was no way a company, or even a platoon, could move quickly through this jungle. If it did not let up soon, Gallagher knew they had a very long day ahead of them. Unbearably hot, most of them had drained half their canteens and there had been no fresh water in the area they were scouting.

Colonel Krulak's Patrol

Krulak's patrol reached the Vagara River and fanned out in the jungle to observe the river mouth and surrounding area. There were no visible enemy troops, so they took in the terrain features.

Directly across the river was Vagara, a small village almost identical to Voza. It appeared to be deserted. Behind the village was thick jungle and a small mountain about a thousand yards away. The entire river area was surrounded by dense jungle. The river mouth appeared to be wide and deep; the Marines would need LCPRs if they were to cross here. With no enemy troops in sight, the patrol followed the Vagara River inland to search for headwaters where they might be able to ford. They were only two miles from the enemy outpost at Sangigai and the Japanese would be foolish not to have lookouts posted along the river. When the paratroopers finally reached the headwaters, they sent a small party across first to draw fire. It was better to risk a few men than the entire patrol to any Japanese guards along the river. Once the point men were across and Krulak was convinced the lead element had forded the river unseen, the rest of the patrol followed. A fortunate topographic feature near the headwaters was another small, steep mountain that shielded them from Vagara Village and distant Sangigai.

Having crossed the river, the men were still at least three miles from Sangigai. Sergeant Mullins approached Major Smoak. The patrol was strung out, single file, and Private Gesch was standing next to Major Smoak when Sergeant Mullins walked up, stopped, and pointed back over his shoulder. "I think we should go that way, major," said Mullins, indicating the overland route toward Sangigai.

"You don't know what in the hell you're talking about," snorted Smoak. "My ass is pointing up into the mountains; we don't want to go that way."

Just then, the Brute walked up. Pointing directly east over the mountains, exactly where Mullins had just indicated, Krulak told Smoak to send men inland to reconnoiter the terrain for the next day's attack. Major Smoak did not say a word.

Krulak divided his small patrol, sending Mullins with three Marines and four natives inland to the southeast. He told them to travel through the jungle and come up from behind the village. They were to note terrain features and difficulty of movement. Once behind Sangigai they would make panoramic sketches of the area that would be instrumental in planning for the next day's attack. Red would be one of the Marines accompanying Sergeant Mullins's patrol but he was present as a rifleman, not an artist.

Meanwhile, Krulak and the others would continue back down the river to Vagara Village where they would follow the coastal trail toward Sangigai and scout the area E Company would take.

Private Hall stayed with Colonel Krulak's patrol. As they moved down the trail, he could not help but admire the tough colonel. Hall was one of the original members of the battalion back in the good old days of Maj. Richard W. Hayward in 1942 and early 1943, when discipline was more relaxed. Krulak came in and made his presence known. The veterans knew immediately that the good times were gone forever. Krulak had earned their respect, not demanded it. Hall remembered watching the little Marine out of the corner of his eye in their first formation. He had to admit that Krulak was the sharpest looking officer he had ever seen. Krulak stopped in front of the man next to Hall, Sgt. Lloyd Swan, and went over him with a fine-tooth comb. He spent a few minutes eyeing Swan's shoes, his own, Swan's, and his own again. Finally, the colonel stepped back and said, "Give this man a forty-eight hour pass. His shoes are shinier than mine."

Krulak had led by example then and he was still doing so on Choiseul as a lieutenant colonel leading the fifteen-man patrol. Hall knew the Brute did things like this because it was important for him to reconnoiter the terrain before he would lead his men into battle.

0800—Voza

The Japanese had strafed Zinoa Island the night before, so it was very likely that enemy intelligence had discovered the battalion's hiding place for its boats. Just as the Australian Coastwatchers used Choiseul's natives for intelligence, the Japanese had their own local assistance. Ordered earlier by Colonel Krulak, Lieutenant Johnston of G Company led a patrol consisting of three Marines—Cpl. Max May, Pfc. Richard Stanley, and Pfc. Harrell Sellers—and one local guide to find a suitable river to conceal the battalion's four LCPRs. Johnston's patrol moved northwest along the coast to the

Baregosonga River where a G Company listening post had been set up the day before. They examined the river mouth and found it choked with debris and logs. If they could clear the obstruction, though, the river was deep enough to move the boats upstream to hide them inland. They simply needed to blow a channel to clear the debris. Johnston sent Sellers back to the battalion to report the information to Hq Company and then return with some demolitions people.

Colonel Krulak's Patrol

Krulak's patrol continued toward Sangigai. It was a top-heavy patrol— thirteen Marines under the command of a lieutenant colonel and a major. Having attained the southeast bank of the Vagara River, they moved back down the river to the ocean. Once at the river mouth they turned left where the coastal trail started again and paralleled the beach, moving southeast toward Sangigai just inside the jungle. They had gone about a mile and a half when the lead element suddenly went to ground.

"Enemy in sight," signaled the point man. Everyone immediately dropped. Colonel Krulak crawled up and saw ten Japanese soldiers on the beach seventy yards away, unloading a landing barge. Up to that point, they had been only recon, but it occurred to Krulak that his Marines had not yet announced their presence. Using hand signals, the Brute placed his men in firing positions. Krulak carried a folding stock carbine and he whispered orders to the men on each side of him.

"Pick out individual targets. When I give the signal, kill them all." The order spread down the line. Hall was farther inland. From where he was in the jungle, he could just barely see the enemy troops. The Japanese must have seen movement because they became alert. Seven of them started toward the paratroopers, obviously underestimating the Marine numbers and firepower.

"Fire!" shouted Krulak as he pulled the trigger on his carbine. The paratroopers opened up with automatic rifles, and at fifty yards killed the seven approaching Japanese instantly. The remaining three Japanese near the barge fled into the jungle without returning fire.

Krulak was certain they had surprised the enemy squad and were not walking into an ambush, and he ordered one of the demolitions men to destroy the barge. Still wary of possible snipers in the trees, they deployed in the jungle while a man with Composition-2 moved over to blow up the landing craft. Krulak ordered his patrol to return to Voza, having left a burning hulk on the beach. First contact with the Japanese had been made and the attack was sure to be announced.

Sergeant Mullins's Patrol

Private "Red" McClure, Sergeant Mullins, two other Marines, and four guides moved through the jungle by the inland route to reach Sangigai the hard way. They climbed and descended countless hills, waded through stream after stream, and chopped their way through some of the densest rain forest in the world. The grueling work took all morning, but they finally reached the area just outside the village. Red was surprised to find it deserted. He had heard that Sangigai was an enemy barge station and expected to see Japanese troops. Not only were there no Japanese, there were not even any natives. "Who will we attack tomorrow?" he thought.

Red was told to take up an ambush position for the afternoon. Sitting idly, watching the little village of Sangigai with its beautiful coconut trees swaying in the breeze, it was difficult to keep focused. Red knew he was in enemy territory, but it was so relaxing and peaceful, it was hard to believe he was in a war. The others were making panoramic sketches of the village and surrounding hills to help in planning the next day's attack.

1400—Lieutenant Averill's Patrol

Averill's patrol had been moving steadily through the jungle all morning and into the afternoon. It was 90 degrees, and the humidity was almost 100 percent. Around 1400 Obrocta began to show signs of heat exhaustion. At first, he had been burning up and sweating profusely, and he began to fall behind. Not long after that, he collapsed along the side of the trail. When they checked him, he had gone from hot and sweaty to cold, clammy, and dehydrated. They gave Obrocta about ten minutes of rest before trying to coax him up again, but he could not continue. If he did not cool off soon, he could die.

This created a dilemma. The patrol had not completed its mission, so they could not go back. They could not take him with them, but they hated leaving him behind. Finally, Lieutenant Averill made a decision: They would leave Obrocta hidden along the trail and return for him after they finished the mission. Averill ordered Pfc. Charles Chergo to take point and the patrol continued.

Gallagher, Obrocta's best friend, loathed the idea of leaving his buddy behind. He tried to coax Obrocta into getting up, but to no avail. He could not stand and had difficulty just responding. Finally, Gallagher gave up.

"Stay off the trail and stay out of sight," he warned his buddy.

Gallagher moved after the others and, taking one last look back at Obrocta, he rounded the bend in the trail, wondering if he would ever see his friend again.

Lieutenant Johnston's Patrol

Private Sellers had returned to the battalion hideout to get some demolitions men who would blow a channel in the Baregosonga. Sellers returned by boat and came ashore with the demolitions squad. They brought all four boats. Lieutenant Johnston and the others were waiting as they came in. The Bn-2 men sized up what looked like a beaver dam and moved in to clear the river. Fastening a liberal amount of explosives to the timbers, they strung a wire back to the shore and detonated them. A huge geyser of water shot up, and timber and debris flew into the air. When the smoke cleared, the mouth of the river was open. The swift current swept the debris out into the ocean. Johnston signaled the boats in and they moved about fifty yards up the mouth where the Marines hid them under huge mangrove and banyan trees. They used branches to camouflage them so they would be invisible from the air. When they had finished, they headed back to the mountain bivouac, leaving the G Company squad sitting at the battalion listening post and the four LCPRs hidden upstream on the Baregosonga River.

Battalion CP

Colonel Krulak had just returned to the battalion camp and was going over maps for the next day's attack when two of his Marines approached him and said, "Sir, can we talk to you?"

"Sure, what's on your mind?" Krulak replied, noting that they seemed nervous.

"We're going into combat tomorrow," said one of the young men, "but we don't have a Catholic priest. Without telling anybody, would you give us a little mass?"

"You're asking me to supplant a priest?" asked Krulak a little surprised. "To try to substitute for him as best I can?"

"Well, yes, anything you can do, you know, to make us feel better."

"Sure I'll do it. When do you want to do this? Now?"

"Okay," they agreed, much relieved.

They went back and got several of the Catholic men together and snuck up toward the back of the jungle camp. The Brute was already there.

He began talking to them about their place in the world and their part in this global conflict. "You should be proud of yourselves," he finished up, "but remember, you have an obligation to God and your fellow Marines. I want you all to know how proud of you I am." They all said the Lord's Prayer and the makeshift mass ended. As his men returned to their bivouacs, Krulak wondered if it had done them any good. Not one of those kids ever mentioned it to him again, one way or another. But the one thing he could not stop smiling about was what they had said: "Don't tell anybody."

Sergeant Mullins's Patrol

Red had been sitting quietly by himself watching the little village for over an hour when Sergeant Mullins came back and told him to gear up again. They had their sketches and were moving back to the mountain hideout. Traveling back the way they had come earlier, Sergeant Mullins and seven other men hacked their way back through the jungle. It had been exhausting work the first time, and during this second pass, with all of them spent, it was twice as hard. They knew they had a long way to go and it was hot. When they reached the headwaters of the Vagara River, Red knew they were still a good seven miles from Voza Village. In all his Marine Corps experience, Red had never felt he had been physically tested—not even in chute school where they ran fifteen miles a day or more—until today. Right then, on that muddy tract of jungle, hot and dehydrated, Red's legs began to cramp up. The pain was worse than anything he had ever felt, and he struggled to keep up. He was in absolute misery. "This happens to the other guys," Red told himself, "but not to me."

He was sweating profusely, and knew he needed to stay hydrated. He dropped Halizone tablets in his canteen and refilled it at every stream they came across. Red would never give up in front of the others; nobody would know he was hurting and wanted to stop, although he was and he did. Struggling on through the worst two hours of his young life, Red finally reached the battalion hideout at Voza along with the others. Barely able to walk another step, Red filled his canteen in the camp stream and collapsed into his hammock.

Mountain Camp

Colonel Krulak held an officers' briefing in his command post to issue an order of attack for the next day's raid on Sangigai. They knew from the information the Coastwatchers provided that at least three hundred Japanese were in the Sangigai vicinity at any given time. Recently, enemy activity had increased as the Japanese relentlessly hunted the Coastwatchers. They wanted desperately to kill the Australians and their native Allies.

Krulak told his officers that the battalion would attack Sangigai the next day at 1400. Their goal was to destroy the enemy garrison and capture as much information as possible before withdrawing to Voza. The order of attack for each company was as follows:

E Company, with one section of machine guns from regimental weapons, two rocket teams from the experimental rocket platoon, and twenty native supply carriers, would also move down to the Vagara River by LCPR. From there they would move on Sangigai thirty minutes after F Company passed their left flank, hitting Sangigai from the northwest and driving the enemy into the waiting F Company ambush. E Company's mission was to destroy the Japanese garrison. They would raze all installations and equipment while assisting in the annihilation of the Japanese forces. Krulak would lead the F Company force while Smoak would lead the E Company force. The TBX radio teams would remain in constant contact with each other and the base during their periodic halts. After the attack was completed, both companies would rally at Vagara Village for withdrawal to Voza.

F Company, with one section of machine guns from regimental weapons, two rocket teams, one additional TBX transmitter, and twenty native supply carriers, would move down to Vagara Village by LCPR and take the overland route to the northeast, flanking the enemy barge station by traveling well inland through the jungle. Once they were north of Sangigai, they would turn to the south and set up ambush positions on the ridge northeast of Sangigai. When they heard E Company's attack, they would ambush from their positions on the ridge, preventing a Japanese withdrawal into the safety of the mountains. F Company would retreat on order from Colonel Krulak.

G Company would stay behind at Voza to guard the battalion camp.

"Remember," repeated Krulak, "do not get drawn into a battle. We hit hard and then we run. After we ambush them, get away clean." The officers concluded their briefing on the Sangigai raid. Shortly thereafter, Colonel Krulak decided to send a squad of Marines down to the Vagara River. The squad would help guide the boats in for the next day's raid while serving as a lookout post along the river. It was more than five miles to the Vagara River and the patrol needed to travel quickly to make it before dusk. To do that they would need to send men who had been there before.

1730—F Company Bivouac

"Gear up, gyrenes," said Sgt. Norman Law to his squad, including an exhausted Red and Hall. "We're moving down to the Vagara."

"What!" exclaimed Hall in disbelief. "We just came from there."

"Then it's your fault," said Law. "Get ready, 'cause you're going back. You've been there and the others haven't."

Red was exhausted from the hike he had made earlier that day and dreaded going back, but he swung out of his hammock while Law briefed the nine other men in their squad.

"We're moving down to the Vagara before dark to set up a lookout post on the northwest riverbank. We're going to stay the night there to guide the landing boats in for tomorrow's assault on Sangigai. Only our squad is moving down tonight, so before we leave, load up with ammo."

At 1730, Law's squad moved out of the battalion bivouac. As they passed through the E Company perimeter, Pfc. Paul Chelf of Alva, Oklahoma, saw his buddy "Ski" (his Polish surname was too hard to pronounce, let alone spell), who was in Law's squad.

"Where are you guys going?" Chelf asked.

"To babysit a river," replied Ski. "The Vagara. See ya tomorrow."

Chelf noticed they were in a hurry because they did not have much daylight.

The patrol reached Voza and turned left on the coastal trail. Cpl. Benjamin F. "Cape" Caperton III was at point. Cape was following the two native guides that had been assigned to lead them down to Vagara Village, even though a few of them had already been there earlier that day. Cape was one of the ones who had not and he was at point. It did not make much sense to him but that was military logic. It was probably because he was the only veteran in the squad. Cape had been a replacement on Guadalcanal and had even been fired on by the Japanese across the Tenaru. He never fired back but a concealed A-4 tore the Japanese machine gun to shreds. That had been the sum total of his combat experience before he was evacuated to Australia with malaria, but it was more than the rest of the squad had.

Cape was five feet eight inches tall, 130 pounds. His name smacked of aristocracy, but that was as far as it went. Cape was from Waco, Texas, with an outrageous accent to prove it. He was Sergeant Law's assistant squad leader.

They moved off down the path until they reached the battalion flank outpost to the southeast. It was five miles to the village of Vagara. Law's squad was making good progress although they had been gone for only fifteen minutes. They were just off the ocean, not even a mile from Voza, when the guides leading them came flying back down the trail, their eyes wide in fear. Cape saw them running right at him. "What the hell?"

"Jap, Jap," hissed one of the natives as he ran past.

It took a second to sink in. "A Jap?" Cape dove to the side of the trail, and the others scattered behind him. Private Caperton scrambled for cover behind the root of a banyan tree and quickly aimed his .03 rifle down the trail, waiting for a target to appear. His .03 had an antitank (AT) grenade launcher attached but, typically, the government had neglected to give him an AT grenade to launch. Cape did not know where the rest of the squad was, but Pfc. Bobby Atkins was just off to his side.

Across the trail, Red melted in behind the roots of another big banyan near his JLMG man, Ed "Prebe" Pryzbyszeski. Both Marines scanned the overgrowth around the jungle trail for targets. While they waited, Red noticed that the jungle had become strangely quiet.

The Marines waited and waited but nothing happened. They were sweating profusely in the humid, hot jungle. They had just started to relax, figuring it was a false alarm, when a Japanese soldier rounded the bend in the trail ahead of them.

Mountain Camp

Private Chelf was lying peacefully in his hammock when he heard rifle fire in the distance. Chelf bolted upright. He knew Sergeant Law had just taken a patrol out. The shots sounded close, maybe half a mile to the southeast. Looking around at the nearby hammocks, he could tell the others heard it, too. Every man was alert. As Chelf listened, the firing became more furious. It sounded like fifteen or twenty rifles and machine guns blasting away at once. It was turning into a massive firefight. Chelf and the men in his platoon lay, sat, or stood listening, waiting for orders.

Sergeant Law's Patrol

Sergeant Law's squad was spread out on both sides of the coastal trail when a Japanese Imperial Marine walked right toward them. He appeared to be completely unaware that he was in mortal danger. Cape sighted in on him and was shocked by the sheer size of this man. He had always heard how short the Japanese were, but this guy was at least six feet tall, and stocky, too. Cape resisted the urge to fire and watched as three more enemy soldiers walked into their firing lane. The others were as tall and as broad as the first.

The squad's plan as they had practiced ambush tactics on New Caledonia, Guadalcanal, and Vella LaVella had been to let as many enemy soldiers move into the killing lane as possible before firing. Someone in their squad either had not been paying attention during their training problems or had gotten nervous; he opened fire after the fourth man came into sight. The noise was deafening. Ten rifles and automatic rifles blasted at once.

Cape had been aiming at the first man. He figured everyone else had, too, because the soldier was hurled backward with half a dozen gunshot wounds across his chest. Right next to Cape, Atkins let go with his JLMG. Everyone else was firing, too, and it looked to Cape as if all four Japanese died right there on the trail. With no visible human targets, the Marines switched to firing low behind the bend in the trail. Cape was working his bolt action furiously and going through so many of his rounds that he considered changing to the Johnson rifle.

Red was firing his M-1 Garand, about ten yards away from Cape. For the first time in his Marine Corps experience, Red heard the report of foreign weapons. There were two distinct noises: the strange new sounds of a machine gun with a very fast cycle rate, punctuated by the loud cracking report of .25-caliber rifle fire. Red heard the "snap" of bullets flying past him and fired at muzzle flashes in the jungle ahead. Beside him, Ski was spreading three-shot bursts with his Browning automatic rifle (BAR). Both Red and Ski were unlike most every other man in the battalion because they did not carry Johnson weapons.

Law's squad threw out a lot of lead and Cape was aware he had gone through one-fourth of his ammo already. It sounded like the others were doing the same. The firing blasted back and forth for ten minutes; then, almost as if they had practiced it, both sides suddenly stopped firing at once.

"Everybody all right?" asked Sergeant Law.

"Yeah," whispered Cape in his thick Texas drawl.

"Yeah," hissed Atkins from close by.

The others sounded off and not a man had been hit. "Get ready. They might *banzai*," warned Law.[3] They had killed four Japanese and hoped they had hit a few more, but nobody was going to go down that trail to find out—yet. Cape wondered if there had been only four Japanese to begin with. He never saw any return fire, and the four men on the trail died without returning a shot. Cape figured they had done all the shooting and everyone just got bang happy, himself included, but when he looked down he saw three bullet holes in the banyan root below his neck. "Goddang," he muttered. Atkins looked over. "Some son of a gun had me lined up," whispered Cape. That was when Cape learned the invaluable lesson about the difference between concealment and cover. He never forgot.

They waited. No one dared move. Sergeant Law was trying to decide what to do. Should they stay right there or should they go back to let the battalion know they had made contact? After about fifteen minutes, Law decided to do both. He would return the short distance to inform the colonel and get orders while it was still light. He ordered Cape to take over the squad and not move until he got back. Their guides had long since disappeared, so Law picked two men to accompany him and went back down the trail toward Voza.

The remaining Marines—Cape, Red, Ski, Hall, Atkins, Pfc. Carl J. Kuehne, and Pfc. Stanley Keller—crawled into a semicircular perimeter facing southeast along the trail, with the ocean off on their right flank, and waited. Everyone knew they had very little daylight left, maybe half an hour. One of them whispered to the others, "Should we go out and check 'em while there's still light?"

"Not unless you want to get shot," whispered Cape back at him. He worried about enemy snipers and possible tricks. "They might be playing dead."

"Then let's just shoot 'em again. Just to be sure."

"Hell, no," said Cape. "If they're already dead there's no use shooting them again. Now keep quiet." Red was quiet by nature. Because he did not want to draw any fire, he never said a word. Neither did Hall.

Lieutenant Averill's Patrol

Miles away from any friendly forces, Lieutenant Averill's patrol, less Obrocta, continued through the jungle in the northwest direction. Past Kuku, but still not quite to Moli, they saw a Japanese landing barge moving to the northwest. Averill's patrol continued through the dense underbrush and suddenly came on what seemed to be an abandoned enemy supply or ammunition dump. It was obvious there was no accessible route through the almost impenetrable jungle, so the only way the enemy could have used this area as a supply depot was by barge.

Just ahead, a few thousand yards off Choiseul's coast, they could see an island with a rocky red cliff—Moli Island. That meant they were getting close, because Moli Island was directly across from Moli Point. They had reached their destination without seeing any enemy ground troops, but dusk was approaching. Although this was supposed to have been a one-day operation, there was no way they could make it back to Voza that night. They wanted to return as far as they could, however, so they turned around and backtracked, hoping to make Kuku before dark. Turning from the setting sun, the patrol retraced its steps to the southeast.

Hewing their way back along the rugged jungle track, Averill's overdue patrol barely reached Kuku before dark. At roughly 1800, as the sun set over the Pacific, they stopped and made a perimeter about forty yards off the ocean, just above a little cove. The Japanese owned the night and there was no way their squad was going to chance moving into it. They had not even dug in yet when the blanket of darkness fell. It was as if someone simply flipped a light switch. The Marines dug their holes blind. Afterward, Lieutenant Averill gave them some last-minute instructions.

"I don't want any talking or shooting unless I do it first, okay?" he whispered. "Go ahead and eat." The famished Marines pulled out their D-bars, ate their meager dinner, and settled in for the night. From where they set up, Gallagher could see the breakers through the trees. In the jungle, the canopy of leaves and branches overhead shut out the light around them, but out on the ocean they could see. Watching the waves had a soothing effect on the weary Marines, and the sound of the surf drowned out many jungle noises. That was relaxing because the jungle was eerie at night. Birds screeched incessantly, and they could hear constant scraping movements, which were probably land crabs. Even with the sound of the lulling surf, they could not get too comfortable. Mosquitoes swarmed, and they slapped at their exposed skin. Because most of the Marines wore their dungarees and shirts cut into shorts and vests due to the heat, the mosquitoes had a field day. Still, aside from the two men on first guard, the exhausted patrol tried to sleep.

As Gallagher closed his eyes he thought about Obrocta, all by himself somewhere along the side of that trail. Gallagher hoped Obrocta would remain hidden and stay off the trail. His main worry was that his buddy would wander in his dehydrated state to search for water. If he did, a Japanese patrol could easily grab him.

1830—Mountain Camp

Private Chelf and the men around him anxiously listened for further sounds of the firefight. None of them had seen combat yet, but they all knew their time was drawing near. The shots had died down more than a half hour earlier. They wondered what had happened. Chelf and the others were concerned, but the officers did not appear alarmed. Nobody had been assembled to rush down to defend the beach, so it could not be anything too bad. Chelf was resting in his hammock when Sergeant Law and two other men from his squad came double-timing back into camp. "Holy shit! Where are the others?" Ten men had left but only three were running back into camp. Chelf's buddy Ski was not one of them. More than one man sat up quickly with his rifle thinking Law's squad had been ambushed and wiped out.

It was 1830 when Sergeant Law arrived at the colonel's CP. He informed the Brute of the ambush and requested orders. Krulak knew there was nothing they could do just then. Dusk was falling and within minutes it would be too dark to send anyone down to reinforce the seven men along the trail. Nobody but the Japanese moved at night. Any Marines moving in the dark might be targets of "friendly fire" before they could even reach the patrol. There were no options. The relief effort to Law's squad would have to begin the following morning. Cape and the others would be on their own for the night, and would be a seven-man listening post farther out from the battalion's southeast flank.

1845—Mountain Camp

Pfc. Donald "Hink" Hinkle, one of Capt. Robert R. "Chesty" Manchester's company scouts, listened as Chesty and Colonel Krulak conferred under a tent. It had started raining for the millionth time. Hink did not ask questions; he just waited for the order that would send them down to Voza. Because of the enemy contact with Law's patrol, Krulak had decided to send E Company down to Voza that night instead of the following morning. Major Smoak, the battalion BN-2 officer, was in overall command of the E Company force that consisted of a machine-gun section from regimental weapons, two teams from the experimental rocket platoon, and Captain Manchester's E Company. They were moving down to the beach to secure it from possible enemy action to the southeast. E Company assembled in the darkness, in the pouring rain.

Private Chelf figured the earlier firefight was the reason they were moving down to the beach. Was that battle with the vanguard of an approaching enemy force? It made sense. Why else would they suddenly have to gear up to move down to Voza in the dark? They were probably moving down to protect the battalion's southeast flank, but there were two regiments of Japanese already on the island and one was at Sangigai. If even one of those regiments' battalions attacked, E Company would have to hold the battalion flank alone.

Iowan Pfc. Rudolph Engstrom was an E Company machine gunner. He carried the heavy A-4 propped on his shoulder. Because he was a machine gunner, Engstom usually walked in the middle of the column. Automatic weapons were too important to risk up front or at the rear where the danger of ambush is highest. Every Marine knew that the most dangerous place in the column was the rear because Japanese snipers or ambush parties often let troops pass before hitting the last men.

Pfc. Robert Brutinel and Pfc. Don Carpenter of Centerville, Tennessee, were two other E Company paratroopers assembling in the darkness for the move down to Voza. Just like the night before, they could not see a thing and stayed in formation by holding onto the man in front of them, connecting the entire company in a long single file. Officers and NCOs went up and down their formation, warning men not to get jumpy.

Brutinel and Carpenter trudged blindly down the mountain path toward the beach. They knew that when they got there they would have to dig another foxhole. It seemed they were always digging holes. On Vella LaVella a few weeks before, after the Japanese had bombed the airfield, Brutinel had turned to Carpenter and said, "You know, one of these days Charlie might come up here. Maybe we should dig a better hole." Carpenter agreed, and the next two days they worked feverishly to dig a deep bunker. They covered it with coconut logs, a foot of earth, and a piece of corrugated sheet metal. For the first time, they slept, confident that only a direct hit could harm them. It was so hot, however, they did not want to sleep in the steamy bunker. Instead, they slept under mosquito netting in their open tent. If the enemy came near, they would hear him and simply run to the bunker.

But they had forgotten they were both deep sleepers because later that night Brutinel was jolted awake by the blast of an explosion detonating nearby. "Don," Brutinel shouted, leaping up. "Let's get the hell outta here!" They both raced out of their tent and ran for their bunker, but when they got there they could not get in. It was already too full. Their buddies were piled inside it. "Get outta my bunker, you sons-a-bitches!" roared Brutinel. A bunch of sweating, scared faces looked up but nobody moved. Bumping into each other like Abbot and Costello, Brutinel and Carpenter ran back to their original foxhole. They would laugh about it later, but during that bombing they were furious.

East of Voza

Seven Marines under the command of assistant squad leader Corporal Caperton were waiting for Sergeant Law to return or for the enemy to come back down the trail at them, whichever came first. They had been keyed up for more than thirty minutes waiting for something—anything—to happen, but nothing had.

Private Hall was on the left side of the trail toward the front. He heard faint whispering in a language he knew could only be Japanese. The sound of movement made his finger tense on the trigger of his Johnson rifle, but the noise faded, and disappeared. Hall assumed the Japanese had just retreated but he was not going to call out to the others and give away his position. Just because he had heard retreating movement did not mean there were not Japanese still ahead. Another half hour passed. Everyone was afraid to speak for fear of drawing sniper fire, but after a while, someone must have been more bored than frightened because he broke the silence.

"I'll claim that first guy. Which one do you want to claim?" To the others in the squad accustomed to the silence of the jungle, his voice sounded like a grenade blast. Cape heard the whisper from across the trail and wanted to tell the wise ass to shut up. Instead, he waited for a Japanese rifle to do it.

"What're you talking about?" whispered someone else. "I got all four of 'em." There was more silence. Cape thought about stepping in to tell both men to shut up.

"You're both wrong," he said instead. "We all shot that first guy. The other three died of heart attacks." The jungle exploded with laughter. It might have been exceedingly dangerous, but they did not draw any fire, and the tension was eased dramatically. Cape sat in the darkness and listened to the jungle. The insects and birds had started to make noises again, and that was a good sign. The men were exhausted and in dire need of rest, although most of them were too excited from their first firefight to sleep. After a while, though, with the quiet boredom of sitting silently in the dark, some of them began to succumb to exhaustion and took Benzedrine tablets to stay alert.

Hall fished in his pocket for a vial of medicinal brandy to help keep him awake. When he pulled it out, though, he accidentally bumped it against his cartridge belt and the vial dropped to the jungle floor. He reached down and pawed through the thick brush at his feet. They had all been warned about poisonous spiders and snakes, but Hall was more concerned about finding the brandy. Hall searched and searched, but try as he might, he never found his brandy.

Enraged, he silently cursed the Japanese, blaming them for everything bad in the world. He fought the urge to shout obscenities toward the enemy position. Sitting alone in the dark, furious with himself for dropping his alcohol, he fished out a D-bar. He was ravenously hungry. As he ate, he remembered a funny incident on New Caledonia. When they first received their new Ka-Bars (knives) he had told Private Keller about them. "They've got those new Ka-Bars in. Why don't you go get yours?"

"I don't like them bars," Keller had replied in his slow, country drawl. "K-bars, D-bars. They all taste awful." Keller was quite a character.

Down the line along the trail from both Hall and Cape, Red sat against a banyan root. It was so dark Red could barely see the phosphorescent watch on his wrist. He knew Kuehne was beside him in the darkness, but he had no idea where the others were.

Then, as happened so often in the Central Solomons, it started to rain. Red began to shiver with cold as he sat in the jungle behind his tree root. The temperature during the day was around 100 degrees, with humidity almost that high. At night, however, the temperature could drop as much as 30 degrees. To anyone inactive, in wet clothing, 70 degrees was freezing. The only thing good about the cold was that it kept Red awake. Unlike the others, he did not take any Benzedrine or drink brandy and just forced himself to stay alert. When the rain let up, the mosquitoes came out in force. The rain came and went all night long. Every time Red's natural body heat warmed him up, it would start to rain again and his shivering would start all over.

Zinoa Island

Just as the Marines and Australians were using Choiseulian natives for their own intelligence, the Japanese were probably doing the same, because Zinoa Island had been strafed the night before. In an effort to stay ahead of enemy intelligence, the LCPRs had been moved yet again from the Baregosonga River, where they had spent the day, back to Zinoa for the night. Lt. Douglas Morton was the ranking officer on the little island and he was in charge of the security detachment. It was another uneventful evening right up until an excited sentry told Morton that an enemy submarine had surfaced two hundred yards offshore.

All the men in their little area crawled over to hug the shoreline, peering out at the enemy sub. It made a beautiful target, but they were under orders not to engage the enemy unless attacked first. It was obvious that the sub had no idea that a platoon of U.S. Marines was on an island two hundred yards away. It was too good to be true. Lieutenant Morton told his TBX operator to call Colonel Krulak immediately and request instructions. "Attempt a rocket attack," said the Brute, as if it were simply a training exercise. "Sink it." Told to raise hell, that was just what the paratroopers would do. The sub attack would just be a prelude to the next day's Sangigai raid.

They had recently been given a new antitank weapon called the bazooka, and Morton told his men to set it up along the beach. Two hundred yards was a long shot for the new weapon. Even one hundred yards was far, but the sub was a big target. They sighted in and, on Lieutenant Morton's command, fired their first round. The rocket sailed out over the surf and just missed the enemy sub, exploding harmlessly in the ocean beyond.

The Japanese responded instantly. The sub went into a dive as the Marines fired a second time. The next round flew straight out and this time the gunner did not miss. The rocket hit the conning tower and exploded against the enemy sub. The tower lit in a quick flash and disappeared in a cloud of smoke. The Marines on shore watched eagerly until the sub moved through the smoke and continued its dive. It quickly disappeared underwater before the paratroopers could fire a third rocket. Strangely, it looked as if the sub had suffered no damage.

Lieutenant Morton was disappointed, and radioed back to Colonel Krulak about the failed attack. The colonel was also disappointed. Although they had not sunk the enemy submarine, Krulak knew that a report would soon be made to the Japanese high command of an American attack from Choiseul. Anything to help the ruse work, even the failed attempt, could have a positive effect. It could mean hundreds of Marine casualties saved on Bougainville.

1930—Mountain Camp

Pfc. George Shively, in Hq Company communications under Captain Bryant, was roused from boredom by Sgt. Harry Walter at 1930 and told to get his equipment together. There was a break in communications with one of the listening posts. Shively would have to find it and fix it. He did not relish his task, but went over to where they cached their supplies. Taking out a length of wire, tape, wire cutters, a tent-half, the portable phone, and the most important item—a Zippo lighter—he followed a phosphorescent vine out of camp and past the perimeter outposts. The most dangerous part of his trip was definitely moving out of and back into the battalion perimeter. Shively worried some bang-happy trooper would take him for a Japanese soldier and start shooting at the sound of his movement.

1950—Lieutenant Averill's Patrol

Miles to the northwest, near Kuku, Lieutenant Averill's squad sat in their semicircular perimeter about fifty yards off the shore. It had not been dark long when, at 1950, they heard the unmistakable sound of a boat engine. Gallagher hoped it was a Higgins boat. It was still early in the night and the LCPRs might be looking for their lost patrol. They were supposed to have made it back to the battalion already. They listened as the boat got closer, but the engines did not sound like those of a Higgins boat. A long, low, concave silhouette appeared through the trees, and the Marines realized it was a Japanese Daihatsu barge. The shadowy silhouette of at least a platoon of Japanese troops was visible on board the moving craft. The boat was heading up the coast but suddenly turned into the cove. Gallagher's finger tensed on the trigger of his Johnson rifle. All the men in Averill's patrol readied their weapons and loosened pins on hand grenades. The barge was barely fifty yards from where they were deployed. It was pitch black in the jungle, and as the enemy craft entered the cove it became more difficult to see. Lieutenant Averill had to make a decision. If the enemy troops came ashore and moved up onto their perimeter, the Marines were going to be in close-quarter combat. Although at first they would have the advantage of surprise, they were outnumbered four to one, and the enemy barge had heavy machine guns.

"We've got to ambush them before they get out of the barge," thought Gallagher. He wondered nervously what Averill was thinking. Their orders were no shooting and no talking unless the lieutenant did either first. Gallagher knew they had three JLMGs and could put a lot of automatic weapons fire into the close confines of that boat. They could also lob in a lot of grenades. If they could get a grenade or two in that boat, they would have a good chance of killing all of them. If their grenades went into the water, though, or if those antiaircraft machine guns on the barge opened up, the game would be over. No amount of cover could protect them long from those heavy machine guns. Under their suppressing fire, the Japanese could hit the beach and spread out in the darkness and the paratroopers would be overrun.

In the darkness of the cove, the barge disappeared from sight and the anxious Marines prepared their grenades, but just then, inexplicably, the barge turned around and headed back out to sea, the drone of its engines slowly fading away. The paratroopers breathed a sigh of relief at their narrow escape right up to the moment when another barge arrived, less than an hour later. Four more barges full of troops followed. The enemy barge traffic seemed to go on all night. Each barge entered the cove, turned around, and left heading northwest up the coast.

As Gallagher listened to the fading sound of the latest enemy barge, he thought he heard voices. They were not speaking English. "My mind's playing tricks on me," he thought, but he continued to hear voices. They were so faint he was not convinced they were anything but the wind, but it prevented him from relaxing and he could not drift off to sleep. "Why did the barges come in and then turn around to leave?" he wondered. "Was there already a barge in the cove? Maybe that was why the other boats always left. They could not find a spot to land or hide." If that were true, there were enemy soldiers fewer than forty yards from them. All night long Gallagher thought he heard voices talking in Japanese, and not just when the barges entered the cove. There was a difference. When the barges came in he could clearly hear Japanese shouted over the roaring engines—those voices carried in the night. It was when the barges were gone that Gallagher heard whispers. It was eerie.

Voza

E Company arrived at Voza and dug in along the jungle, with most of their firepower covering the approaches from the southeast and the ocean. There was a whispered rumor that the Japanese were planning to move on Voza. Everyone speculated about how they would come—by barge right up Voza Beach, or along the jungle trail where the firefight had occurred a few hours before? Only the officers had any real knowledge of what was going on. Squad leaders set guards and the Marines waited for something to happen or for the sun to rise.

Pvt. Richard Reneau was one of those Easy Company paratroopers wondering what was going on. The officers were not passing along any information, so once again the men dug in and waited. Ever since he had been in the Marine Corps, which was more than three years, it seemed all Reneau did was dig holes and wait for orders. The only good thing was that he had complete trust in his leaders. The Brute was sharp, too sharp, to lead them into something they could not escape.

Reneau thought that Captain Manchester was even better, the best officer he had ever served under. Chesty was extremely intelligent and had gone to law school. He was tough as nails on his men, but he was also fair.

In college, Chesty had been an outstanding wrestler, and in the Marine Corps he took on all comers. Reneau never saw him lose; he pinned everyone. On New Caledonia, the captain had started a boxing and wrestling program for the Second Marine Parachute Battalion and, as an outstanding all-around athlete, he pushed his men into all types of sports.

Reneau was an athlete too, so Chesty asked him to run for E Company at the battalion track meet on New Caledonia. Reneau ran the 100- and the 440-meter races. He was surprised when Chesty also asked him to run the 10-kilometer race. "Sir," protested Reneau, "I'm a sprinter. I can't run distance."

"I know that, Reneau," said Chesty. "When we get on the line and take off, I want you to run like a rabbit. I want you to run as fast as you can for as far as you can."

"Why?" asked Reneau. "I'll conk out even faster that way."

"You're the rabbit," explained Chesty. "You draw them out and make everyone run. When they tire out, I'll pass them all and win the 10K."

Sure enough, the race started and everyone ran to catch Reneau. When they tired, Chesty won.

Reneau had a reputation as a troublemaker, but he wanted a chance to clean it up. That 10K seemed to put Reneau on his captain's good side. He also admired Captain Manchester, and it was important to him that Chesty like him. When it was time to run the 440 relay, Reneau was determined to win. Reneau was again surprised when Chesty came over to him and took him aside.

"Reneau, there's only one guy we need to worry about," he said, pointing to a lean, muscular Marine from F Company. "That guy runs like a cheetah. You're going to need to give it everything to beat that guy."

Reneau was the anchor and there was no way he was going to let his captain down. The race started and Reneau watched his three teammates give him at least a forty-yard head start. When Reneau took the baton, he flew like a gazelle down the track. He was surprised to see Captain Manchester running beside him stride for stride, looking back. "You're doing fine, Reneau," Chesty coached as he ran. They raced about twenty more yards and Chesty added, "You better step it up a little, he's gaining on you." Reneau was already running as fast as he could. They ran another twenty yards and Chesty calmly said, "Pick it up a little more. He's coming." Then Chesty's voice rose in panic and he yelled, "Run like hell, Rich!" The F Company kid passed Reneau like he was standing still and won the race. Reneau's attempt to stay on Chesty's good side ended right then and there.

Reneau was sitting in the mud under his poncho in the pouring rain waiting for orders in the pitch-black jungle night. "How the hell did I get here?" he asked himself, knowing the answer. "Like every raggedy-assed gyrene, I volunteered."

Reneau was a six-foot, 185-pound blond, blue-eyed Marine. His father was French, his mother Norwegian. He had lived a hard life, so it was not the bugs or the mud or the small quantity and poor quality of the food that he disliked—it was the monotony. That was why he had already made four separate trips to the brig and was a private after three years in the Marine Corps. Every man that joined the Marine paratroops was instantly made a private first class, so Reneau had really been underachieving to get demoted to private. He was frequently bored, and craved action. That was why he came to Choiseul in the first place instead of going to sick bay on Vella LaVella because of his jaundice.

Reneau's mother had died when he was a young boy in Nebraska, and Reneau and his father hit the road as migrant workers during the Great Depression. Jobs were hard to come by, but there were always apples to pick in Washington, pears in Oregon, grapes in California, cotton, corn, wheat, you name it. They went hungry a few times, but Reneau's dad always kept his sense of humor and he passed that on to his son.

When war broke out in Europe in 1939, Reneau decided to enter the service, but he was just seventeen and needed his father's signature. Expecting a flat-out "No," Reneau surprisingly heard his father sigh and quietly say, "Yes, there's going to be a war. I'd like to see you get all the training you can." Reneau's dad had fought in World War I and had seen the horrible reality of combat. Since he could not spare his son the violence of war, he hoped early and thorough training might spare his life.

Close beside Pvt. Reneau, Private Hinkle also sat and waited. At twenty-four Hink was older and wiser than the young teenager, but Hink could not help but like the gutsy Marine. Reneau was a stocky, fearless kid, the type you wanted beside you going into combat. It was often that way with brig rats.

A few months back Hink had stood guard over Reneau when Reneau was thrown in the brig on New Cal for fighting. Every three days a prisoner was entitled to a bath, so Hink marched him out of his small cell down to the Tontua River to clean up. As they walked, Hink could see Reneau was thinking about something. "What would you do if I just took off?" Reneau asked with a sideways glance. Reneau looked like he was going to make a break for it any second. Hink simply worked a bullet into the chamber of his gun. He did not know whether he would shoot the big teenager, but he knew if a prisoner got away, the guard had to stand his time in the brig. Reneau just grinned, stripped down, and happily dove in the river for his bath. After a while, he swam out and called back to the beach. "If I just went under and swam away, what'd you be able to do about it?" Hink just patted his .03.

Hink knew Captain Manchester had taken Reneau under his wing to bring the young Marine along, and he also knew the stocky young leatherneck had a lot of potential if they could just channel his energy. Hink thought Reneau was a better Marine than Reneau ever gave himself credit for being. Hink also knew how hard it was to put up with some of the military bureaucracy. Months earlier, in New Caledonia, he had had a run-in himself. Hink was standing guard at the main gate when Major Smoak drove up in a jeep with another officer and a couple of nurses. They were all in their bathing trunks. Hink did not recognize who they were so he did not salute. Major Smoak became angry and reprimanded Hink.

"Why didn't you salute me, private?"

"I'm sorry, sir, I didn't recognize you." Then he saluted the major.

"Yes, you did," said Smoak without returning the salute, and he drove away. Hink thought it had ended there, but later that day Captain Manchester called him in to his office.

"Why didn't you salute Major Smoak?"

"I didn't see him, sir," said Hink.

"It's the uniform you salute," replied Chesty, "not the man."

"He wasn't wearing a uniform, captain," replied Hink. He never heard anything else about it, but he was sure Chesty had kept him out of the brig. Like Krulak, Chesty was fair and looked out for his men.

Pfc. Harold N. "Hal" Block, another E Company Marine, was huddled under a poncho just off Voza Beach. The rain was so intense he could not have been more wet if he were lying in the ocean, which was about ten feet away. Suddenly he noticed something dark in the surf not fifteen feet out. Each wave seemed to push it closer to shore. Block's curiosity got the better of him and he went over to see what it was. It looked like an enormous black bowling ball with multiple prongs protruding from it. "Holy shit, a mine!" he exclaimed.

Block backed away quickly and moved up the beach. He found his platoon sergeant and told him about the mine, but he did not go back over to see who had the job of trying to defuse it.

Jungle Trail

It was not yet midnight, and Private Shively of the Hq Company communications platoon was moving at a painfully slow pace through the jungle, still searching for the broken wire between the listening post at Krulak's CP and Voza. Alone and blinded by the darkness, he was feeling his way through the pitch-black night by following the telephone wire hand over hand. He felt much safer away from the Marine perimeter, and he knew he was less likely to draw friendly fire. He moved along at a snail's pace because he had to walk on all fours or crawl on his knees to feel the wire as he moved. It was taxing, backbreaking work. He moved as cautiously as possible, protecting his eyes so they could not be poked by a stick. Every so often he would stop, put the tent-half completely over himself, and strike his lighter just long enough to connect the phone. Once he had the phone hooked up, he would try to contact both the beach and the colonel's CP. "Come in, beach," he whispered into the phone. "This is George."

The men never worried about talking in formalities or code because the phones were sound powered and could not be intercepted. The only way the enemy would be able to hear it was if they had killed the guards at the other end and picked up the phone. "This is Harry," came the bored, tired voice of Sergeant Walters back up at the CP. "I hear you, George."

Shively listened for another response, but he could only reach the CP, so he knew the break was farther down. He could tell by the sound the phone made that there had been a break; the phone made a different noise when it was working. Shively figured an animal had broken the wire, or one of the E Company Marines had accidentally severed it on his way down to Voza.

George moved on another sixty-five feet, feeling the wire as he went. Then he pulled the tent-half over himself to repeat the process.

"Come in, beach. This is George."

"This is Harry. I hear you, George."

Sergeant Walters sounded like he was dying of boredom. Shively listened for another response but there was no answer from the beach. He would have to keep working his way down the mountain.

Chapter 4

BAPTISM OF FIRE: OCTOBER 30 (MORNING)

It was the Johnson Rifle that should have been the weapon of the United States Soldier in the Second World War. There was no better rifle! But lobbyists and politicians had money to make so the Garand won out.

Sgt. Thomas Siefke, G Company

0015—Jungle Trail Near Voza Beach

Well past midnight, Pfc. George Shively was still moving through the jungle blindly following the telephone wire with his hands. It was a torturous task. The jungle teemed with life. Shively could feel insects and anonymous creatures scurrying away from his fingers. Sometimes he got tangled up in giant spiders' webs, and jerked back in fear.[1] The webs were incredibly strong and would completely stop his momentum. He would try to pull away but the webs always clung to him, making him swipe, struggle, and flail at the strands stuck to his face and neck. The spiders were huge, as wide as a man's fist. They scared everyone, but luckily they rarely bit and were not poisonous.

It was nerve-racking work and not just because of the spiders, scorpions, and snakes. Every time he whispered into the phone, Shively worried that he would draw a grenade from a Japanese soldier, or feel a knife blade in the dark. He worked all night, and finally found the break at 0350. For the last time that night, he pulled the poncho over his head, lit his lighter, and found the damaged wire. He removed a length of the damaged wire and connected a new piece. After taping it securely, he tested the phone. "Come in, beach. This is George," he said into the phone.

"This is Harry. I hear you, George," came the exhausted voice from the colonel's command post.

"This is Dan. I hear you, George," answered the hushed voice of Pfc. Daniel Schlesinger from the Voza end of the line.

"Thank God," said Sergeant Walter on the mountain.

The listening post was restored. Private Shively moved back up to the Hq Company area, looking forward eagerly to crawling into his hammock.

73

As he neared the battalion perimeter with its many outposts, however, he knew the most dangerous time of the night was approaching.

0500—Battalion Camp

It was almost dawn and the streaks of light from the east lit the jungle plateau just enough so that the Marines could see silhouettes in the darkness. At 0500 Fox Company assembled for their move down to Voza where they would link up with Easy Company for the assault on Sangigai. As the long single file formed, Pfc. Bynum Jacobsen of Des Moines, Iowa, was standing in the muddy trail beside his buddy PM1 Clay Dunigan of New Orleans, Louisiana.

"Dis what you went into da corps fo, Jake?" asked Dunigan in his outrageous Cajun accent. "Da travel?"

"No," replied Jacobsen, "the money. My recruiter back in Iowa had a strange accent," (punctuating the remark with a look at Dunigan) "and when he said 'Semper Fidelis,' I thought he said 'seventy-five dollars.'" It was an old joke they had all heard a hundred times, but it never failed to bring a laugh.

Jacobsen and Dunigan went way back. Before they had shipped overseas, they had met one morning when Jacobsen was preparing for morning roll. Jacobsen's face was black and blue and covered with blood blisters from a beating he had taken the night before. He had been sneaking back into camp when another guy came up to him out of the darkness to do the same thing. They were both in composite battalions waiting to ship overseas. The guy said he was a Raider. They decided to sneak back in together, but the guy was making so much noise Jacobsen shushed him. The next thing he knew, he had been coldcocked, and the Raider was on top of him, pummeling his face. He woke up alone in the dark with a blistering headache and the taste of blood in his mouth. He snuck back into camp and went to sleep, but soon reveille sounded. Dunigan spotted him as he prepared to go out. Dunigan was their corpsman and he told Jacobsen he better not go out looking like that. Using a needle, Dunigan lanced every blood blister on Jacobsen's face. After that, they became friends. When they shipped overseas to New Caledonia, they stole lumber and built a shed out of pieces of boards. It looked like something in a shantytown, but it had a wood floor and was a lot better than sleeping on dirt. Everyone used to come over to play cards in their nice little home. They would have given anything to have it here on this miserable, muddy island.

Another F Company trooper, Pfc. Earl "Ed" Cassaday of Crown Point, Indiana, fell in for the march down to Voza where they would join E Company. As he lined up, his buddy Pfc. Leo Gruidl fell in beside him. Gruidl wore a .45 colt in a tanker's shoulder holster across his chest.

"You know, Gruidl," teased Ed as he always did when he saw him, "one-a these days some Jap's gonna zero in on ya 'cause-a that .45 you're wearing. They're gonna take you for an officer."

"Maybe, Hoppy," joked Gruidl, "but not 'cause-a the pistol."

The column was ordered to move out, and they took the jungle trail down to Voza. At the tail end of the long column, Pfc. James P. Dugan brought up the rear. His buddy, Jerome M. Clarey of New Jersey, was walking just in front of him. As they followed the others, Dugan would often turn and walk backward because the Japanese often let patrols pass by to ambush the last man.

"Hey, Dugan," said Clarey in his thick New Jersey accent.

"What?"

"Who's that behind you?" Clarey would always tease whenever Dugan brought up the rear.

0600—Lieutenant Averill's Patrol

It was almost dawn, and Averill looked around for their native guide. Not seeing him, Averill stood up and raised his hands to his mouth to call out for him. Suddenly the guide stood up in the bush near the beach, motioning wildly for Averill to get down. The lieutenant crawled over to him. The native quickly flashed both hands with extended fingers, four times. "Jap. Jap. Many-many," he hissed. He then pointed south of the cove. "Same-same. Many-many."[2]

Averill had heard the barges all night, but he didn't realize any of them had stayed in the cove. Perhaps they had been there all night. Even worse, the Japanese were between the Marines and Voza. Averill didn't know what to do until the guide pointed behind a small ridge and began moving silently toward it. Averill followed, crawling lightly through the Kunai grass. Soon thereafter, the native paused and pointed through the bush at a now clearly visible beach on either side of Kuku cove. Two Daihatsu barges were beached, one on each side of the cove. Beside each craft was a platoon of Japanese soldiers cooking rice. More than eighty enemy troops were less than a hundred yards away. The native moved off slowly toward the small hogback to worm around the enemy troops. Averill motioned for his men to silently follow.

Suddenly the roar of an engine turning over shattered the morning silence. The unmistakable noise of orders shouted in Japanese rose over the drone of the engine, and Averill's patrol scrambled to bring up their weapons. Their hearts were pounding. "Oh, my God," thought Pfc. Roy J. Gallagher, "there were Nips here all night long."

The Marines readied their grenades and sighted in with their weapons as a barge full of at least forty Japanese troops moved out of the cove. Gallagher wondered again if they could hit this barge and get away clean, but the antiaircraft machine guns decided the question for him. Also, just because that barge left did not mean there were not enemy troops still in the area. There were just too many Japanese, and the Marines were on a mission of stealth, not power. The patrol had a large amount of information about enemy-troop movement and terrain features to report to Lt. Col. Victor H. Krulak; they had to get back. Lieutenant Averill ordered the exhausted group back to battalion. The patrol left Kuku at 0600 and followed the rugged jungle tract back along the coast toward Voza.

Jungle Trail

Fox Company arrived at Voza and assembled with Easy Company. With the exception of George Company and Hq Company, who would stay behind to hold the fort, today would be the battalion's baptism of fire.

The paratroopers waited for the LCPRs to come in from Zinoa Island. Suddenly, they heard the drone of airplane engines. Looking to the southwest in the direction of Vella LaVella, the Marines saw four Corsairs flying toward them. The Marine paratroopers got an unexpected morale boost as they saw they were going to have air support for their attack. The planes had almost reached them and were flying over tiny Zinoa Island when they abruptly broke off their course and went into a dive right on Zinoa. Private Cassaday and the men in his squad watched as the planes made a strafing run and shot up something. Zinoa Island was only two thousand yards off Voza, so they each had a front-row seat for the show. The Corsairs came back for another pass, but suddenly they pulled up. Instead of firing, they tipped their wings as if to say, "Sorry."

Just then the colonel's TBX team got a call on the radio from Zinoa, and it was not good news. The Corsairs had strafed the LCPRs. Three of the four were damaged and could not be used for the day's attack. Without the boats, the Marines would have to march down to Sangigai on foot.

So much for their morale boost. This was not the auspicious start they had hoped for. The two companies fell in and turned to the southeast along the coastal trail. It was ten miles to Sangigai and they would have to make it in good time if they wanted to keep their 1400 scheduled attack time. The Coastwatcher intelligence had told them that an attack any later in the day would not give the Americans sufficient daylight to make their escape. They did not want to spend even one night in the area, so the officers needed to stay on schedule. The columns formed up behind their native guides and, with E Company in the lead, they moved down toward the Vagara River and Sangigai.

Pfc. Donald "Hink" Hinkle of E Company, Capt. "Chesty" Manchester's platoon scout, was in the long single file when he saw Cpl. "Baron" Hoffman moving down the line against the grain. Hoffman was Krulak's runner and he claimed to be a nephew of German Field Marshall Erwin Rommel, the Desert Fox. Why he was moving down the line Hink did not know, but Hoffman was rebuking the paratroopers in his comedic German accent. "If ziss ting does not turn out juz right," he threatened, "ich vil report you all to mine uncle."

As the southern task force moved to the southeast they passed the G Company lookout post. PM1 John Holland was sitting quietly with his buddies at the outpost watching the Marines pass. Holland watched Hoffman move by and bark his orders in his Hitler accent, wearing some kind of fake mustache. Holland wanted to tell him to shut up, but since so many others seemed to get a kick out of Hoffman's Hitler routine, Holland did not say a word.

Colonel Krulak watched his men pass and heard Hoffman ranting, as he often did. He had picked Hoffman as his runner simply because he was brave. He would do what he was told and he would do it well, but he needed a lot of supervision. The Brute had to keep him close or he would get in trouble. The Brute knew he had good men, although they were a little wild at times. They loved throwing grenades, especially into the privies. Krulak never could catch anyone doing it, but on the two occasions men rolled grenades down the Company Street, he threw the book at them. It was one thing to have fun, but that was dangerous. The perpetrators were promptly reduced, brigged, and placed on bread and water. Although he had to corral his high-spirited men from time to time, Krulak had the utmost confidence in them as they marched toward their first battle.

0600—Jungle Trail

A bleary-eyed Pfc. Bruce "Red" McClure was still sitting behind his root just before dawn on the morning of October 30. He was thinking about the last time he had slept: the night of October 26. Since then he had not had more than two hours sleep at a time. The day before, he had marched more than twenty miles in the mud down to Sangigai and back. Last night he had been awake all night waiting for the Japanese to *banzai* after their firefight. Like most of his fellow Marines, though, Red's fear of the unknown, the firefight, the cold, wet night, and the powerful instinct of self-preservation had temporarily wiped away all traces of fatigue. He and the others became aware of the sound of movement and they became alert. A large party of troops was approaching from the northwest—their rear.

"Halt," challenged Cpl. Benjamin F. "Cape" Caperton III. "Who's there?"

"Lollipop. Who's asking?"

"Lulu Lady. Advance and be recognized."[3]

The leading elements of E Company moved into sight along the trail and Corporal Caperton and his men breathed a sigh of relief.

Pfc. Paul Chelf was walking along the trail and saw Sgt. Norman Law's squad waiting in the brush to fall in with F Company, which was behind Easy Company. He saw his buddy Ski and wanted to ask him what had happened the night before, but he only waved a hello. Chelf had not gone more than a dozen yards down the trail when he had to step over four dead Japanese lying on the path. It was then that he realized what the firing had been about.

Red watched the E Company guys pass and noticed an unusually large contingent of natives supporting the Marines. There were almost as many as when they had landed. They carried huge loads of ammunition, supplies, and rockets.

After E Company passed, F Company filed out. Capt. Spencer Pratt moved near the head of his company. When he passed the area where Law's squad had fought it out, he took in the scene before him. "Good job, Cape!," said Pratt nonchalantly. Cape suddenly felt very good about his squad's work. He and the others got up from behind their tree roots and fell in with their platoon. Sub-Lt. Carden Seton ordered some of the natives to move the dead Japanese soldiers off the trail and a few others to search the nearby area. They reported that there were no other living Japanese in the area but that three more enemy dead were in the jungle just off the trail. That put the total enemy dead from the firefight at seven.

So far, since the time the Marines had landed on Choiseul, they had killed fourteen Japanese soldiers. Fortunately, they had done it at a cost of zero Marines—not bad. But if they were going to be believable as a division-sized invasion, they were definitely underachieving. The single file continued to the southeast along the coastal trail moving toward Vagara Village. At roughly 0600, they heard the drone of airplane engines approaching. "Uh-oh," thought Ed.

James Dugan had the same thought. Every time they heard airplane engines something terrible happened. Not sure which was more dangerous, friendly aircraft or the Japanese, the entire column prepared to dive for cover as they looked out over the ocean. A squadron of navy Dauntless dive-bombers and their fighter escort was heading northeast toward them, probably from Vella LaVella.

Pfc. Norman Dibbens was between his JLMG man, Pfc. Frank Rodgers, and Pfc. Reece Canady. The three listened as the drone of the planes got louder. "That's music to my ears," Dibbens said.

They knew that the dive-bombers were part of an orchestrated attack ordered by the colonel, because a division on the attack would have air support. Not long after that, Dibbens heard the explosions and felt slight tremors in the ground from the 500-pound bomb blasts. "Good," he thought, "pour it on 'em."

The Marine force continued on to Vagara Village with Easy Company in the lead. Pfc. Harold N. "Hal" Block of E Company was moving as the point of the entire force because his element was point for his platoon, which led the raiding party to the southeast. Coming upon a small stream, Hal tried to look across at the trail. There was a bend in the path on the opposite side that prevented him from seeing anything. "This is a perfect spot for an ambush," thought Hal. "This is where I'd wait." Hal reluctantly moved down the stream bank and waded across to the other side. Once there, he climbed the opposite bank and carefully lifted his head above the lip. About twenty yards down the jungle trail were two of the largest men he had ever seen. They had stars on the front of their helmets but they were not generals—the stars were a reddish color.

He quickly ducked back down, his heart pounding, and turned to the men behind him and signaled "Enemy in sight." His platoon leader was not far behind and immediately crawled to him. "There are two Japs standing just down the trail," whispered Hal.

The two readied their weapons and went up for another look. Lifting their heads just enough to see above the bank, they saw nothing but empty trail in front of them. The enemy soldiers were gone. Without a moment's hesitation, the lieutenant motioned his men to continue. The battalion could not stop their mission because of two Japanese soldiers. Hal and his element prepared to go but nobody wanted to be first. They assumed they had been spotted and a sniper would shoot the first man down the trail. They decided to settle who would be first up the stream bank by drawing blades of grass. Hal lost.

He was sweating profusely and as alert and nervous as he had ever been in his life. Hal lifted his head up for the third time and peered down the trail, but the jungle path was still. There was no movement or sign of the two Japanese soldiers. Holding his weapon ready to fire, he stepped up onto the trail expecting a bullet to crash into his skull any moment.

BLAM! Hal's heart stopped. He knew he had been shot. Instinctively, he dropped to the ground. At first he assumed he was dead, but then realized he had not even been hit. The rifle shot had come from behind him. It scared the hell out of him, though, and he wondered who was doing the shooting. No other shots followed and, not one minute later, word passed up that someone had misfired his weapon.

"Dumb son of a bitch," seethed Hal.[4] "Who's the stupid bastard that misfired?" Hal still had to continue down the trail, but by then the Japanese would be alert. Anyone within a mile had heard that shot. He crept down the trail, expecting to die with every step he took. He had gone about ten yards when he saw the end of a sniper rifle sticking up from behind a mangrove root just ahead. Sighting in on the root, he waited for the sniper to rise. He was sweating bullets. Where was the other man?

The big root extended across the trail and Hal wondered if he should go around it or over it. Finally, he decided to continue straight down the trail, and aimed just above the root where the rifle stuck out. The other men in his element were behind him and he hoped they could see the other sniper. Hal wondered why the Japanese did not try to rise to shoot him, or at least look out from behind his spot. When he was close enough he saw why. It was not a sniper; it was a stick protruding from behind the root. Wiping the sweat from his eyes, Hal breathed a sigh of relief, but his relief was short lived. In the next instant, he saw the bunker.

Dropping instantly behind the root, he motioned to the others. The bunker was made of logs about five yards off the trail. Hal realized the only reason he was still alive was because the bunker was empty. Shaken, he continued and entered the Japanese camp. He could see small tins of food and medical supplies as he moved through it. The camp was along the coast and gave anyone there a commanding view of the ocean. It looked as if it had only recently been abandoned. Hal saw a Japanese boat far to the southeast in the distance and reported it to Captain Manchester, but it was much too far away to fire. They continued down the coast on their way to the Vagara River, E Company in the lead, with F Company in single file just behind.

0800—Mountain Camp

Lieutenant Averill's squad was more than sixteen hours overdue and the battalion feared that the Japanese had hit them. Earlier that morning, Colonel Krulak had left instructions to send a patrol out to find them if they were not back by 0800. It was past that time and there was still no sign of the lost patrol. Lt. Donald Castle was ordered to lead a search patrol to find them; he was instructed to go all the way to Moli, if necessary.

Battalion Southeast Listening Post

G Company parachutist Pfc. Jack Carns of Branson, Missouri, was squatting behind a tree root in the jungle, covering the coastal trail that led to Voza from the southeast. His position was good because it gave him enfilading fire across the river and down the trail, while providing defilade for most of his body. Half the battalion had recently passed and was moving toward Sangigai to attack the Japanese barge station while Carns's squad pulled guard duty on the battalion flank.

Carns and the other Marines in both G Company and Hq Company were disappointed because they were missing the attack. Many of the parachutists, Carns included, had been in the Marines since just after December 7, 1941, and had still not seen any real action. Chasing half-starved, ill-equipped enemy troops on the Canal and Vella LaVella did not really count. Carns was wondering when he would finally see action when a flicker of movement on the trail ahead caught his eye.

Carns could see a Japanese Imperial Marine moving cautiously toward his squad's position. The man seemed to see something he did not like because he raised his rifle to fire just as Carns let go with a short burst from his JLMG. The enemy soldier took the bullets across his torso and dropped on the trail. Carns and the other Americans along the listening post readied for an attack, but the jungle became silent. There was no further sound or movement. It baffled Carns. Where had this Japanese soldier come from? Four hundred Americans, forty natives, and one Australian had just passed down that trail not an hour before, but here came a Japanese soldier along the same trail moving in the opposite direction. Carns wondered how many more Japanese were hiding in the jungle in front of him.

1030—West of Vagara River

Private Dibbens heard the report of gunfire behind him and the entire column stopped. They waited while the officers sent a runner back to find out what the shots were about. Soon word passed back up the line that the rear guard had shot a Japanese lookout. Was this a lookout from the camp they had just passed or a straggler from last night's firefight? Easy Company continued toward Sangigai and their first combat action. Pfc. Robert Brutinel and Pfc. Don Carpenter were two of those E Company paratroopers. Both men were in the same squad and shared a memory on Vella LaVella that was as infamous as it was secret.

A few weeks before, Brutinel and Carpenter were on garbage detail on Vella LaVella. They drove their six-by-six truck into the New Zealand–run garbage dump to unload it. The New Zealanders disposed of the trash by burning it and used bulldozers to cover the ashes with sand. Brutinel backed the truck up to a big pit and dumped the trash in. After they had unloaded their cargo, the Beach Master tried to light the trash on fire, but he could not get it lit—the garbage was too wet. Brutinel watched him try repeatedly, and finally made a suggestion. "Why don't you get some of that gas?" There were at least fifty barrels of high-octane aviation fuel about one hundred feet from the trash dump.

"I would if I could," said the New Zealander.

So Brutinel decided to help the guy. He took a big wrench out of the truck, walked over to the aviation fuel, and unscrewed the cap on one of the barrels. Meanwhile, the New Zealand Beach Master grabbed one of the five-gallon cans that was in the Marine garbage and walked over to fill it with gas. He dunked the can in the barrel, filled it, and walked quickly back over to the trash. He threw the fuel on the pile, stepped back, lit a match, and tossed it on. WHOOSH! The pile went up in flames, but to the horror of Brutinel, Carpenter, and the New Zealander, a small line of flame ignited and raced back toward the fuel barrels with unbelievable speed.

What the New Zealander had not known was that the Marines, as a force of habit when disposing of trash at sea, punched a hole in their gas cans so their garbage would sink, to prevent leaving a trail for enemy submarines to follow. Habits die hard, and even on land, the Marines punched holes in the cans. When they filled the five-gallon container, Brutinel and Carpenter forgot they would be leaving a trail of high-octane fuel from the fuel drums to the trash.

The ocean was fifty feet away from the trash pit; both men took off sprinting as the flames raced back toward the fuel barrels. Brutinel shouted a warning and hoped the New Zealander was behind them. The Marines dove into the water just as the fuel ignited. The explosion was tremendous. Every barrel of fuel exploded and burned, spreading flame all across the trash dump. Brutinel and Carpenter's six-by-six truck caught fire, exploded, and partially melted from the heat. Amazingly, not one of them had been hurt. The three men stood in the water and watched the inferno. When they arrived back at camp they pretended nothing had happened, and word quickly spread that a Japanese air attack had destroyed the fuel dump. About an hour later, though, Colonel Krulak summoned both Brutinel and Carpenter to his office. Brutinel was called in first. He was terrified.

"What happened?" asked Krulak.

"I was on garbage detail and this New Zealander tried to light the trash on fire. Somehow the barrels blew up," Brutinel explained, neglecting to tell the colonel that he had suggested using fuel to light the trash in the first place or that he actually unscrewed the cap on the fuel barrel. Krulak dismissed Brutinel and called Carpenter in. "What happened?" asked the Brute.

"An unidentified Marine unscrewed the cap on one of the fuel barrels. The New Zealander tried to light the trash on fire and blew all the barrels up."

Krulak also dismissed Carpenter. Although Brutinel was convinced he would be court-martialed over the incident, neither heard another word about it.

Almost two weeks later, both men were on the island of Choiseul traveling along the coastal trail. They came across another Japanese camp that appeared to be recently and hastily abandoned. Brutinel saw all kinds of junk lying around the Japanese bivouac. He kicked at some empty fish tins lying on the trail and kept moving. Carpenter saw the same discarded items and decided to souvenir hunt. Finding a strange mallet that was probably a Japanese hammer, he stuck it in his belt, and took some unopened cans with Japanese writing on them as souvenirs, not food. As hungry as he was, he was not famished enough to try Japanese army cuisine. Besides, an identical opened can lay strewn in the mud and its spilled contents did not look good. Carpenter thought the size of the camp probably meant a platoon had been there.

Just behind them, machine gunner Pfc. Rudolph Engstrom picked up a few souvenirs, too. A small container about the size of a mint tin with Japanese characters written on the top fascinated him. He assumed the tin held malaria or dengue fever pills or something. He pocketed it and continued with the others.[5]

One man who was not afraid to eat from the Japanese tins was Hink, who was both hungry and sick and tired of D-bars and K-rations. He opened the tin and although he was at first apprehensive about eating fish heads, he was so hungry he popped one of the little heads in his mouth. It was not bad, and he finished the rest of the can. Just ahead of him, he saw one of the other Marines stop and bend down to grab something. It was a small watch. Remembering his first day on Zinoa Island when they found the dead body of what he believed to be a young Korean "comfort girl," Carpenter wondered if this watch had once belonged to a woman, and how many such women had been on the island.

The southern task force passed through the abandoned camps getting progressively closer to the Vagara River. To augment both E Company's and F Company's strength, a rocket platoon from regimental weapons had been attached to the battalion. Gen. Alexander A. Vandegrift had hung the rockets on Colonel Krulak against his will. Krulak knew his Marines would already be loaded down with weapons, ammunition, supplies, and equipment. The rockets were unrealistic for both jungle movement and fighting. If it were not for the natives, they would not have been able to even move them without stripping Marines of their weapons and ammo. Besides, the dense canopy of trees overhead probably meant that the big weapons would be useless or severely hampered. The general wanted the loud, powerful rockets to help lend credibility to the ruse, to imply that a much larger, stronger force was on the attack.

Brutinel and Carpenter were walking fairly close to the rocket guys. Although they were officially designated as a "platoon," Brutinel did not see more than a half-dozen guys—a lieutenant and maybe five or six men—with more than forty fin-stabilized rockets. Brutinel noticed that the natives were carrying almost all of the 43-pound rockets and firing stands.[6] The supports were simply folded pieces of metal and wire, but they looked heavy and cumbersome. Brutinel was amazed at the natives' strength. They seemed to know every inch of the island, which was obviously invaluable to the Marines. Having the guides moving confidently in front was very reassuring for the Marines because every step brought them closer to Sangigai Village and their first encounter with enemy troops.

Based on the intelligence gathered by the Coastwatchers and the reconnaissance sketches from the patrol of the day before, Colonel Krulak had devised his attack plan. At the Vagara River, the column would split. Krulak would take F Company and move inland to the headwaters where they could cross and continue through the jungle toward their ambush position northeast of Sangigai. It was the same difficult route that Sgt. Paul Mullins and Private McClure had taken the day before. It was vital to the plan that Krulak's force be in position to ambush by 1400.

Maj. Tolson Smoak and Captain Manchester would wait half an hour before taking E Company with an attached weapons and rocket platoon section across the Vagara River. They would move southeast and attack Sangigai at 1400, supported by mortars and rockets. The company would drive the enemy troops into the prearranged ambush site where F Company would be waiting. It was a classic pincer movement designed to trap the enemy forces and make them think that multiple large units on a broad front were hitting them.

The paratroopers were making good time. Considering that Corsairs had literally shot up their original plans earlier that morning, the battalion was making progress. They had almost reached the Vagara River and it was not yet 1100.

Lieutenant Averill's Patrol

All morning, Gerald Averill's patrol retraced the path back to Voza. Just before they reached the Baregosonga River, their native guide motioned that he was leaving. Every man shook his hand, knowing he owed his life to this native. As Averill shook hands with the guide, he thought of the quotation from Kipling that his father had taught him as a child. "There is neither East nor West, Border, nor Breed, nor Birth, when two strong men stand face to face, though they come from the ends of the earth."[7] The native disappeared into the jungle. The Marines continued toward Voza.

The day before, Pfc. Andy Obrocta had fallen out of their column because of heat exhaustion. When they reached the spot where they had believed they had left him they began to search and call out. However, the jungle looked the same everywhere, so they were not even sure they were searching the right area. They had told Obrocta to stay put until they returned but he was nowhere to be found. Assuming the worst, they feared a Japanese patrol got him. If so, they were sure he was dead. Gallagher hung on to the hope that his buddy had made it back to camp on his own. If Obrocta kept his wits, all he had to do was follow the coast to the southeast. If he did, he would eventually reach Marine lookouts on the Baregosonga.

South Pacific Command

To lend credibility to the diversion on Choiseul, Adm. William F. Halsey gave a press release from his headquarters informing the media of the Allied invasion of Choiseul. "A division of Marines, twenty thousand men, has landed and is moving on their objectives." Never, since the outbreak of World War II, had the United States media been purposely misled. Up to this point, every operation reported was factual. This, more than anything, was meant to make the Japanese believe that the invasion of Choiseul was the real thing. The Allies knew that very soon the enemy spy network back in the United States would report the news to Tokyo.

Colonel Krulak's Force

When the lead element reached the Vagara River, the Marines and their guides fanned out along the edge of the jungle to observe the other side. They signaled back that they had reached the river, and the entire column took the prone position. Within minutes, Colonel Krulak and Captain Manchester were crawling up front to peer through the brush with their binoculars.

The Vagara River was a natural defensive position. After the previous day's firefight, the enemy would be foolish not to have posted lookouts hidden along the southeast side. This posed a problem for the Marines. If they were seen crossing the river, they would move into a meeting engagement, or worse—a Japanese ambush. It was important to get across the river undetected. It was also time for the two groups to split. If they were successful, they would be in position to continue with the plan. The two forces would split here and hit Sangigai at 1400. They would catch the enemy completely unaware by an overland attack behind them, especially if they slipped past a hidden Japanese listening post along the enemy flank. If they were unsuccessful, they would cross that bridge when the shooting started. For the moment, however, they had no other choice because the boats had been shot up. Although they had made good time moving down the coast, more than one Marine worried about their timetable.

Colonel Krulak called Major Smoak and Captains Pratt and Chesty together. This was where the two columns would divide. Krulak and Pratt would move inland with F Company while Chesty and Smoak would wait a half hour and then cross the river to attack Sangigai Village along the coast with E Company. The half hour wait was to enable F Company time to get inland. If E Company moved right then, they would reach Sangigai before F Company was in position. Krulak repeated that he wanted the two groups to stay in radio contact and to coordinate during their brief halts. With that, the colonel told Seton to lead them up to the headwaters. F Company moved out, leaving E Company and its attached sections waiting in the thick jungle northeast of the Vagara River. F Company headed inland to the headwaters where Krulak had crossed the day before. From there they would be able to ford the river behind a small mountain that obstructed any watchful eyes.

Red, in the long line of troopers behind Krulak, knew that the difficult part of their journey was just beginning. He had been over this terrain the day before when they went down to scout Sangigai for the attack. Red also knew they were planning to coordinate their attack with E Company at exactly 1400 hours. He looked at his own watch, and doubted they would be able to stick to their schedule. They would really have to push it if they had any hope of getting to that ridge behind Sangigai by 1400. The terrain was just too difficult. Having been there before he thought the timetable was unrealistic, but nobody had asked him. He also wondered if the village was still deserted.

Lieutenant Averill's Patrol

The lost patrol under Lieutenant Averill stumbled back into camp at 1100 hours. While Averill went to report in at the battalion CP, the others went immediately to their hammocks. The camp was practically empty with only G Company holding the fort. The returning Marines wondered if something big was happening right then.

Gallagher returned to a sight that made him exceedingly happy: Obrocta was lying in his hammock! Elated that his best friend was okay, Gallagher hurried over to him, but when he got to him, he was suddenly mad. "You were just an ol' fuckoff," accused Gallagher. "You were lazy. There's no reason you couldn't keep up with us."

"I couldn't move, Roy," said Obrocta slowly and not too kindly. "I couldn't walk."

"How'd you get back?" retorted Gallagher.

"I was just sitting in the jungle by the side of the trail," said Obrocta. "Suddenly, two natives were looking down at me. One minute I was alone, the next minute they were standing over me. Luckily, they were Seton's men. They led me back to camp."

When Gallagher got to his own hammock, he realized he had been hard on his friend. For anyone to fall out and be left alone on an enemy island, miles from help, well, that man had to be hurting. He also knew that Obrocta was lucky it was one of the Seton's men that found him and not the Japanese. Otherwise, he would be dead.

Colonel Krulak's Force

When F Company reached the headwaters, Colonel Krulak ordered a squad across the river to reconnoiter the opposite side. Everyone knew this was really a test to see if they would draw fire from an enemy ambush. Nobody knew it better than the unlucky men that drew the assignment. They knew they were living bait. If they were shot up, the rest of the company would know not to cross. They started across in water up to their chests. The headwaters of the Vagara River were much more claustrophobic than down near the ocean and Vagara Village. The jungle pressed in on both sides of the river, which was only about a hundred feet across. The squad reached the southeast bank without taking fire and reconnoitered the opposite side. After a few minutes, they signaled for the others to come across. Soon F Company had crossed the river.

Captain Manchester's Force

While Easy Company sat waiting at the Vagara River, preparing to cross, the first sergeant passed word down the line for all the troopers to send up their toggle ropes.[8] The first sergeant assembled the five-foot cords into one long line they would use to span the river. The plan was for a squad of Marines to ford the river towing the rope. Once across they would tie it to a tree so the rest of the company could pull themselves across the river where it might be too deep to ford with their heavy equipment—the machine guns, mortars, and rockets. The appointed half hour passed and they prepared to continue their mission.

The ten Marines forded the river and waded up to a big banyan tree on the opposite side. They spread out and made a quick recon of the area. Once they were certain there were no Japanese in the immediate vicinity, they tied the rope to one of the banyans and Captain Manchester sent his men across. Sgt. George Tovrea crossed with another squad to form a small bridgehead, followed quickly by another squad. They continued this procedure until the entire reinforced company was across the river in surprisingly little time. There was still no sign of the enemy. Either there were no enemy scouts on the southeast riverbank, or the Japanese lookouts were cool customers. If that were the case, the paratroopers could be walking into an ambush.

Colonel Krulak's Force

As paratroopers, the battalion had trained knowing they would fight surrounded by the enemy. Although technically they were already behind enemy lines just by being on Choiseul, they were well inland and behind the Japanese forces stationed at Sangigai Village. Fox Company was hacking their way through the jungle trying to stay on time for the coordinated assault, the point men slashing a trail through the thick foliage with their machetes. It was hot and humid. The Marines struggled under the weight of their weapons and ammunition to keep the pace the officers were pushing. Everyone was angry with the Corsair pilots who had strafed their own LCPRs back on Zinoa Island. Because of that accidental strafing, they had an additional five miles carrying all their heavy weapons and equipment, and they were dangerously behind schedule.

Cape was in the long line of Marines between Pfc. Bobby Atkins and Pfc. Stanley H. Keller, swatting at insects while he fought through the brush. Cape saw Sgt. George Gerarden urinate. "Sergeant," said Keller in his slow country drawl as he passed Gerarden, "don't walk off and leave that thing running."

Everyone within hearing distance burst out laughing. They were all tense and nervous, keyed up about the attack and constantly being wary of ambush, and the humor eased the tension. Cape thought Keller, young and green as could be, was a good kid. Both Cape and Sergeant Law had told the rest of the squad to go easy on young Keller and help bring the awkward eighteen-year-old along.

As the men trudged along, the NCOs moved up and down the line, pushing the men. "You're lagging," they would say when a trooper let the space between himself and the man in front increase too much. "Keep up."

While the column continued, the TBX team stopped from time to time and tried to raise E Company. Cpl. Roy Homerding and Jacobsen fiddled with the radio, but they were unable to raise either Easy or Hq Company back at the mountain camp, possibly due to the interference of the jungle mountains. Jacobsen and Homerding strapped the heavy radio on their backs once more and rejoined the line of paratroopers.

Dibbins was hacking his way through the dense underbrush and thought how terrible it was to travel in the jungle as opposed to the coastal trail. He had serious doubts they would make their rendezvous time, even at the man-killing pace they were moving. Looking at his watch, he saw it was already close to 1330.

They waded through countless streams, climbed huge roots, and crawled under fallen trees. Everything seemed to snag on their shirts, belts, and straps, slowing them down. The terrain was an unforgiving wallow of jungle and mountain. Men tripped and slid in the mud, their arms flailing to grab branches or something to stop their fall.

Dibbens thought how eerie the jungle was. What he had thought was a tropical paradise was obviously something else completely. At that moment, that paradise struck him as sinister, fetid, and vile. The rotting branches and vines seemed to move above a ground that oozed mud. A humid and dank smell of decay permeated the heavy air. Even in broad daylight it was dark under the canopy of trees. There were venomous brown snakes, spiders, and millions of insects—centipedes, mosquitoes, scorpions, ants, flies. It seemed like every ravenous insect on earth was on Choiseul. Even the nonpoisonous insects were maddening. If the Marines sat down to rest, they found themselves covered by hundreds of biting ants. When they opened a K-ration, swarming flies landed on it as they ate. Whatever it was, it was not a tropical paradise.

Dibbens was following behind his buddy Canady. The two had met on February 19, 1943, the day they were both sworn into the Marine Corps in Kansas City, Kansas. They had gone to boot camp together at Camp Gillespie and were shipped out to New Caledonia together. Then they were assigned to the same squad in the Second Marine Parachute Battalion.

Canady was just turning to speak to Dibbens when something fell out of a tree onto Dibbens and covered his face. A huge spider had fallen from a branch and its front legs caught the lip of the Marine's helmet and held on. The rest of the spider's body and legs swung down into Dibbens's face. The spider was so big it blocked his vision. All the Marines had been warned about the poisonous spiders and snakes in this part of the world, and Dibbens had been terrified of them long before the spider's legs wrapped around his cheeks and jaw. He would have yelled if he had had time to register the horror but the spider was just as suddenly gone. His buddy had seen it and slapped it away.

Jungle Trail

As E Company continued down the coastal trail approaching Sangigai, Hink, the scout, was moving quietly by himself to reconnoiter their left flank. The battalion scouts such as Hink, Pfc. Billy Joe Cagle, Cpl. William R. Zuegel, and others were often alone on recon patrols. If Hink saw anything, he was to report in immediately via walkie-talkie and beat feet back to the company. He was extremely quiet as he moved through the jungle. Suddenly, the silence was shattered by his radio.

"WHAT IS YOUR LOCATION?"

Hink scrambled for his walkie-talkie so fast he juggled it and almost dropped it. Fearing an enemy sniper was going to shoot him any second, his eyes darted from tree to tree as he whispered into the radio. "This is Hink, I'm about . . . "

"SAY AGAIN?" blared the voice at the other end before he could finish.

Hink had to resist the urge to throw his radio to the ground and jump on it. It was so loud, the jungle echoed. Hink knew that if he wanted to remain alive much longer he had better turn it off. After he signed off, he turned the walkie-talkie off. From then on, he would call them.

Captain Manchester's Force

The scouts indicated that they were nearing Sangigai, which was just about 330 feet ahead through the jungle. Captain Manchester immediately ordered the weapons platoon mortar crews to begin setting up and once again told his TBX team to try to raise F Company.

Pvt. Richard Reneau was standing in the column about five men down from Chesty. Chesty was conferring with the point men and the native scouts, his eyes searching the line of Marines. When they fell on Reneau, they stopped searching. "Reneau, come over here," he ordered.

"Yes," said Reneau as he approached his captain, fighting the urge to call him "sir."

"You always want to fight. Now here's your chance. You'll get all the fighting you want," said Chesty. He told Reneau to go forward to Sangigai with two other Marines to scout the village. Their native allies would lead them through the jungle but not into combat. The Marines would move on Sangigai without guides. At first Reneau thought it was an honor to be picked, but he realized that he and the other two Marines were basically just bait. If they drew fire, the rest of the company was walking into an ambush. It made sense to Reneau. Why endanger the entire column when three men could find out if it was a trap?

As Reneau and the other two moved forward, Captain Manchester ordered the rest of the column to spread out by platoons into a skirmish line. The mortar crews set up their stands in a small clearing and adjusted for range while the rocket platoon prepared their firing stands. The natives began to stack the rockets nearby. Lt. John Richards briefed his squad leaders and told them the mortars would start firing in ten minutes. He wanted them ready to jump off when the barrage started. So far, everything was going by the numbers, just like in training.

1345—Colonel Kulak's Force

The Marines were dehydrated, struggling to keep the pace the officers were pushing. They needed to step it up if they wanted to reach the ambush site before E Company began their attack. As they pushed through the jungle, they loosed a stream of curses at the Corsair pilots who had shot up their landing boats, forcing them to walk the extra miles.

Private Dugan was hacking his way through the thick jungle when he passed Captain Pratt.[9] Knowing they were in danger of failing to meet their timetable, Pratt had stepped out of the line to urge his Marines on to greater speed. Pratt was tall, slender, and athletic, a no-nonsense maverick who had worked his way up through the ranks. His men liked him well enough, but more importantly, they respected him. The unassuming captain was businesslike, quiet, and never shouted. He expected the men to obey his orders, and they did. Just then, he was pushing them to the limit.

Private Cassaday was up front behind Lieutenant Seton. Seton was moving along carrying his carbine like a pistol with three of his men, Lt. Samuel Johnston, Peta Kiri, and Peta Nu. Unbelievably, the natives carried his pack, extra ammunition, and equipment while Seton just carried his little carbine and nothing else. "K'mon, mates," Seton called back in his Aussie accent, "clows it up." They were running out of time. It was already 1345 and Sangigai was nowhere in sight. Their line was strung out and they needed to close ranks and move faster. The men were thirsty, hot, and physically drained from lack of sufficient water, diet, and sleep over the past few days. Many of the Marines carried up to 50 pounds of weapons and equipment, and some of them only weighed 140 pounds to begin with. Here was

Seton acting the proper English gentleman, carrying nothing but his carbine, which looked like a toy gun in the big man's huge hand. Colonel Krulak weighed less than anyone else, yet he carried his own pack and ammunition. It really made Cassaday mad every time Seton turned to prod the Marines to move faster. "Why you son of a bitch," he thought, "if you carried your own pack and ammo, you wouldn't be so spry, either."

Chapter 5

BAPTISM OF FIRE: OCTOBER 30 (AFTERNOON)

We were elite. We were trained professionals, conditioned like professional athletes.
In all my military service with the Marines and the army, in World War II and
Korea, the Marine paratroops were the best I've ever been associated with.

Pfc. Howard "Barney" Baxter, G Company

1400—Captain Manchester's Force

Pvt. Richard Reneau and the other two scouts moved cautiously to the
edge of the jungle just northwest of Sangigai and, peering from the trees,
scanned the huts for enemy troops. Reneau could not see anyone, but that
did not mean there were not Japanese soldiers watching him. He carefully
searched the trees beyond the village, then he focused again on the village.
Sangigai was just like Voza and Vagara: a half-dozen thatched-roof huts that
had no sides, so the people inside could be sheltered from the sun, but catch
the cool breeze off the ocean. A few of the huts appeared to have caches
of supplies and medical satchels.

Reneau was worried that an enemy sniper had him in his sights, and
moved reluctantly out into the flat, open ground of the village between the
two NCOs. "Be careful," he thought, "this place might be booby trapped.
But where are the Nips? Who are we going to attack?"

It was 1400 and Reneau and the E Company scouts were the first to
pass through the deserted village. Just like the day before when Pfc. Bruce
"Red" McClure had been there, they found the village empty. They backtracked immediately, and reported to Capt. Robert R. "Chesty" Manchester,
who subsequently ordered E Company to move on Sangigai in a long skirmish line by platoons. "From here on, hand signals," directed Lieutenant
Richards.

The platoons moved forward. The first platoon was closest to the ocean,
and the others were in a line moving inland. Pfc. Robert Brutinel's platoon
was just off the beach, and Pfc. Don Carpenter was beside him. When they

reached the open area of the village, they saw their platoon leader pump his fist up and down, signaling for them to move quickly. Staying low, weapons ready, they approached the open ground near the huts on the run.

Pfc. Billy Joe Cagle, a battalion scout and Captain Manchester's runner, was ordered to take a three-man patrol farther inland along Easy Company's flank. From where he was inside the jungle, Billy Joe could not even see the village.

1415—Colonel Krulak's Force

The paratroopers nervously watched the hour of 1400 come and go, but Sangigai was still not in sight. They knew Easy Company was attacking right then and were worried because they could not hear the sounds of the firefight. If they could not hear anything, maybe they were farther away than they should be.

One-hundred-foot banyan and mangrove trees blocked out the sun, and smaller trees below them obstructed sight and movement by vine, limb, branch, and root. In an effort to push his men faster, Lt. Col. Victor H. Krulak moved to the front of the column. It was almost 1415 and Krulak was up with Captain Pratt trying to will his men to move faster.

Jungle Inland

Pfc. Donald "Hink" Hinkle, the solitary battalion scout moving on the extreme flank of Easy Company, was well inland of the others, moving cautiously. Suddenly the jungle opened up to an area of low vegetation about as wide as the length of a football field. Hink stopped at the edge to scan the jungle at the far end of the clearing. He did not see anything at first, but then the slightest flicker of movement caught his eye, and he saw three of the biggest men he had ever seen.[1] He was suddenly aware of their uniforms—Japanese uniforms. Hink slowly moved behind a tree, watching the men from across the tall grass. They must have seen him, too, because they also faded into the trees, their eyes in his direction. The two sides watched each other for a few minutes before Hink got low and backed off, keeping the tree between him and the enemy troops. He moved back, pulled out his compass, shot an azimuth, and headed south toward E Company. He was just pulling out his walkie-talkie to call Captain Manchester when he heard rifle and mortar fire.

Sangigai

Spread out in a skirmish line, Brutinel, Carpenter, Pfc. Harold N. "Hal" Block, and the other Easy Company Marines passed quickly between the huts of Sangigai. Like Private Reneau before them, they did not think it was much of a village. It looked like a series of shaded spots with four poles in the ground covered by palm fronds. It was very hot, though, and as Brutinel passed through the village, he thought the water offshore looked cool and refreshing.

Hal ran through the empty village scanning the few huts that had satchels and supplies. He saw surgical equipment and medical satchels beside burlap bags that looked like they might hold food. In no more than a few seconds, Hal, Brutinel, Carpenter, and the rest of the platoon were through the village and into the trees on the opposite side. They had not gone far when the jungle opened up in front of them again to reveal the ocean and sandy beach of a curved bay or an inlet. That was when they saw the Japanese along the narrow strip of beach. As soon as they saw them, Lieutenant Richards raised his hand in an extended fist and his men immediately went to ground.

Brutinel had never seen Japanese troops before but there was little doubt as to their nationality. It looked like about two companies of infantry, at least three hundred men. They appeared to be cooking and eating just off the beach and some of them were splashing around in the cool surf. They were spread out along the shore, anywhere between fifty and three hundred yards away from the Marines. The Japanese did not appear to see the Marines, but suddenly everyone was firing.

The company had been in an extended skirmish line but not all platoons were in position to attack. Private Cagle moved through the jungle on the company's left flank. He, Reneau, and two other men came up on one of the many small streams that bubbled out of the ground and crossed it one at a time before continuing. The jungle was very dense and visibility was almost zero. They were moving parallel with the coast through a well-worn jungle trail when Billy Joe saw movement in a tree about thirty feet in front of him. He moved his head to the side to check it and locked eyes with a Japanese soldier. The soldier had probably leaned out from behind his tree to do the same thing. Billy Joe did not know who was more surprised, him or the enemy, but they both reacted quickly. He brought his scoped .03 rifle up for a quick shot and hissed, "Jap," to warn the others. Meanwhile, the enemy soldier had ducked behind the tree. Billy Joe did not have a shot, so he went to ground. One of the other Marines fired a couple of shots, but the bullets hit the tree trunk. At that moment, they heard the sound of roaring gunfire and mortars and knew the rest of the company was engaging the enemy. The Marines did not want to move into sniper fire, so they stayed behind cover and waited for the enemy to appear.

Back in the area of the thinning trees where the paratroopers had come up on the enemy troops on the beach, Pfc. Robert Zimmerman of Burr Oak, Michigan, was one of the closest Marines to the Japanese. Just before the shooting started, he sighted in on an enemy soldier who was squatting down eating food from a can. Zimmerman chose this man for one obvious reason—he was closest. There was no signal, the shooting just started. Zimmerman pulled the trigger and the Japanese soldier slumped to the sand and did not move. Zimmerman was aware of roaring gunfire as his fellow Marines blasted away around him. He aimed at another Japanese soldier, but after the initial fusillade, it was hard to hit the scrambling targets. Like a surging wave, the enemy troops were rushing madly toward the jungle along the beach.

Pfc. W. Garth Bonner of Salt Lake City, Utah, shot two Japanese soldiers with quick shots before the enemy became a mass of sprinting bodies. He sighted on a man who was flying for the safety of the tree line. The man was stark naked but for his boots, and he was holding his rifle in one hand and his helmet in the other. Bonner emptied his magazine but his bullets only seemed to spur the man on to greater speed because he made it into the trees.

Private Brutinel fired continuously but he could not tell if he had hit any Japanese. So many men were blasting away that it was chaotic, and after the first seconds of shock, the Japanese had run for the safety of the jungle. The Japanese troops in the water fared the worst, shot dead before they could reach shore. Those along the beach were hit hard, too, but the majority of the Japanese infantry made it safely to the tree line, although some of them made it without weapons or clothing.

Sgt. Oscar Frith was in charge of an E Company machine-gun section. Frith's section had not been in position when the firing started, and they scrambled to set up. The enemy troops were scurrying behind the trees and Frith's men did not have the clearest field of fire. Frith began pointing and calling out where he wanted his men to direct their shooting. The A-4 began raking the trees where the Japanese had fled Easy Company's 60-mm mortars. Explosions flared up inside the jungle. The small amount of return fire slackened and then stopped.

Carpenter saw few enemy soldiers but he raked the tree line with his JLMG anyway. With no visible human targets, he saw a barge and riddled it with machine-gun fire, aiming near the water line to sink it.

Private Engstrom did not see many Japanese, either. The Japanese had mostly fled into the jungle by the time his machine-gun section set up to fire, but he raked the tree line, hoping to catch stragglers as they fled inland to the east.

The paratroopers had not been firing long when an experimental rocket screamed overhead. Brutinel looked up as the first rocket went over, but instead of roaring toward the Japanese, it tore out over the ocean to explode harmlessly about two hundred yards out, in the surf. Brutinel turned to look back at the rocket platoon, surprised at their poor accuracy.[2]

The rocket platoon continued to fire all thirty-six of the experimental explosives. Most roared off to explode in the jungle where the Japanese had fled and were thought to have rallied. They could not tell how effective they were, but they were blowing huge chunks out of the jungle. If any Japanese were still there, they were dying.[3]

1430—Colonel Krulak's Force

Less than two hundred yards from the crest of the hill, F Company was nearing its appointed ambush site directly north of Sangigai when they heard distant rifle fire and the explosions of E Company mortars.

It was 1430. With less than two hundred yards to go, Colonel Krulak and his officers were pushing their paratroopers to the limit, trying to get them in position before the Japanese arrived. Otherwise, their ambush would turn into a meeting engagement. On the run, Krulak passed an order back to his TBX crew to try to raise E Company again.

F Company raced down a little valley, crossed a small stream, and began climbing up the very hill from which they were to ambush the fleeing Japanese. Colonel Krulak began issuing orders for the company to split up by platoons and move on the hill. Running quickly to gain the top of the ridge, the point men surged forward. Strangely, the area they were moving into was relatively barren of cover compared with the rest of Choiseul. The top of the ridge was thick with vegetation, but the slope they were moving up was lightly wooded or had been cleared. The leading element was gaining the top of the ridge when point man Pfc. Frank Augustine dropped like a rag doll. A split-second later the report of a rifle made everyone hit the deck. Not a second later, Pfc. Herbert "Blacky" Bell of Bartlesville, Oklahoma, was shot in the back of his helmeted head and Pfc. Kurt

Garbuschewski of Saint Joseph, Missouri, took a bullet to the hip. Blacky went down and lay still, but Garbuschewski was still moving. Writhing in pain, he dragged himself over to what little cover there was. Three men were down and the Marines realized they were in a major ambush.

Sgt. Joseph Martin saw three of his men go down in as many seconds and saw that only Garbuschewski was still moving. It looked like both Augustine and Blacky were dead, with bullets to the head. Snipers in the trees around them had let the Marines pass underneath before springing their trap. From their prone positions, the Marines were reacting quickly, though. Looking almost directly overhead, Martin saw one of the snipers already shot to pieces. He saw another sniper in a different tree, but within seconds that man, too, was killed, riddled with bullets. Martin took aim at the ridge ahead but he could not see any living Japanese. He knew there were many Japanese soldiers around, though—he could smell them. Because of their diet, they had a fishy odor—and the smell here was strong. Martin waited for a target to appear.

The Marines were taking fire, spread out by platoons in a one-hundred-yard radius. They had eliminated the snipers directly above them and began putting suppressing fire on the ridge. The rest of Martin's squad had been just behind Augustine, Blacky, and Garbuschewski, spread out in a staggered column with Captain Pratt, their company commander. Martin was aware of his assistant squad leader, Pfc. Victor Drabecki, and his buddy Pfc. Bill Dolan next to him firing away. Everyone was prone, throwing as much lead at the enemy as possible.

Not far down the hill, Pfc. Orrin Hall was the point man in his squad. Once the shooting started, he hit the deck and searched for a target. The last thing Hall expected was a Japanese ambush. The Marines were the ones who were supposed to be doing the ambushing.

Someone shouted and Hall turned to see Captain Pratt holding a bloody wound, cursing angrily in pain. Pratt was on the deck near his platoon sergeant, James Gibson, and he had been hit in the upper arm or shoulder. Everyone was flat on the ground, firing up at the ridge, as bullets kicked up around them.

Pfc. Robert Adams was approaching a big tree behind which Sub-Lt. Carden Seton and the natives were conferring. Adams and his fire team of Pfc. J. Lloyd King and Pfc. Glenn Barbee had just split up from Pfc. Ed Mach, Pfc. Albert Hyle, and Cpl. Frederick Akerson in an attempt to spread out. Colonel Krulak was leading them with Sgt. John Baker, their squad leader. They had crossed a small stream and were moving up to the military crest of the hill when the sniper fire broke out, followed by the return fire of the Marines at the head of the column. At the sound of the shots, Adams saw Seton, holding his tiny carbine like a pistol, race around the tree heading up toward the fighting. Both Peta Kiri and Peta Nu were right behind him.

Not far from Adams, Krulak was sprinting up the hill calling his men forward. Pfc. Chris Kosma was just ahead of Adams, and Colonel Krulak was ahead to his right side. As they neared the large tree, rifle fire erupted from behind and to their left. Simultaneously, Adams saw bullets tear into the tree in front of them; Private Kosma was struck in the back and went down. Adams dropped instinctively, but as he did, the barrel of his JLMG exploded. It had been hit by a bullet and split into steel shards like the tip of an exploding cigar. Turning to the sound of the firing, Adams saw two Marines about forty yards away aiming at them.

"Hold your fire, knock it off, cease fire!" shouted Adams, waving his free arm.

Just behind him, Cpl. "Baron" Hoffman shouted, "Sniper!" and began firing up into one of the trees. Adams looked but he could not see what Hoffman was shooting at. Everything was happening so fast. He turned back toward the top of the hill to see Colonel Krulak on one knee leaning against the big tree. The Brute looked surprised. He had blood on both checks. "We gotta go," he said, recovering quickly. Waving the others forward, he shouted, "Get up. Let's go." Krulak disappeared around the tree, running toward the ridge.

His JLMG useless, Adams drew his .45 but did not know what to do. He wanted no part of a firefight holding just a .45. He saw Pfc. Glenn Barbee standing next to him, looking confused, and realized why. Training was so instinctive that Barbee stayed with his JLMG man—Adams—even though Adams did not have a weapon. Adams watched Hoffman follow Krulak around the tree and saw everyone moving up the hill.

"Go with Hoffman," Adams told Barbee. He knew Kosma had been Hoffman's assistant JLMG man, and because Kosma was dead and Adams's own gun was useless, Hoffman would need ammo. Barbee turned and raced after Hoffman, with Adams following cautiously up the hill behind them.

Pfc. Earl "Ed" Cassaday was below and to the side of Seton when the first shots were fired. As everyone went to ground, Ed watched Seton and the two natives sprint toward the firing. "He's brave but stupid," thought Ed. He figured the big Coastwatcher was going to be killed for sure—he was just too big a target. But for such a big man, Seton could really move. Seton charged ahead and Ed lost sight of him in the confusion.

Suddenly, he saw Colonel Krulak in front of him, about fifteen yards away.

All the Marines in the vicinity had gone to ground and Krulak was yelling at them to get up and get moving. The Brute ran ahead. Ed followed him and leaped down behind some fallen branches. He saw a dead sniper hanging limply by the ropes that tied him to the tree. The sniper's blood was running in trails down the tree; Ed figured every Marine that moved up the hill must have shot him.

The firefight was gaining intensity and Ed blasted back with his JLMG. There was at least one coconut log bunker on top of the hill and Ed pumped bullet after bullet into it. His fire team had crawled next to him and they all concentrated their fire at the bunker. Everyone else must have been firing at it, too, because it was being shredded by gunfire. Ed spotted another sniper in a tree not too far away, but that man had already been shot dead, too.

Pfc. James P. Dugan had been filling his canteen in the small stream when the firing broke out. The officers were shouting for the men to move forward, and just as they always did in training, they ran up the hill toward the fighting. A line was taking shape and Dugan ran up to join the Marines forming it. He took cover behind the spider-like roots of a banyan tree, and returned fire kneeling close to his buddy Pfc. Herbert Bell. Seeing muzzle flashes firing from the trees ahead, he could hear at least one Nambu machine gun, firing from a concealed bunker. Dugan could not see any living Japanese troops, but he returned fire at the muzzle flashes.

Pfc. Robert Dubson of Naperville, Illinois, was next to his JLMG man, Pfc. Melvin "Barney" Boe of Joliet, Illinois. After the officers roused them, they moved up the hill to the invisible line that the Marines seemed to have deployed along. They were caught on a hill with high ground on three sides of them, and Dubson thought the enemy could not have found a better spot on the island to ambush them. Off to his side the Brute, bleeding from both cheeks, was about fifteen yards away firing up at the ridge and shouting commands to the men. Putting suppressing fire on the top of the ridge, Dubson fired his Johnson up at the tree line and Pfc. Melvin "Barney" Boe let go with his JLMG. Being Barney's assistant, Dubson stayed close so he could provide ammunition for their light machine gun if needed. Suddenly, Barney cursed in pain. One look told Dubson all he needed to know; Barney was out of the fight with a gaping hole in his hip. He did not look good. Wanting to help his friend, but knowing they had to kill the enemy first, Dubson crawled over to Barney's JLMG. Firepower would decide the issue, and Dubson knew they needed to put more fire on the Japanese than the enemy put on them.

Colonel Krulak ran forward and hit the deck near his lead paratroopers. Everyone was firing madly at the top of the ridge. Krulak shouted for his platoon leaders to get their men into action. He pumped a few bullets from his carbine up at the enemy and felt a searing pain in his arm. A bullet had hit his left forearm, passing under his skin paralleling the bone. It exited behind his triceps, blowing out the back of his arm. Krulak continued to fire and shouted for his men to get in position. He was pleased to see them reacting just like it was a training exercise, working together. Their fire-power was devastating the top of the ridge.

Pfc. Norman Dibbens and his fire team of Pfc. John Buckley and Pfc. Frank Rodgers ran up the hill toward the fighting. Dibbens's squad had been farther back in the line, and as he rounded a big bush in front of him, his foot came down on a pile of excrement. Dibbens had no chance of avoiding it but had enough time to wonder, "Either that Jap is sick as a dog or he's been eating the damnedest food." His boot slipped and brought him down. He landed flat on his rear end in the mess, smearing the back of his dungarees. When he fell, his Johnson rifle buried itself barrel first in the ground. It was packed with mud like an old muzzle-loading flintlock that had not been loaded properly. Dibbens could not believe it. In his first fire-fight, before he could even fire a round, he slipped in filth and temporarily disarmed himself. He immediately set to cleaning his weapon as bullets and machine-gun fire exploded all around him.

Pfc. J. N. Clark was working his way forward with his squad. Rifle fire was exploding from everywhere up ahead of them; everyone was lying prone facing the top of the hill.

"Skirmish line," shouted Lt. William King, "spread out."

Clark moved up the hill with his fire team, and his squad automatically fanned out. When he reached the line where most of the platoon was deploying, he put fire on the ridge ahead. Bullets and tracers cut the jungle around him as hundreds of men fired rifles and machine guns back and forth. "The shit has hit the fan," said Clark.

Pfc. Reece Canady had been moving next to one of the native supply carriers when suddenly the man disappeared. It was broad daylight and he was right beside Reece—and then vanished. Canady was taking fire, so he ran and leaped between the roots of a banyan tree, finding himself right next to the native. The man was wedged like a pretzel between two roots. Canady's first thought was that this guy would make a great contortionist.

He could see from the man's expression that he was very unhappy about having a Marine right next to him at that particular moment. Like many of the others, Canady returned fire at sounds and muzzle flashes. The noise was getting louder and louder as men from both sides entered the firefight.

The officers and NCOs were shouting for everyone to get up and move forward. Cpl. Benjamin F. "Cape" Caperton III and his squad followed Sgt. Norman Law to where Sergeant Gibson was firing up at the ridge. Cape took the prone position close by.

"What's going on?" yelled Cape.

"Captain Pratt got hit," yelled back Sergeant Gibson. "Auggie [Private Augustine], too."

The scene was chaotic. From the sheer sound of battle, Cape had expected to see hundreds of enemy troops on top of the ridge. Like many of the others, because of the smoke, the jungle, and their enemy's skill at concealment, Cape could not see a single Japanese soldier. "What the hell do I fire at?" he shouted to Gibson.

"Shoot at ground cover and the base of the trees. Look for smoke or a muzzle flash."

Unlike the top of the hill and the rest of Choiseul, the area they were moving through was relatively barren of vegetation. The Japanese could not have engaged the Marines in a better spot. It dawned on Cape that they had been ambushed. The entire island was teeming with lush vegetation, but here Cape could pick out at least five separate firing lanes. He scanned the trees for snipers, rotating his shooting between each firing lane. He was unable to see any that were not dead, so he went back to the tree line. Unlike the firefight along the trail the day before, Cape knew they were taking fire. He could hear the snap of bullets passing his head. He fired low at the tree line in likely spots before rolling onto his back to search the trees above for snipers.

Red was also in Sergeant Law's squad. He was following his JLMG man, Ski, when he saw one of his fellow troopers, Pfc. Stanley H. Keller, hung up in a bunch of vines.

"Help me," gasped Keller to Red. "I'm stuck. Help me get out."

"Get yourself out."

"I can't. I'm stuck."

Red did not even pause; he kept moving up the ridge toward the line of Marines, following his JLMG man. Red would come back and get Keller out after the fight. Red's job was to follow his JLMG man—who was pounding away at the Japanese. Colonel Krulak and the officers were barking commands, calling up and placing the regimental weapons A-4 machine guns. Red was getting closer when he heard a warning shout. "Stay down! That's a machine-gun lane."

Tracers spit and flashed in front of him and he saw that he had almost stepped into the firing lane of a Japanese Nambu machine gun. He crawled back along the side of the visible firing lane and crossed behind a small rise. Red would be forever grateful to A-4 gunner Pfc. Ralph Nield of Lincoln, Nebraska, who had shouted the warning and spared Red a violent death.

Pfc. Andrew O'Guin of Rockford, Illinois, was in the weapons platoon, so he was farther back in the line. He could not see much through the foliage as he looked up the hill, but he could hear that the lead platoons were in a huge firefight. Pfc. Roger Kirkpatrick was moving just ahead of him when suddenly a rifle fired and Kirkpatrick went down. The shot had come from the tree almost directly over O'Guin. The Marines ahead whirled around and blasted up into the tree. To O'Guin's surprise, a Japanese sniper fell down next to him. The man had a stunned expression on his face. Andrew had always heard how the Japanese had slanted eyes, but this guy's were round with surprise. The man had been shot in the waist and looked as if he had been stunned. O'Guin was so close he did not think to step back to shoot. His hand just reacted and flashed the Ka-Bar from his belt. Slashing out with his knife, he laid the enemy soldier's neck open to his spinal cord.

"Give him one for Kirk," shouted a nearby Marine. O'Guin's knife flashed out a second time and the enemy soldier slumped dead against the side of the tree, a second gaping slash across his throat. O'Guin stepped back to wipe off his Ka-Bar as another trooper ran over and stabbed the dead man, too.

Up toward the ridge in the midst of the raging firefight, Private Hall was busy cleaning his rifle. It was clogged with at least two inches of muck, and Hall was out of the fight until he could clean it. Hall could not have been more grateful to be carrying a Johnson rifle instead of an M-1. He simply took the barrel off (the Johnson rifle came apart in three pieces), pushed a cleaning rod through it, and put it back on. Even though it was not completely clean, he knew it would not jam like a Garand would. He began firing, and sure enough, dirty barrel and all, the Johnson did not fail him. Bullets zipped and tore the jungle around him while he fired at muzzle flashes along the crest of the ridge.

Private Bell, who had been shot in the back of the helmet, regained his senses and got back in the fight. He had no idea how long he had been out.

It could have been seconds, minutes, or half an hour; he did not know. When he recovered he was mad, and turned to fire on the sniper that had shot him. Sighting in, he prepared to shoot but stopped. The man was already dead, shot many times over. Turning back up toward the hill, he could not see any clear targets to fire at so he just shot at smoke. There was not much difference between the sound of opposing rifles and the Marines', but the quick chatter of the Nambu machine guns blasting away in front of them was something new.

Clark still could not see any Japanese to fire at. He turned left and right to see what was happening around him just in time to see Pfc. Gerald Harbert get shot between the eyes. Harbert dropped lifelessly, and a stunned Clark turned back to fire on the ridge. Clark had known Gerald since chute school. They had been in the same training platoon back at Camp Gillespie.

Pfc. Thomas Preston stayed right next to his JLMG man, Pfc. Ralph Bagwell of Arab, Alabama, and kept his eye on the top of the ridge. Pfc. Gilbert DeVault was the third man in their fire team and he was just off to their side. Clark, Pfc. Raymond Hoskins, and Pfc. Earl F. Nevins were on the other side of Cpl. William D. Cole, their squad leader, and everyone was firing up at the ridge. It had been crazy at first, but everyone soon settled down and was reacting as though it were one of their many training problems. Pfc. Mel Lavine was farther over with his two men, so each fire team in the squad was functioning together and Cole was instructing the squad as Lieutenant King, their platoon leader, had ordered.

Dibbens sat furiously cleaning his weapon as leaves and branches shorn off the tree above him by machine-gun fire fluttered down around him. He quickly finished cleaning the rifle and worked a bullet into the chamber. Leaning around his tree, he fired a shot up at the ridge to make sure his weapon worked, and it did. He was too far back, though, and knew he needed to get up on the line. Dibbens looked for his fire team of Buckley and Rodgers and saw them ahead near Pfc. William Alexander. He sprinted and dove at a spot between them and began firing at the ridgeline.

Pfc. Victor Drabecki, a JLMG man, was lying next to one of the native guides who had helped carry supplies. Hugging the deck, Drabecki and his assistant JLMG man, Pfc. Thomas Cloud, were firing up the hill, carefully picking their shots through firing lanes, sometimes even between their own platoon members. The native on the ground next to them suddenly started pointing to a tree ahead and to their flank. Drabecki could not see what he was pointing at, but he unloaded a full magazine into the tree anyway. He figured the man knew something he did not.

Then Drabecki heard a thunk from behind him and turned to see a mortar team set up and firing on the ridge. They were lucky in one respect, thought Drabecki. They had been ambushed in the one spot on Choiseul where they could actually fire a mortar because there were so few trees. When Drabecki turned around, his helmet accidentally slipped off and rolled down the hill toward the mortar team. A Marine from the weapons platoon was about ten feet to the side of where his helmet landed, and Drabecki shouted down to him, "Hey, grab my helmet for me, will you?"

"Get it yourself."

Drabecki crabbed backward, grabbed his helmet, and heard another thunk. Glancing over, the mortar team was firing with their tube almost vertical. He heard thunk, thunk, thunk as the crew fired rapidly again and again. It gave the Marines around them confidence. Drabecki watched the round shoot skyward, but he lost sight of it when it finished its arc. An explosion rose up on the back of the hill followed by another. It looked like the blasts were tree bursts; that was a good thing because shells exploding aboveground maximized casualties. Drabecki climbed back up the hill and moved forward with his squad while the mortar crew fired at impossibly close range. The Japanese were responding with their own knee mortars, and soon the entire hillside and ridge were fogged by smoke from explosions and gunfire.

One of the coconut log bunkers on the top of the ridge concealed a Nambu machine gun that was raking the Marine line. Private Cassaday was pounding the bunker with his JLMG when Pfc. Leo Gruidl jumped up to charge forward. The Nambu machine gun was directly in front of them and it cut loose on automatic, almost chopping Gruidl's legs off. He went down hard with what looked like multiple hits to his thighs. Falling backward with his head down the hill, the machine gun kept firing at him, its bullets kicking up dirt around his feet. Every Marine in the vicinity opened up again, firing right at the aperture of that bunker, and it practically exploded. Bullets chopped it into shards of chipped wood. The machine gun never fired again.[4]

Colonel Krulak gave orders to his runner to tell Lt. Arthur H. Naylor and Lieutenant King to prepare their platoons for a flanking movement. Hoffman crawled off with the orders as Krulak turned back to fire on the ridge. Just then, a Japanese knee mortar dropped ten feet in front of Krulak. The explosion burned his face and threw him backward. He was aware of shrapnel embedded in his jaw, cheeks, and forehead.

"My God," he thought, "I'm blind." He was stunned but came out of it lying several feet down the hill, facing upward. Krulak was surprised to find he could still see. He felt his face and knew he had multiple shrapnel wounds, but he pulled a large piece of steel from the left side of his face, grabbed his carbine, and continued firing on the ridge.

Private O'Guin was still farther down from the leading elements. He scanned the trees above and behind them looking for more snipers. The entire company was spread along the side of the hill and a huge battle was raging. Grenades were exploding and automatic weapons were blasting, but O'Guin could not see anyone except the guys right next to him. He was convinced that the trees in his area were clear of snipers, so he began searching the jungle around him. His eyes immediately were drawn to lateral movement. Someone was sneaking around behind and to the left.

"They're everywhere," thought O'Guin. The man was crawling up at them through the jungle when O'Guin sighted in on him. Just as O'Guin began to squeeze the trigger, he realized it was not an enemy soldier at all but his squad leader Sgt. Richard N. Sullivan. He had almost shot Sullivan dead.

Pfc. Bynum Jacobsen and Cpl. Roy Homerding were F Company radiomen. They had stopped halfway up the hill to try to raise E Company by radio. Homerding started cranking the radio while Jacobsen adjusted the settings. They lost track of time in the adrenaline rush of the firefight, but Jacobsen and Roy were unable to raise E Company. As the battle raged above them on the hill, for the first time since he became a radioman Jacobsen wished he carried the Johnson rifle. Up until that time, he had not wanted to carry any extra weight. His radio was heavy enough, and because he was in the communications section of Hq Company, he figured he would never fight as infantry anyway. All he carried was a .45 pistol. At that moment, however, he wished he had bothered to carry the extra ten pounds. As the firefight rose to a crescendo, word passed down from Colonel Krulak, "Call battalion for more corpsmen."

Soon the hill was wreathed in smoke and there was nothing they could see to fire at. Colonel Krulak was worried his men would expend all their ammo. Many of the men were already bang happy, blasting away at anything along the top of the ridge. For most of the Marines, this was their first combat action and they did not know from experience that they should conserve ammo.

"Cease fire," Krulak shouted over and over. Soon, all of the officers were yelling, "Cease fire, cease fire. Conserve your ammunition." Finally, the shooting began to fade.

The firefight gradually died down and both sides regrouped to prepare for the second round. The strange silence that followed seemed unnaturally loud after the violent battle. Suddenly, the Japanese started shouting at the Marines in English from across no-man's-land.

"Marine, you die tonight."

"Go back, Marine. The bastards of Bataan are here," shouted another. That told the Americans facing them that they were the Japanese Imperial Marines that had stormed the Philippines.

Not to be outdone, the Marines responded with their own insults. "*Notendahakabaka*," yelled Private Dibbens back at them. He had been told that meant, "Your leader is an ass." He hoped he had been given the right translation.[5]

"Marines kill mothers," screamed a Japanese soldier from the top of the hill.

"What the . . . " muttered Private Keller looking over at Cape. Both men were lying on their stomachs. Keller did not seem to understand the slur so Cape explained it to the green paratrooper.

"They're told that in order to be a U.S. Marine, you have to kill your mother. They tell them that to keep them from surrendering." Noticing the confused look on Keller's face he added, "Would you surrender to a man that killed his own mother?"

Hall was lying close to Sergeant Gerarden and his buddy Pfc. Kenneth Twigg. They listened to the insults and laughed. Nobody yelled louder at the Japanese than corpsman PM1 Clay Dunigan. "Tosho each it," roared Dunigan at the enemy line.

After the slur, a Nambu machine gun opened up and raked the berm in front of Dunigan, kicking dirt and leaves into the air. He was not going to be intimidated by that, however, and shouted, "Maggie drawers," and waved his poncho from side to side. He shouted again, "Tosho each it."

"What the hell is he yelling?" asked a paratrooper.

"Tojo eat shit," explained Dugan, laughing. Dugan did not know what was funnier—what Dunigan was saying or what the Japanese could decipher, because most of the Americans did not even understand him. Once again the Nambu machine gun opened up, making the leaves dance above the mound Dunigan was lying behind. "Damn it, shut up and leave 'em alone," laughed Dugan. "They're mad enough now." Then he shouted, "Eat spam, you sons-a-bitches."

The slurs and taunts echoed off the hills. There were all kinds of words thrown at the Marines in Japanese they did not understand, but often English would echo down to them. Private Adams sat behind a tree listening to the curses and saw Pfc. Kenneth Andrews lift his head to shout up at the hill.

"Come and get us, you Jap sons-a-bitches!" roared Andrews.

"Fuck you, Marine," shouted back a Japanese Imperial Marine.

"Fuck Tojo," volleyed back an American.

"Fuck Roosevelt."

"The Emperor is a queer."

"Babe Ruth is a son of a bitch."

Dibbens broke out into laughter at that. He had been so anxious about his combat debut, but it could not have been farther from how he imagined it would be. First, he had slipped in excrement and disarmed himself. Next he had spent part of the firefight cleaning his rifle, all the while his dungarees smelling like a latrine. Then some Japanese soldier calls Babe Ruth a son of a bitch. So far, combat was funny.

While the opposing sides shouted insults at each other, Colonel Krulak was busy thinking about winning the battle. His only thoughts were that soon the Japanese would be making their second attack, so the Brute was helping place their A-4 machine guns. When the enemy came, his Marines would shred them, but he wanted to limit their survivors. He used runners and sent word to his officers again. He wanted Lieutenant Naylor's platoon to flank the Japanese on one side and Lieutenant King's to hit them on the other. Lieutenant Cook's platoon would hold this center. If they could get behind the Japanese after their attack, they might be able to get most of them. The Brute wanted to kill as many as he could. Only a handful needed to escape to report that two large Marine forces had hit them—one along the coast and the other farther inland.

Voza

Pharmacist's Mate Holland was boarding one of the battalion's four Higgins boats with a half squad of Marines that were going to accompany him down to Sangigai. Navy mechanics had repaired the boats. Holland had been sitting around the battalion mountain bivouac when word passed for him to get his medical bag and get down to Sangigai. They had learned via radio that F Company was in a big firefight and had wounded. He and the Marines made the quick trip to the Vagara River. Once there, they followed the coastal trail to the southeast and cut inland just before Sangigai to find F Company.

Captain Manchester's Force

Easy Company had been firing sporadically into the jungle where the enemy had retreated after the initial attack. Dead Japanese lay along the beach and in the water and one of their barges was half sunk in the surf, riddled with bullets. The distant firing of F Company ambushing the Japanese overshadowed the lull in the shooting. The fight seemed to have stopped, so Private Zimmerman ran down to the clearing where he had shot a Japanese soldier at the start of the firefight. It was a good fifty yards, and a number of Marines shouted at him to come back. Zimmerman ran over to the dead soldier and started going through his pockets, looking for a souvenir. He could not find anything, so he switched to the man's pack. He was elated to find a rising sun flag. Stuffing his trophy in his shirt, he ran back to the Marine line. "Zimmerman," chastised one of his fellow Marines, "you dumb bastard. You're damn lucky a sniper didn't kill you."

"Yeah, but look at this," said Zimmerman, proudly holding up the flag.[6]

Farther inland from the others, Private Cagle waited by that little stream alongside the other two men in his reconnaissance party. It was a standoff, and neither side wanted to move first. Billy Joe had his scoped .03 pointed right at the tree where the Japanese soldier had been, but the man never leaned out. He was patient and Billy Joe figured he was waiting for them to move toward him. The Marines did not dare move. For the last half hour, they heard firing coming from both flanks and assumed both companies were engaging the Japanese. The jungle popped with rifle fire, accentuated by the extended bursts of automatic weapons. Explosions sounded off to both sides and he recognized the sounds of the 60-mm mortars easily enough. Those incredibly loud blasts had to be the big experimental rockets the natives had been lugging on their shoulders all morning. It sounded like a huge battle was going on, but Billy Joe, Reneau, and the others were not about to advance blindly in the jungle. They waited patiently for the enemy to come to them.

Back at the former enemy position, Marines in Lieutenant Richards's platoon were moving through the area checking the enemy dead for information and souvenirs. One of the Marines found a pouch and opened it to find papers and documents inside. He knew immediately he had found something that had belonged to an officer. He pulled the papers half out of the pouch to get a look at them and saw a number of hydrographic maps. The maps showed the water routes of Bougainville and its surrounding islands. Every Marine in the Second Marine Parachute Battalion knew that the only reason they were on Choiseul was to take attention away from Bougainville and the invasion scheduled for November 1. Excited about having found something he thought might be important, the Marine ran the maps over to Lieutenant Richards.

The rest of the E Company Marines were having a field day destroying the stores of supplies and ammunition the enemy had abandoned when they fled into the jungle. The paratroopers destroyed everything—nothing remained. They even burned the natives' huts and everything else the Japanese might have found useful in the area. Soon all that remained was the shot-up barge lying half sunk in the surf, but even that would not last. A Bn-3 man was sent out to put C-2 on the sunken barge to make sure it never floated again. Pfc. Frank Dudek, a demolition man, carried all kinds of explosives, but he could only watch with jealousy as one of his buddies waded out to blow up the barge.

Colonel Krulak's Force

Round One had ended, and the Marines had no idea if they had inflicted any casualties on the Japanese other than the dead snipers in the trees. It sounded to them like Round Two was about to begin. From the Japanese line, the angry shouts and screams grew in volume and tempo until the jungle reverberated with the sounds. The paratroopers waited for the assault, fingers tense on triggers. It was so hot and humid that sweat was running down every face. Many of the men knew that the Japanese held the high ground and had ambushed them. Dead and wounded Marines along the hill attested to that unpleasant truth. The enemy had even had time to tie at least three snipers up in the trees—each slumped dead against the ropes that held them suspended.

Private Clark was rechecking his JLMG when he heard moaning coming from the jungle in front of him. The area was lightly wooded where he was, but thirty feet ahead it became jungle again. It sounded like the man was very close. Even with all the screaming and yelling farther up on the Japanese line, Clark could still make out the sound of a man in a lot of pain. With the impending attack moments away and convinced it was a wounded Marine making the noise, Clark got up slowly and crept forward, his JLMG ready to fire. He had not gone five feet when his squad leader Corporal Cole snarled in his slow Tennessee drawl, "Clark, you stupid sombitch. Git yer ass back here."

Clark dropped and crabbed back to where he had been. He suddenly realized he was in the forward Marine line. The only Marines in front of him would be Japanese Imperial Marines. He had barely reached his old position when he heard a command that made him turn cold.

"Fix bayonets," yelled Colonel Krulak.

The officers and sergeants were shouting commands to the F Company paratroopers.

"Check your ammo," shouted Sergeant Gibson. "Use grenades."

"Get ready, they're coming," yelled Lieutenant King along his platoon line. "Jar's on full automatic. They're gonna *banzai*."

The Marines checked and double-checked their ammo, loosened pins on hand grenades, and put Ka–Bars where they could use them. At only fifteen to twenty yards away, it was very likely the *banzai* would end in hand-to-hand combat. The Japanese on the ridge above had kept up a constant barrage of screams and curses that began to grow still louder. The noise was bloodcurdling and eerily high pitched. Soon it was difficult to make out single voices. The increased arpeggio of more than a hundred men shouting and screaming at once drowned everything else out. The Marines below knew the attack was coming at any moment. The enemy could not possibly hold their thundering volume much longer. This was the Japanese prelude to battle.

"*Totsugeki, totsugeki!*"[7]

Hurtling down at the Marines, screaming at the top of their lungs, Japanese Imperial Marines rushed at the Americans, roaring, "*Totsugeki!*" They stormed out of every bush and tree, incredibly fast, and the noise was deafening. Throwing grenades and firing on the run, they poured out of the jungle with long bayonets sticking out from their rifles.

The F Company Parachutists opened fire almost as one. A wall of bullets met the enemy infantry head on, decimating their ranks. Clark was firing furiously and went through his first magazine in seconds, with just a few quick sweeps. Everything was happening so fast he had difficulty processing it. Up to that point, he had not seen a single enemy soldier; then, suddenly, they came pouring out of the jungle in front of him, charging wildly down the hill. He popped in another magazine and held down the trigger on his JLMG as he swept it back and forth.

An enemy soldier burst from the jungle in front of Private O'Guin and banged a grenade against his helmet, activating it. Just as he brought his arm back to throw it, O'Guin heard a Thompson submachine gun fire from his side. The Japanese soldier flew backward as a burst of three .45 slugs climbed up his chest and neck. The grenade that he had been preparing to lob flipped lazily into the air and came back down to explode harmlessly in no-man's-land.

Pfc. John Erotas, Private Cassaday, and Pfc. Milton O'Neal were on line firing at the charging Japanese sweeping down at them. Erotas emptied a magazine from his M-1 Garand and dropped three Japanese in a quick burst of semiautomatic fire. Three more were right behind them. Erotas went to reload when Private O'Neal cried out in pain. Erotas looked over and saw O'Neal holding his stomach. O'Neal was writhing in pain and obviously out of the fight. Erotas reached over, took O'Neal's automatic weapon, and resumed firing. Japanese troops were being shot to pieces as they ran out of the jungle ahead, and Erotas and Cassaday emptied their magazines again. They both went to reload at the same time when a Japanese soldier that had gone to ground lifted up on one arm, banged a grenade against his helmet, and threw it the fifteen yards down onto the two Marines. Cassaday saw the soldier rise up and slammed his magazine in fast, but he was not fast enough. The next thing he knew he was lying face up with his head toward the bottom of the hill. The grenade had blown him backward. His head was ringing and he did not know where he was. He grabbed his JLMG and looked up just in time to see the same Japanese soldier rise up to throw a second grenade. Cassaday knew he would never be able to aim and fire in time, but just then the unmistakable sound of a Thompson submachine gun went off to his side. The Japanese soldier fell dead. The activated grenade detonated in his lifeless hand.

Pfc. Carl Desanto was off on the company flank. From his angle, he could not see any Japanese because the jungle was too thick, but his fellow Marines were in a lightly wooded area and he could see them clearly. Colonel Krulak was beside an A-4 machine gun feeding ammo to the gunner. The Brute's face was a mask of blood. The big weapon he knelt beside was chewing ravenously at the ammo belt, spitting empty cartridge casings out like popcorn.

Private Canady saw a Japanese soldier appear out of the jungle some ten yards in front of him. He fired his M-1 rifle point-blank and hit the Japanese Marine in the stomach. The man crumpled and dropped in his tracks. Canady's magazine pinged, signaling he was empty, so he quickly slapped a new one in and resumed firing.

Privates Dugan and Bell blasted away at the charging enemy troops but the Japanese kept coming. The Marines threw grenade after grenade at the surging Japanese, and their ranks blew apart or were shot down.

Jacobsen, the radioman armed with only a .45, saw a Japanese soldier come screaming out of the jungle. Jacobsen fired his pistol, but so many men fired at once, it was hard to say who brought him down. Still, he was surprised when the man fell just as he fired.

Private Dibbens fired and fired into the jungle in front of him, but all he saw was swirling leaves flying in all directions. Heavy smoke covered the jungle floor. Dibbens heard his JLMG man Private Rodgers cry out in pain and looked over to see him holding his hand in surprise. His thumb had been almost blown off by a Japanese .25-caliber exploding round. Rodgers had been firing his JLMG right next to Dibbens, using the same banyan tree root to hide behind.

A *banzai* attack is a frenzied and terrifying experience for the men it is directed toward. But the reality of a charge straight into automatic weapons is almost always the slaughter of the attacking infantry. The *banzai* was shredded and the few remaining Japanese broke and ran, disappearing into the jungle. Some four-dozen dead Japanese Imperial Marines lay scattered throughout what had previously been no-man's-land. The valley was shrouded in gun smoke and the shooting again died out as the officers shouted for the men to conserve ammo.

Private Cassaday looked over and saw Sgt. John C. Strange grinning at him. It was Strange who had shot the Japanese soldier preparing to throw that second grenade. "Thanks, Sarge," said the private, knowing that the second grenade might have killed him.

"We sergeants have to take care of you boots," replied Strange.

Cassaday remembered then that Private Erotas had been next to him when the grenade went off. Cassaday looked over at his buddy and saw that he had been hit. Erotas's helmet had a hole in the side of it, and his ear, neck, and hair below the helmet were covered in blood. He was not moving and did not look good.

"Corpsman!" someone shouted. A dozen feet to his side, Cassaday could see Rodgers holding his hand.

"What's the matter?" asked Cassaday.

"This," winced Rodgers as he moved one hand to expose the other. Rodgers's thumb appeared to dangle by a strand of tendon. "Corpsman!" he shouted again.

The Marines took stock of their casualties and prepared for the next attack. Private Dibbens looked over at gut-shot Private O'Neal and thought he looked as frightened as any person he had ever seen. O'Neal was in great pain, and Dibbens figured he probably knew he was dying. Nobody came back from stomach wounds.[8]

Dr. Richard Lawrence and the corpsmen were doing what they could for the wounded. Dibbens saw that Colonel Krulak had been hit at least twice. He had wounds on both sides of his face and appeared to have taken a bullet through the arm. It did not seem to affect him, though, and the Brute was going about business as usual.

1530—Captain Manchester's Force

Private Hinkle had reported his sighting of three enemy infantry to Captain Manchester and was standing near the ocean with a number of Easy Company paratroopers, the battalion chaplain, and Major Smoak. It was after 1530, and they wondered what was happening with F Company. They could hear a huge fight coming from the ridge. The clearing they were passing through gave them an unobstructed view of the hill, and they could not help but pause to see what was happening up there. The ridge was wreathed with hazy smoke and that meant F Company was really slaughtering the Japanese. It looked like the ambush had worked perfectly. As Hink, Smoak, and the other Marines watched from the small clearing, they began to take fire from the hilltop. Everyone scrambled for cover, and some of the men began returning fire on the ridge. Hink was behind a fallen log near the battalion chaplain and Major Smoak. Smoak was muttering angrily and reaching for the American flag the battalion chaplain carried.

"Cease fire!" roared Smoak at the Marines firing up at the ridge. "That's F Company firing at us." Hink listened to the report of the incoming gunfire and swore it did not sound like any weapons used by the U.S. Marine Corps. He could hear others saying the same thing, but Major Smoak was convinced it was F Company. He moved back out into the clearing holding the Stars and Stripes, and standing erect, he waved the flag back and forth in big sweeping motions.

"He's going to get his ass shot off," thought Hink. However, as soon as Smoak waved the flag, the shooting abruptly stopped. "I'll be damned," thought an amazed Hink, "Smoak was right." They stopped taking fire from the hill and, because everyone knew F Company was supposed to be on that ridge, it made sense. It was just that those weapons sounded different from anything Hink had ever heard before.

Not three seconds passed when a torrent of rifle fire chewed up around the major's feet. The hill rattled with .25-caliber rifle and Nambu machine-gun fire. Hink watched as the six foot, two inch, 210-pound Smoak did a mad dance back toward the cover of the jungle, the flag trailing ingloriously behind him as bullets kicked at his feet. It was all Hink could do to keep from laughing.

Colonel Krulak's Force

Aside from the terrifying sound of the attack, most of the Marine paratroopers suddenly thought a *banzai* charge was the best opportunity to kill Japanese at relatively low cost in Marine casualties. The Japanese, for their part, probably thought they were facing a much larger force of Americans than they had anticipated. What they could not know at the time was that they were facing more firepower per squad than any military in history, and they had run headlong at almost a dozen of those squads.[9] The Japanese rifle fire ceased, and the taunts and slurs began anew. The enemy troops were trying to psych themselves up for another *banzai* attack, but as the Marines listened they could tell this new round of shouting and cursing did not have the same intensity and volume as the first. After a few minutes, it died down completely. Private Dibbens thought the Japanese must have realized their nineteenth-century tactics were mass suicides against twentieth-century automatic weapons.

After this second half-hearted attempt to *banzai*, Sergeant Martin was still lying flat on his stomach waiting for the enemy to do something. He was near two native guides who had been on point and who had gone to ground. Suddenly, almost as one, the two men pointed at a distant tree. Martin did not even wait to see what they were pointing at; he just opened fire with his Johnson. Both Private Dolan and Private Drabecki did, too, and the tree was riddled with bullets.[10]

"Cease fire, Martin," shouted Lieutenant King from behind them. "Cease fire."

"Look," said Martin pointing. "The guides are pointing up at that tree." Martin put a new magazine in and started firing again.

"Cease fire," ordered King. "Conserve your ammo." Everyone stopped firing and waited, lying on the side of the hill scanning the trees for the enemy. "First platoon, skirmish line, let's go," shouted King.

The time was right for the Marines to go on the offensive. First Platoon leader Lt. Col. Richard "Dick" Cook heard Captain Pratt shout, "King, left end run," then, "Naylor, right end run." These orders sent King's Second Platoon to the left and Naylor's Third Platoon to the right. Cook's platoon would hold the center with the regimental machine guns.[11]

The Marines had greater firepower and put the Japanese in a withering crossfire. The enemy fire lessened considerably and the Marines moved up the hill firing at anything that moved.

Sergeant Martin and his squad held their weapons aimed at the trees as they advanced on the hill. Dolan, Cloud, and Drabecki were spread out beside him as they flanked the hill to the left where there was better cover. They turned, advancing on the ridge from its side.

Private Canady moved forward searching the base of the tree where he had just shot a Japanese soldier. He had seen him go down fifteen minutes earlier. As he moved along, Cassaday stepped over many dead enemy soldiers. He was surprised to see how big the dead men were and even more surprised to see how some of them had no rifles. He knew there was no way the survivors could have collected the weapons before their retreat. Why did these not men have weapons? Something else was puzzling, too. Some of the Japanese infantry were dressed in Imperial Marine uniforms, but others were naked or wearing only loincloths. The whole scene baffled him.

Private Dibbens was advancing on the Japanese flank, and he figured there were still snipers in the trees. He kept his Johnson rifle aimed high as he moved forward with his fire team. They entered the area of the Japanese line and Dibbens saw enemy dead littering the ground ahead of them. Private Nield's A-4 had eaten them alive during the *banzai*. Suddenly, the report of a Japanese rifle fired just ahead made every Marine in the first platoon go to ground. The jungle was very thick in the area they had moved into and nobody had seen the sniper. Several Marines fired at the same tree, but they were firing blindly. The entire platoon was ordered forward again; Dibbens and Buckley began crawling ahead. They came to an area in the jungle where the ground dipped in front of them like a poor man's trench or a dry streambed. Dibbens reached the low area and crawled down into it. What he saw gave him an instant shot of adrenaline. A Japanese soldier was in the same low ground not twenty feet away from him, crawling away toward the lip of the hill. Dibbens quickly fired twice and put two bullets in his torso. The crawling enemy soldier jerked and dropped facedown in the mud. Not long after Dibbens fired, a Japanese rifle spoke again. Dibbens and Buckley exchanged worried glances.

"Did you see him? Where is he? I don't know," they whispered back and forth.

None of them had seen the sniper, although they had an idea of where he was by the sound of his weapon. They also could not really tell whom he had been shooting at. Barely moving, Dibbens crawled forward again.

There were Marines off on both flanks and Dibbens knew someone was going to draw fire any minute. He thought he knew what tree the sniper was in and crawled behind the roots of a banyan tree to try to flank him. He reached the tree trunk and slowly brought his rifle up. When he leaned out to get a look, a .25-caliber bullet tore into the root three inches from his face. A split second later, he heard the crack of the sniper rifle as his reflexes jerked him back.

Private Dibbens had been in combat less than an hour and he realized he had almost been killed. That bullet had just missed his head. Suddenly things were not as funny as they had seemed before. He was furious at the man who had shot at him, but he was also afraid. He still had not seen the soldier, but he was sure of the tree he was in, about twenty-five yards ahead. Dibbens brought his rifle up in anger and, without looking, stuck the barrel around the tree. He fired a full magazine, and brought his weapon back down for fear he would get his hands shot off. He popped a new magazine in. He had no idea if he had hit anything, but he was convinced the sniper was in that tree.

When Dibbens crawled to his new spot, he found himself next to Private Alexander. Alexander rose up to fire and when he did the sniper shot again. CRACK! Dibbens saw the flash and was certain where the sniper was. He brought up his rifle again and pumped another full magazine into the tree at the spot he had seen the flash. Ducking back behind cover to reload, Dibbens turned to Alexander to ask if he had seen the muzzle flash, but he stopped short. Alexander's right shoulder was a bloody mess. A Japanese .25-caliber exploding round had torn it to shreds. Dibbens stayed low and crawled behind the spider-like root to his wounded buddy. He pulled out his first aid kit, exposed the wound, and dumped sulfa powder on it before slapping a field dressing on. After that, aside from telling Alexander he was going to be all right, there was not much Dibbens could do.

There was still the sniper, though, who had pinned everyone down in his area. Even though they had not seen him, they knew where he was. Dibbens and Buckley pumped round after round into his tree but they were just spraying blindly. If they peeked out, they might get their faces blown off. This sniper had already gotten Alexander, almost shot Dibbens, and had temporarily halted the advance. Off on the flanks, though, leapfrogging in twos and threes, the Marine fire teams continued moving on the hill.

Pfc. Thomas Preston was approaching the military crest of the hill and was next to Pfc. Ralph Bagwell and Pfc. Gilbert "Gilly" DeVault. Preston kept his weapon on the tree line and moved in a crouch. They soon cut into what had been the Japanese line. Suddenly, Preston saw movement to his side at the base of a tree. It was the same tree DeVault had fired at before, but Preston could not see anyone. Both DeVault and Bagwell opened up with their automatic weapons, peppering the tree with bullets. Convinced nothing could live through that fusillade, the Marines moved forward again. As they got closer, Preston saw two dead enemy soldiers lying at the base of the tree. Because of the angle, Preston figured DeVault had killed both of them. Near the top of the hill they got down and crawled the rest of the way. There was a third dead soldier lying on the ground in front of them, but they could still hear sniper fire from the jungle ahead, so they did not move any farther. When they received word to pull back down the hill, they were only too happy to follow that order. Although they had obviously won the battle, Preston never believed they had killed all the Japanese.

Private Dibbens heard the order for the First Platoon to pull back. This particular sniper was lethal; even though they had pumped magazine after magazine into the area where they saw his muzzle flash, they still had no idea if they had hit him. Nobody was willing to stand up to find out, either. Dibbens crawled back, keeping the big banyan tree between himself and the sniper's tree, helping Buckley pull the wounded Alexander with them. Private Canady was just off to their flanks, and he could not reach the enemy soldier he had shot. He wanted some souvenirs or at least the man's rifle, but the sniper was too dangerous. With the others, Canady pulled back and moved down the hill.

1600—Jungle Trail

Pharmacist's Mate Holland and the five men assigned to escort him down to Sangigai had reached the Vagara River by LCPR and landed on the southeast side of the river near the village of Vagara. It had taken the Marines almost two hours to travel the five miles down to the Vagara River, but Holland and the others had done it in twenty minutes in the Higgins boat. When they pulled up to the shore the village was deserted and there was no sign of either the Marines or the Japanese. Holland and the five Marines escorting him moved quickly down the coastal trail to the southeast and cut inland, moving toward the large hill in the distance where F Company had ambushed the Japanese. It was 1600 and Holland could hear sporadic rifle fire. He figured the battle was all but over and knew he was needed.

Cautiously but quickly the six men moved inland through the dense jungle to find F Company.

Captain Manchester's Force

While F Company was mired by sniper fire, E Company was preparing to move back over the same trail they had come down earlier that day. They had been waiting for more than an hour in a defensive perimeter that would keep the Japanese penned against F Company. By then, the firing on top of the hill had died down, so everyone figured F Company must have slaughtered the Japanese. Captain Manchester ordered his men to torch Sangigai and destroy anything the enemy could use. He ordered his company to fall back and form up for the trip back up to Vagara Village where the LCPRs were supposed to be repaired and waiting.

They made considerably better time on their return trip. As they passed back through an abandoned Japanese camp Sgt. Philip Romero told Private Dudek to destroy it. A demolition man, Dudek had been champing at the bit to blow something up. One of his buddies had just blown up a Japanese barge, and Dudek was fiercely jealous. He took out his primer cord and a block of C-2 as the others moved through the camp. Dudek was salivating with the thought that he was going to help destroy the enemy logistically, but as he looked around the camp, he soon lost his enthusiasm. It already looked like it had been blown up. The only thing to destroy was a Japanese field kitchen and some tools lying around a fire spit with a hanging pot. He would be a laughingstock if he blew up a field kitchen, so he tossed the spit into the jungle, broke the pot, threw the tools in the ocean, and kicked the field kitchen in. Then he moved to catch up with the others.

"Why didn't I hear an explosion?" demanded Sergeant Romero.

"To blow up a field kitchen?" retorted Dudek. "Hell, I'm not gonna waste my C-2 on that. I'd never hear the end of it."

F Company

Throwing his wrecked JLMG to the ground, Pfc. Robert Adams looked down at the eighteen-year-old Private Kosma and shook his head. He felt terrible at the death of this young replacement. Kosma had been killed by friendly fire. "What a fiasco," he thought. "One man killed by our own guys." Adams had been with the Second Marine Parachute Battalion since its inception and he had still not seen combat. Through the entire hour-long firefight, Adams had never even fired a shot. How could he? His JLMG had been destroyed. All he had was a .45 pistol and he had not seen any Japanese close enough to shoot at. Two men came over and lifted the fallen Kosma to carry him over to where the other KIAs lay. When they lifted him, Adams looked down at the perfectly good Johnson rifle that had been lying under the dead man. He could have armed himself. Further sickened, he picked up Kosma's weapon and slung it over his shoulder.

"Where's Kenny?" asked Pfc. Bernard Best at his side. Adams looked around but he did not see Private Andrews. Andrews was in a different platoon, but he and Best were good buddies. All Adams saw were Marines spread out on the hill. "Kenny?" shouted Best, looking around.

The company was trying to organize and others joined in. "Kenny? Andrews?"

Colonel Krulak was moving back down the hill. He had blood all over his face and left arm. A corpsman moved over to treat him and started to pull steel fragments from the Brute's face. "I'm not even going to try to get that one near your eye," said the corpsman. "If I do I'm liable to blind you. Maybe Dr. Lawrence can get it, but I doubt it." The corpsman finished dressing the colonel's face and went to work on his left arm.[12] This was a flesh wound. He dumped Sulfa liberally on entry and exit wounds and bandaged both.

"Gear up," ordered Krulak. "Police the area and don't leave anything behind. Prepare the wounded for travel."

The Marines were going back to the Vagara River for LCPR extraction to Voza. The reinforced company was spread out along the top of the hill, moving the wounded over to a makeshift triage the corpsmen had set up. Dibbens and Buckley brought the wounded Alexander down and turned him over to a corpsman. They laid the dead next to each other in an area of low ground. The demolition men came over and put a large amount of explosives beside the knoll.[13] The Marines did not have time to bury them with entrenching tools; the TNT would cover the fallen men with earth.

Many of the Marines felt good about their first combat action. They had chewed up the enemy pretty good during the firefight and took a body count of seventy-two confirmed enemy dead with an undetermined number of wounded. There were probably more dead Japanese, but they had not searched the entire hill because of the enemy snipers. Some five thousand living Japanese were still on Choiseul, however, and they would be in hot pursuit. The Marines needed to get out of there.

Private O'Guin sat next to his wounded buddy Private O'Neal and waited for the order to move out. "You're going to be okay, Milt," O'Guin lied.

Private Cassaday moved over to help with the wounded and he could hear his buddy Private Gruidl pleading with Dr. Lawrence, saying, "Don't leave me."

"I'm not going to leave you," Lawrence reassured him. He stooped and picked the young man up, carrying him to a makeshift stretcher. Lying the wounded Marine down on a poncho, he adjusted the tourniquets on both legs to make sure the private was ready for travel.

Private Jacobsen finally contacted Easy Company over the radio and learned that they had accomplished their mission. They had also captured what appeared to be important documents. Jacobsen was told it was something the colonel would definitely want to see immediately. The documents appeared to contain information that would greatly assist the Bougainville invasion. Jacobsen hefted the radio, slung it over his back, and checked his pistol, which felt strangely light. Jacobsen was surprised to find the magazine empty. He only remembered firing one shot during the *banzai* but apparently in the frenzy and adrenaline rush, he had emptied the magazine. Jacobsen went over to tell the colonel about the captured documents and saw Dr. Lawrence working on a man who apparently had stepped in front of his own machine gun.

What a man Dr. Lawrence was. Jacobsen had seen him crawl down into a muddy hole in the rain to help a private suffering from malaria stay warm. Lawrence would give his men the shirt off his back. What was ironic was that of all the Marines too sick to be there, nobody was worse off than Lawrence. He should have been relieved. Lawrence had malaria and dengue fever. Cassaday knew there was no way the doctor would leave his men, though. He had asked him about it once, and Dr. Lawrence just laughed. "As far as the Marine Corps knows, I'm the healthiest man in the Parachute Regiment. I have better physicals than any of you virile young bucks."

"How?" snorted Cassaday.

"Because I write them myself," replied Dr. Lawrence. "That's how."

Not far away, Pfc. Robert Dubson was helping his buddy Pfc. Melvin A. "Barney" Boe over to where Dr. Lawrence and the corpsmen were treating the wounded in their makeshift jungle triage. Barney had been shot in the hip and was in a lot of pain, although he could stand with help. Dubson had an arm around Barney to help hold him, and he carried Barney's JLMG besides his own Johnson rifle and their ammo.

Corporal Caperton assembled with the rest of Sergeant Law's squad and watched Captain Pratt walk by with a bloody bandage on the muscle between his shoulder and neck. It looked like he had been shot right through his trapezius muscle. Cape had never seen Pratt so visibly shaken, but it was not from his wound. Pratt was trying to cope with the loss of Private Augustine, who had been like a son to the captain and had been his company clerk. Augustine's lifeless body was stretched out on the side of the hill. Cape had just talked to the corpsman who was closest to the private when he got hit. The corpsman told Cape that Augustine had been on point with Pratt just behind him. When Augustine was first shot, Captain Pratt froze in his tracks; then he, too, was shot in the shoulder and went down. Before the corpsman could get to him, the wounded captain crawled up to check on Augustine. The corpsman crawled up, too, but Augustine was already dead. Lying beside his fallen clerk, Pratt's face conveyed how he was grieving inside.

Private Hall moved back through the area where the KIAs were being stretched out, side by side. They were Private Kosma, Private Harbert, Pfc. Kemper Biggs, and Private Augustine. On his way, Hall passed the wounded Milton O'Neal, who was still alive, but for how long?

The wounded were being put on makeshift stretchers while the corpsmen were doing the best they could to patch them up. It had been a bloody baptism of fire for Fox Company and the attached weapons sections. Colonel Krulak had taken multiple shrapnel to the face and was shot in the arm. Captain Pratt was shot through the shoulder. Private Rodgers was shot in the hand and Private Boe in the hip. Private Erotas had taken shrapnel to the head. Private Gruidl was hit badly in both legs, Private Slivkoff was shot through the buttocks, Private Garbuschewski was shot through the hip, Private O'Neal in the stomach and shoulder, Private Kirkpatrick in the back, and Private Alexander in the shoulder. The list went on, with Pfc. Anton Wrobleski, Pfc. Lowell Shelton, Pfc. James Fisher, and Pfc. Ray Roucher all hit and needing to be carried out.

A man that did not make the casualty list but should have was Private Bell. He had a raging headache, the worst he had ever had. By all rights, he knew he should be joining that big Marine Infantry Regiment in the sky because a sniper had shot him at point-blank range in the back of the head. When, an hour later, he took his helmet off to examine it, however, he saw that the bullet had entered the back and somehow ricocheted around between the liner and the helmet and had stopped in the front. A huge dent indicated where it had lodged when it stopped. It was a miracle Bell was alive. As he examined his helmet, some of his friends came over to see it. "It doesn't come any closer than that," said Dugan.

Blacky Bell took the liner out, and when he did, a flattened .25-caliber bullet fell to the mud. He put his helmet back on, and his buddies laughed at the effect of a puncture hole in the back and the dented protuberance in the front. Blacky became the brunt of a great many jokes. "Yep," joked Dugan, "went straight through."

"Rang his 'Bell,'" joked others.

Blacky was to be ribbed about the incident for the rest of his life but he never—ever—underestimated the importance of wearing a helmet. Before they headed back, Blacky took one last look at the sniper that had almost killed him. His body still hung lifelessly from a tree as the last of his blood dripped down the branches to the jungle floor.

"Kenny?" shouted Private Best, looking around for his buddy Private Andrews. Private Adams was standing beside Best, who looked like he was dying inside. "Kenny? Kenny?" Best shouted again as he started moving back up the hill.

"Where are you going?" asked Adams.

"I'm not leaving without him," replied Best, without looking back.

Word passed to move out. Picking up their wounded, F Company assembled by platoon and began moving in single file back along the jungle in the direction of Vagara Village. Twenty paratroopers carried ten wounded Marines on makeshift stretchers. It would have been difficult to carry them on the coastal trail let alone the dense, hilly jungle. The men slipped in the mud, were slapped in the face by branches that swung back after the man in front had passed, and ducked under fallen, rotting tree limbs. They had to stay alert for enemy ambush, and the men at the back of the column tried to walk backward, alert for counterattack.

Private Adams was a stretcher bearer who helped carry out the wounded Private Gruidl. Adams was carrying the front end of the stretcher. As they moved down the hill, he had to lift his end to keep the wounded man level for the descent. Adams was tired, demoralized from missing the fight, and sick about seeing Kosma get killed by friendly fire. F Company carried their wounded in a long column, slashing and hacking their way to the northwest toward Vagara Village. Every time Private Adams went down a hill or crossed a stream, he had to hold the stretcher high on his shoulder. Going down a particularly steep hill, he was unable to keep the stretcher level. A rush of warm liquid soaked his neck, back, and butt. He just assumed it was sweat that had pooled on the stretcher. He was exhausted by the time the column finally stopped and the officers ordered the bearers replaced. When two men came up to take over, Adams turned around to look around at his back. He was covered in blood, his dungarees crimson. He realized then that it had not been sweat that had poured over him—it was Gruidl's blood.

The column started moving immediately and stopped again in about twenty minutes. The arms of the stretcher bearers were quickly fatigued, and so the men needed to rotate often. Private Adams was surprised when he was told to get back on for another shift as a stretcher bearer for the wounded Private Gruidl. Private Dibbens was the other stretcher bearer. It was 1700, and he worried they would not be able to get out of the jungle by nightfall. Dibbens was carrying the back of Gruidl's stretcher and could not help but look at the poor guy's wounds, where Nambu machine-gun fire had stitched him across the legs. It looked like someone had ripped open his pants and stuffed them with bowls of dark red jelly where his thighs should have been. In fact, they had not traveled fifteen minutes when the wounded Marine bled to death. Private Dibbens had never watched a man die before but he was so exhausted from the physical strain, mental fatigue, and anxiety stretched over a sleepless seventy-two–hour period that he was strangely removed from this man's death. He told Private Adams, and they simply rolled Gruidl off the stretcher. They informed one of the officers and left the dead man for the demolitions people to take care of. With Private Gruidl's death, the Fox Company KIAs totaled five.

Pfc. Albert Hyle of Cleveland, Ohio, was tired before he picked up one end of a stretcher made from two large branches and a poncho. He and another stretcher bearer lifted wounded Pfc. John Slivkoff up and moved along the line of paratroopers. Everyone was connected—hand on shoulder or hand on belt—to the man in front. Men walking between stretchers had to use both arms to keep the line together. Down every hill, Hyle had to lift the poles onto his shoulder to keep Slivkoff level; up every hill, he had to walk bent over. It was murder on his lower back and shoulders. Hyle was exhausted in no time. To keep his mind off the aching pain in his arms while he trudged along, he thought of the firefight. He had blasted away at the tree line like everyone else, but he had never seen anything but an occasional muzzle flash from behind a tree. He never even saw any Japanese during the *banzai*, only dead ones, but he had been off on the flank.

"Give up your shirts, the wounded need them," passed down the line. Private Drabecki took his shirt off and handed it to Pharmacist's Mate Dunigan who came around to collect them. A motley-looking crew marched along in the late afternoon of October 30. They were all filthy, and those old enough to have facial hair were growing beards like mountain men.

Private Dibbens took his dungarees off and threw them away. They were covered in human excrement and smelled awful. A corpsman came by and handed out medicinal brandy and Benzedrine. Dibbens watched one guy take two of the uppers, wash them down with brandy, down two more vials, and stick himself with a syrette of morphine. "Good God, this guy's gonna kill himself," thought Dibbens. But the Marine seemed fine, and when the column started moving again, he walked just in front of Dibbens, none the worse for wear.

Captain Manchester's Forces

As they approached Vagara Village, Easy Company's platoon scouts carefully moved through the jungle paralleling the shore inland of the coastal trail. The main column was spread out by platoons behind them. The scouts moved uncontested all the way to the edge of the village. Major Smoak and Captain Manchester knew that there could be enemy troops in the area, so they set up a defensive perimeter at the village and sent scouts to search the surrounding jungle. They had only to wait for Colonel Krulak and F Company to show up and for the LCPRs to come get them.

It had been a successful day for Easy Company. They had caught the Japanese completely by surprise and forced them up into the F Company ambush exactly as planned. They had shot up the enemy and left their dead scattered along the sand and surf. A Daihatsu barge was half sunk, and they had destroyed all of the enemy's supplies, munitions, and medicine. More importantly, they had not taken a single casualty, and had captured what appeared to be documents that might assist in the Bougainville invasion. Both Smoak and Chesty had looked at the maps and believed they appeared to show Japanese barge routes and mined channels. The real invasion was coming in less than forty-eight hours, so this was deemed invaluable information that IMAC needed immediately. If it proved accurate, the Bougainville invasion fleet would be able to avoid the mined channels.

Colonel Krulak's Force

While F Company stopped to change stretcher bearers and see to the wounded, the lead element heard approaching movement ahead in the jungle and prepared to fire.

"Halt. Who goes there?"

"Lollipop," came the reply. "Who's asking?"

"Lulu lady. Advance and be recognized."

Pharmacist's Mate Holland and the half squad of Marines with him had found F Company. While the column was stopped to switch stretcher bearers, Holland moved over to check with Dr. Lawrence. The wounded men lay along the ground, and Lawrence and the corpsmen treated men by priority of wounds. At that moment, Lawrence was trying to keep Private O'Neal from bleeding to death. Because the doctor had his hands full, Holland began looking for a stretcher that did not have a corpsman kneeling beside it. As he did, he opened his pouch.[14]

Holland approached a stretcher bearing Private Slivkoff, who had been shot in the buttocks. Holland pulled his bloody compress back to examine the wound. Slivkoff had a nice neat hole completely through one of his cheeks. He was lucky. It was not even bleeding that much. Holland dumped sulfa powder on it and bandaged his patient's wounded posterior. While he did, Slivkoff looked over his shoulder at him.

"I'm dying," he said. "Please, get me a priest."

"Dying?" snorted Holland, feeling torn between humor and disgust. "Hell, you're not even hurt. You shouldn't have left the line."

"No," insisted Slivkoff, "I'm dying. Please, get me a priest."

"We don't have a priest here," said Holland. He would have grown impatient with the young man but for the fear in his voice. "It isn't even a bad wound," he repeated. He knew it was probably a painful one, but it was not bad as far as gunshot wounds went.

"I'm dying," insisted Slivkoff, slipping into shock. Holland immediately put an IV in the private's arm and started giving him plasma to bring him out of shock.

"You're not hurt that bad, Slivkoff," he said soothingly. "Calm down. You're going to be fine."

"I'm dying," the private repeated. "Please, get me a priest."

"We don't have a priest," explained Holland, "and the battalion chaplain's not here."

"I'm dying," persisted Slivkoff, with anguish in his voice. "Will you hear my confession and give it to a priest?"

"Sure," said Holland, thinking he would do anything to calm him down.

The wounded man confessed his sins to Holland, who could not help thinking that Slivkoff did not have anything to worry about. He obviously led a very clean life. Compared with Holland's own experiences, it was not much of a confession. What was he worried about? As soon as Slivkoff finished his confession, he slipped right back into shock. "What in the hell?" muttered Holland in frustration. He had the terrible thought, "Did I miss something?" He carefully rechecked the body, removed Slivkoff's shirt, cut his dungarees open, and checked his head. Nothing. The man was not hurt anywhere else. Convinced he had not missed anything, Holland called for Dr. Lawrence. By the time Lawrence came over, Holland was worried Slivkoff was going to die.

"I can't keep this guy out of shock."

"Are you sure he's not hit somewhere else?"

"Yeah, I'm sure. I've checked him twice and someone saw him before me 'cause he's already been treated with sulfa. He's only got a flesh wound in the butt. It's not even bleeding bad."

"Let me see," said Lawrence. He turned Slivkoff over and checked his entire body. After he had made a thorough examination he agreed. "Hell, he's not even hit that bad."

They tried to bring the wounded man back but were powerless to do anything but watch him die. In frustration, they pulled the poncho over his face. That meant a total of six Marines killed during the day's action. As he moved on to another wounded man, Holland saw them take Private Slivkoff off the side of the trail to be buried. "He willed himself to die," thought the pharmacist's mate.[15]

The exhausted company continued through the jungle. It had been hard for them to move earlier; carrying the wounded made it even harder. Most of them were undernourished, sustained merely by D-bars. Also, many of them had not gotten more than four hours of sleep in five days.

Private Clark was one of those fatigued stretcher bearers. In addition to his own weapons, ammo, and equipment, he was helping haul out Pfc. Roger Kirkpatrick, who had taken a .25-caliber exploding round in his back. It seemed to Clark that he had been carrying the private for miles. His arms were about to fall off. He thought he could not go much farther when, mercifully, the column stopped and another Marine showed up to take his place.

Pharmacist's Mate Dunigan came by to check out Kirkpatrick, and when he did, he saw just how bad Clark looked. He reached into his pack and took out a vial of medicinal brandy. "Drink dis," he said extending the vial. "It'll help." He reached into his satchel and pulled out something else. "Take dis, too," he said extending his hand palm up to reveal two tablets. "It's Benzedrine."

Clark took the tablets, popped them in his mouth, and used the brandy to wash them down. Then he moved over to where Corporal Cole, Private Bagwell, Private Lavine, and the rest of his squad were resting. In the last minutes of light, he saw a sight he would remember the rest of his life. The battalion doctor was carrying a dead man piggyback in the long column of men. Dr. Lawrence was covered in the man's blood. Lawrence was as torn up as Clark had ever seen a man look. Clark wondered how long Lawrence had been carrying the dead man, for they had been moving through the jungle for more than an hour.[16]

Two Marines came and took the dead man from Lawrence. The exhausted doctor did not resist. The two guys propped the dead man against a tree and in morbid fascination Clark watched them place him in a lifelike position, and put a rifle across his lap, as if he were resting. "Maybe he'll buy us some time," said one of them. The dead Marine looked like he was merely sitting guard, looking back down the trail.

Private Preston was behind Clark and he, too, saw the dead man. If he had not seen them place the man against the tree he would have thought he was alive, just another Marine resting with his weapon in his lap. The single file began moving through the jungle again.

Private Drabecki knew they only had a few minutes of sunlight left before night dropped, and then they would all be blind. He noticed a Marine sitting against a tree, relaxing along the side of the trail with his rifle on his lap. He looked like he was on a field problem back in California. The guy was smiling and looked content, even happy. "What the hell are you so happy about?" snorted Drabecki. Suddenly he realized the man was dead. He continued marching, but he thought about the dead Marine and the peaceful, pleasant look on his face. It looked, he said, as though the man had "just passed over to somewhere good."

Dusk fell and it was like someone had turned off the lights. Within seconds, it was impossible for them to see the man in front. Private O'Guin was carrying one end of the stretcher that held his wounded buddy Private O'Neal. O'Guin had serious doubts his friend would make it. He and O'Neal had gone through boot camp and chute school together, and were put in the same squad in New Caledonia. They were both tall, skinny Irishmen who loved to play basketball. On Vella LaVella, O'Guin had been transferred to the weapons platoon and that was why he was not next to his friend during the firefight. O'Neal looked bad, his upper body covered in blood. Dr. Lawrence had been working on him, but he said O'Neal had to get to a field hospital fast.

That was the toughest day of Private O'Guin's life, watching his buddy slowly bleed to death while trying to fight his way through the jungle to get him to help. O'Guin's arms burned from the weight, and it seemed he always had another hill to climb or another stream to cross. It had been difficult enough to move in the jungle when he could use his arms. Every step he took with his new burden was a struggle. The jungle was so dense with trees whose branches stuck out in every direction that passing unhindered was impossible. During one of their frequent stops to change stretcher bearers, an officer came by and handed O'Guin a vial of medicinal brandy. "Don't take it until you have to," instructed the officer.

"I have to," said O'Guin, downing the liquor immediately.

1830—Voza

The LCPRs finally arrived, and Major Smoak and Captain Manchester had to make a decision. They had already waited almost two hours for F Company. It was going to be dark soon. They had not heard from F Company on the TBX for a while and did not know what was keeping them. Finally, with dusk approaching, Major Smoak made the decision to withdraw to Voza. They could not remain at Vagara Village to keep a corridor open for F Company. E Company was already low on ammunition and rations and, more important, they needed to get back to protect Voza. G Company alone was holding down the fort, guarding the entire battalion's supplies. If Easy Company stayed at Vagara Village waiting for the colonel, they might return to find the smoking ashes of their battalion bivouac and their logistical ruin. Loading the repaired LCPRs with a platoon of men each, Easy Company shoved off from the mouth of the Vagara River and moved back up to Voza. They arrived around 1830 and moved immediately up to the battalion hideout. By then, they were accustomed to traveling that trail at night because they had done it so many times. They assembled in another connected single file and moved up the mountain in total darkness. Tired but pleased with their first combat action, all but the assigned guards climbed into their waiting hammocks.

Colonel Krulak's Force

An exhausted F Company was connected hand on shoulder or cartridge belt, stretching through the dark jungle, led by Lieutenant Seton and the native guides. They moved blindly, at a snail's pace. They had been backtracking through the jungle for more than two hours, trying to reach the

Vagara River. They had already covered more than fifteen miles that day and had fought a pitched battle. Immediately thereafter, they had moved out, carrying their wounded. All of this was accomplished on little sleep or food. Private Dubson concentrated on the bobbing phosphorescent smear on the back of the Marine in front of him. Dubson had been helping Private Boe for most of the way, and he was exhausted. Barney was doped up on morphine, but he could still walk, barely. It was nerve-racking and tiring, because Dubson could hear engines that he assumed were Japanese barges ranging up and down the coast looking for them. Sangigai was a base for a Japanese regiment of more than fifteen hundred men and they would be bloodthirsty for revenge.

The column stopped to replace exhausted stretcher bearers; it was taxing to carry so much weight for an extended time in the jungle. The colonel and Lieutenant Seton were up under a tent-half again checking map and compass, using a lighter for illumination. Private Dibbens felt very confident in both his leader and their guide, and he was grateful for another rest.

Suddenly, he heard noise directly behind him and the hushed whispers of irritated men. He listened and knew instantly what was wrong. The guy who had taken the uppers, brandy, and morphine was starting to act irrationally. He kept trying to wander off into the jungle. The man holding his shoulder was getting angry because he did not want to get separated from the others. Dibbens feared this guy would get him lost. The column waited and waited. It was a good thing the men in front and back of the drugged-up man seemed to like him because they did a great job keeping him in the column and preventing him from wandering away.

Private Jacobsen was squatting with his heavy radio on his back, waiting silently for the line to move again. Everyone knew better than to talk at night, but some of the men wondered if some snafu had separated the column. Would they wait all night before the others figured out they had left them? Jacobsen knew his mind was his own worst enemy. Dr. Lawrence was right next to him working on somebody that had been shot up bad. During the breaks, Lawrence would move back and forth checking the wounded under a tent-half, a lighter supplying him light. Pharmacist's Mate Dunigan and the other corpsmen were doing the same thing for other wounded. Jacobsen heard a hushed whisper, "Keep it quiet. A Jap patrol is passing on our left." He held his .45 ready to fire. Their column was long—almost two hundred men—and it seemed unlikely to him that they would be able to warn everyone in time. He expected gunfire at any moment. Long minutes passed and nobody moved. After five minutes, the "all clear" came and the line started moving again.

The parachutists soon came across another of the dozens of streams that seemed to bubble out of the island, but this time they entered it. Following the shallow water path made traveling a bit easier and reduced the odds of getting lost. They followed the stream for twenty minutes before stopping again to switch stretcher bearers. Private McClure was exhausted as he stood in the flowing water. In two days, he had made two trips through the jungle to Sangigai. It had been rough, but at least his legs were not cramping as they had the day before. The night before, his squad had been in a firefight, and since the Japanese were famous for night fighting, he had expected the enemy to probe them. He had stayed awake all night.

The seemingly endless halt continued and Red stood in the stream waiting for the order to move. His boots were full of water and felt like lead weights. He held a wounded man on the stretcher, but it was too dark to see who he was or where he had been hit. There was nothing Red could do. He did not dare break from the column to get out because they might leave any minute. The orders were "No talking and stay ready." Red could not put the wounded man down either because they stood up to their knees in a stream. He hoped someone would remember they needed to be relieved, and sighed gratefully when he felt the tap on his arm. "I got him," said a voice in the darkness.

Carefully, Red let go only when he knew his relief had a good hold. That was the second time he had been a stretcher bearer, and he hoped there would not be a third. As he waited for the column to start moving again, an officer came by and handed him a vial of medicinal brandy. Red took it, but he never drank it. Instead, he offered it to the Marine behind him who gratefully accepted it. Red was not opposed to drinking and could have used it, but he was convinced that they were not out of this yet and he wanted all his mental faculties unhindered. There was no telling how many Japanese might still be between them and the Vagara River.

Once again, the line moved forward and the paratroopers started sloshing their way along the stream. Moving through the water offered them one real advantage in the darkness—it was difficult to get off the path and not know it. If they just followed the rivulet and held to the man in front, it was hard to get separated from the others. Red could not even see the phosphorous patch on the man ahead of him. He figured the phosphorous only worked if there was some form of natural light. He was unable to see the water, so he simply felt and listened as he walked. The man in front of him rose up and Red stepped up to solid ground as they left the relatively easy movement in the stream to trudge back into the jungle.

Private Dibbens was holding the line between two stretcher bearers; he had his hands on the shoulders of both the man in front of and the man behind him. They had all been trained that if the man behind lost his grip, the man in front would stop. That way the column would not get lost. Well, that was what was supposed to happen. When Dibbens slipped and fell getting out of the stream, however, he got back up and reached for the shoulder that was supposed to be in front of him, but it was not there. He did not dare call out and figured the man would realize the column was broken and would stop. Dibbens and the others waited. Soon five minutes passed, ten, fifteen, but nobody came back for them. Dibbens began to worry. They had wounded and were stranded in a stream. Someone else must have had the same thought because he whispered forward, "What's the hold up?"

"We're separated from the column."

"Ohhhh shit."

The rest of the column, unaware that Private Dibbens, Private Buckley, Private Canady, and a dozen other Marines had been separated and were standing in a stream far behind them, snaked on until Seton and the guides successfully led them out of the jungle and into Vagara Village. E Company and the navy LCPRs were long gone and F Company found the area deserted. They tried to make radio contact but Private Jacobsen and Corporal Homerding could not raise either E Company or battalion head-quarters. Because he was unable to raise anyone by radio, Colonel Krulak sent Lieutenant Cook and his own runner Corporal Hoffman up the coastal trail to Voza to get the boats and bring them back.

Meanwhile, the Marines were ordered to set up a perimeter defense around Vagara Village and dig in. Private Clark was hewing at the earth in the hastily formed F Company perimeter and he was mad. Here they were, outnumbered, on an unfamiliar enemy island, running low on ammunition and practically starving, and the navy, as usual, was not there to pick them up as had been planned. Clark was not surprised they were left high and dry, though. That was just the lot in life of Marines. Private Adams dug in and his buddy Private Best dug a hole beside him. Best was torn up because he had not been able to find his buddy Private Andrews, who was missing in action.

Jungle East of Vagara

Private Dibbens was still waiting in the darkness. He and the dozen Marines carrying a wounded man were conferring in whispers about what to do. The highest rank among them was a private first class, and not only did they have no idea where they were, but they also really had no idea where they had been. No one even had a compass. They had come to the unfortunate conclusion that nobody knew they were missing and therefore nobody would be coming back for them. They knew what direction they had to go in order to get to Voza, but that was almost ten miles away through the jungle at night. What should they do? Should they stay right there and move at dawn, or should they keep moving and try to find the coast, hoping to run into the others? The only decision they had made so far was to get out of the stream.

They stood close and whispered in the darkness. To compound their troubles they had a wounded man, no corpsman to look after him, and a man who had overdosed on drugs and alcohol. It was worse than having another wounded man because he kept wandering off, or worse, talking in a normal voice. They all hissed at him to be quiet, and he tried, but his flagging attention span resulted in his talking again. It got to the point where they had to assign a permanent guard to hold onto the man at all times. Suddenly they were aware of a boy standing in their midst.

"It's a kid. A native kid."

"He can lead us back to the others."

"How do we know he doesn't work for the Japs?"

As far as the Marines had been told, most of Choiseul's natives were just as likely to kill Americans as Japanese. Only a small percentage of natives had picked sides in the conflict. The Sangigai villagers were friendly to the Japanese, that much they knew. They would lead any Americans into an ambush. The people of Peta Kiri and Peta Nu's tribe, however, would aid the Marines. But how could they know who this boy was? Could they trust him to lead them to the coast and north to Voza? Or was he a Sangigai native who would lead them to the Japanese? The one obviously incriminating fact was that the closest village was Sangigai. What would a kid from a hostile village be doing here at night?

The Marines tried to communicate with the boy in the darkness, but his English was only slightly better than their Melanesian. They could barely see him; Dibbens had to stand very close to try to get him to understand. He figured the young boy was probably only ten or eleven. He had intense, extremely intelligent eyes. With crude sign language and Pidgin English, they finally seemed to get through to the boy that they wanted to get to the ocean.

Shoulder to shoulder behind their young guide, the men in the lost group snaked through the jungle in what the men prayed would be the direction of Voza or Vagara. Each man was privately worrying that the guide was leading the Marines to the southeast, deeper into enemy territory. As their minds played tricks on them the Marines could not help but think they should have just stayed put until someone came back for them. It was possible they were being led into an ambush. Dibbens was close behind the boy when he suddenly stopped. Dibbens could feel his small shoulder tense up; Dibbens instinctively went down. Like dominoes, the rest of the hand-on-shoulder line of troopers followed him down. Someone was obviously ahead of them in the darkness. But who? Were they Japanese troops or Americans? Suddenly there was an intense challenge in the dark.

"Halt. Who's there?"

"Lollipop," said Dibbens quickly. "Who's asking?"

"Lulu lady," said a relieved voice. "Advance and be recognized."

Dibbens and the others had made it. The Marines were lucky to have had that young boy come out of nowhere in the darkness. They were also lucky that the sentry was on the ball. A nervous man might have started a firefight that would have probably killed Dibbens's entire group and some of the Marines in the F Company perimeter.

Dr. Lawrence, Pharmacist's Mates Holland and Dunigan, and the other corpsmen were working to stabilize the wounded men. Dr. Lawrence worried they might have more KIAs. Private O'Neal was not expected to live, and some of the other men were hit bad, too. Lawrence worked on the wounded O'Neal, trying to stop the bleeding from his multiple gunshot wounds, and Holland assisted.

Lieutenant Cook's Patrol

Moving blindly through the darkness, Cook, Hoffman, and two natives headed for Voza. They had backtracked up the Vagara River to cross at the headwaters before moving back down to the coast again. Cook had decided against traveling along the jungle trail for fear of a Japanese ambush. With only two Marines, he thought it would be suicide. Instead, Cook and his small party moved along the coast, walking on the coral reef. Sometimes they were forced to walk chest deep in the surf; other times they were able to move along the sandy shoreline. They made slow progress, always wary of an enemy ambush.

Wondering how much farther they had to go, Cook whispered to the native, "How much farther to Voza?"

"Voza four hour," the guide replied. They continued up the coast for several hours, at which point Cook asked again, "How much farther to Voza?"

"Voza four hour," the guide repeated.

Cook realized that the native, who did not speak English, had been told that it took four hours to reach Voza from Vagara. Thus, every time he asked how far, he got the same reply. Just then the lieutenant saw the silhouette of an island against the ocean to his front left. He knew instantly it was Zinoa. They were getting close.

But they would soon have the problem of being safely identified. The password changed every day at midnight, and because it was then just after midnight, the Marine sentries would fire on anyone that didn't use the correct countersign. Cook talked it over with Hoffman and they decided to sing "One Ball Riley" aloud. Any Marine who heard the lyrics "Sitting around Old Riley's store, telling tales of blood and slaughter" would know instantly that other Marines were coming through. No Japanese would sing "One Ball Riley."

The sentries challenged Cook, who replied, "It's Lieutenant Cook and Hoffman. We're coming through." They were admitted and went immediately to the Voza phone. They called up to the mountain camp and told them Krulak needed the boats. Cook was told the boats would head back down first thing in the morning. It was too dangerous for them to leave right then.

Chapter 6

THE CALM BETWEEN THE STORMS: OCTOBER 31

They didn't make 'em any better than Sam Johnston.

Sgt. Thomas Siefke, G Company, of his
platoon leader, Lt. Samuel M. Johnston

0630—Colonel Krulak's Force

Dawn in the Solomon Islands is breathtaking. For the tired, hungry Marines of F Company the blazing reds and oranges in the sky went unnoticed. At roughly 0630, eleven hours after their scheduled extraction, the U.S. Navy LCPRs finally showed up to get them. The Marines quickly boarded, carrying their wounded, and disembarked at Voza. Once on shore they made the thousand-yard hike up the mountain.

When they approached the battalion bivouac and its perimeter defenses, Pfc. J. N. Clark and his element were on point. As he approached the camp, Clark saw the unmistakable jacket of an A-4 machine gun just barely protruding from the dense foliage in front of him. The machine gun covered the trail that led into the battalion perimeter and was aimed directly at him. If it fired, he was a dead man. "Get that damn machine gun out of my face," he said loudly in clear unmistakable English.

"Okay, Clark," said a voice from behind the thick bushes, "come on through."

Clark could not even see the man who had spoken. The jungle was so thick that even when he walked abreast of the machine-gun position he still could not see who was manning it. The reason he had spoken like that was to let any Marines, especially the jumpy ones, know that it was a friendly coming in. Private Clark had been training in the jungles of New Caledonia, Guadalcanal, and Vella LaVella and learned that although they might not be able to see someone, it was possible to tell a friend from a foe by the sound or tone of their voice.

At 0800, the Marines reached their hideout. Except for the unlucky few who had to stand guard, most of the men climbed into their hammocks and fell asleep. Pfc. Norman Dibbens and some of the other men were sitting around their camp talking about the firefight, trying to wind down. As tired as they were, a few of the Marines were insomniacs.

"I got one," said Pfc. Reece Canady. "I shot him in the stomach during the *banzai*."

Not far away, another group of F Company troopers was sitting around chewing the fat. "Hoppy," said Sgt. John C. Strange to Pfc. Earl "Ed" Cassaday, "get over here and work on these follicles." Strange was as bald as a white bowling ball and hoped his hair follicles would grow back when his scalp was massaged.

"I don't know, Sarge," said one of the others. "You've had Hopalong do that ever since we got to Vella and we haven't seen a whisker yet."

"Shaddup. I didn't ask you."

Cassaday started massaging Strange's scalp. Everyone was talking about the firefight and it was pointed out that Strange had saved Ed's life from a second Japanese grenade. "The massage is the least you can do," said one of the paratroopers.

"Jus' think of yerself as a bald man's barber," said Strange. After a few minutes went by, Strange asked his standard question. "How's it lookin', Hoppy?" There was hope in his voice.

"Boy, Sarge, your hair's sure coming back," lied Cassaday. "Looks like you're gonna have a full head-a hair soon."

0900—Mountain Camp

At 0900, in a poncho-covered dugout, Pfc. Eugene Gesch pounded away on his typewriter. A clerk had just handed him a few sheets of paper and Gesch was typing them up. Gesch had been picked for the Bn-3 section simply because he knew how to type.

The assault on Sangigai had been a great success. They had destroyed all the Japanese fuel, food, communications equipment, medical supplies, and ammunition in the Sangigai area, had scattered the Japanese forces to the winds, and had confirmed seventy-two Japanese Imperial Marines killed. Marine losses were six dead, one missing, and twelve wounded. The raid was considered a material success and definitely served its diversionary purposes. They had also destroyed one barge (the equivalent of an LCPR) and captured what appeared to be valuable Japanese documents.

Being in Hq Company meant Gesch was constantly around the brass, something he could have done without. Gesch was Maj. Tolson Smoak's runner and Smoak was always saying, "Gesch, get your ass over to . . ." running him back and forth, often to Lt. Col. Victor H. Krulak. Gesch liked the Brute, but Krulak was just like every other officer: gung ho and out to get ahead. Like every enlisted Marine, Gesch and the other NCOs would sit around and laugh at the idiosyncrasies of the officers. Gesch's best friend was Pfc. Gene Hood, Major Bigger's runner. Gesch particularly enjoyed when Hood cracked jokes and did impersonations of Bigger and Smoak.

At 0930 the captured documents were turned over to Major Smoak's intelligence section. The maps were thought to be hydrographic charts of the Bougainville, Shortland, Fauru, and Bailale sea-lanes. Naval Lt. (jg) Richard Keresey was with the battalion to check for possible PT boat bases; he was called in because of his expertise and experience as a PT skipper in these waters.

The Second Marine Parachute Battalion was on Choiseul temporarily, but depending on the weakness of the enemy response, the Allies might stay or even return. Keresey was to check the coastline, water depth, and accessibility to the Vagara River for the viability of a base. Keresey agreed that the maps were indeed what they appeared to be, and pointed at what he thought were the graphic location of minefields and barge routes. The documents were bundled securely and labeled for shipment to IMAC Headquarters. A navy PBY would arrive that afternoon to pick them up.

Private Gesch was typing in his dugout when Lt. Samuel Johnston walked by, heading down to Voza for a recon patrol. Johnston was a very impressive officer and someone Gesch respected. The lieutenant was also one of the few officers that Gesch enjoyed talking to. Like Krulak, Johnston was fair and treated everyone well. Johnston was engaged to be married to the daughter of George Marshall, a big-time producer in Hollywood. That was fitting because Johnston himself looked like a movie star. He was tall and handsome, and always appeared immaculate in his tailored uniform. His fiancée had sewn a stenciled paratrooper into it; it was the envy of the parachute regiment. Of course, it was back on Vella LaVella. None of them brought anything but combat clothing and gear to Choiseul. Back on Vella LaVella Johnston had even offered his uniform to Gesch just before they made their Choiseul landing.

"Hey, Gene, if I ever get hit, you can have my uniform."

"Are you serious?"

"Sure," he said. "If I get hit."

"Well, okay."

Gesch worried about Johnston. The lieutenant was too eager to get into combat. A lot of guys thought they were missing out on the war and Gesch believed Johnston was one of them.

Not far away, up toward the ridges behind the camp, on a makeshift alter in the jungle, the battalion chaplain held services for all denominations. Pfc. Rudolph Engstrom and several other paratroopers stood around listening to those services. It was very comforting for the Marines to know that even on an enemy island they had a few peaceful moments to give thanks.

U.S. Marine Corps Headquarters, Washington. DC

To help cement the ruse and convince the Japanese high command that Choiseul was the actual invasion site, the military released communiqués to every newspaper in the United States telling about the Allied invasion of the island of Choiseul in the British Solomon Islands. From coast to coast, newspapers ran the headlines; one Chicago paper even ran a sketch with the article that depicted Marine paratroopers descending from the sky. The Marines hoped that every spy in America was sending back coded messages about the division-sized landing on Choiseul.

1000—Voza

At 1000 Major Bigger, Lieutenant Johnston, and the First Platoon of G Company, under Lt. Donald Justice, made a patrol to the northwest, toward Nukiki. They were reconnoitering the Birumbiru River, Nukiki, and the Warrior River area with orders to make contact with any Japanese forces there. The day before, Lt. Gerald Averill's patrol had determined that movement by land was unrealistic, so the patrol moved out from Voza by LCPR to make the quick twenty miles up the coast. Averill's patrol also alerted the Marines of the possibility that large numbers of enemy troops might be concentrated in that area. They had seen six or seven barges with a platoon of infantry on each one.

One of the men accompanying Major Bigger's patrol was Pfc. Charles Allman. He felt packed like a sardine into the crowded boat that held close to forty men. Allman stood next to his squad leader, Sgt. Frank Banner, for whom he had a lot of respect. Banner was tough as nails, and hard on his men. Not one for spit and polish, Banner was truly a combat Marine sergeant.

Pfc. Norman Wurzburger also accompanied the patrol. He was a radio operator from Hq Company, and lugged the TBX on his back.

The LCPR moved northwest along the coast past Moli Point until they reached the mouth of the Birumbiru River. There, Lieutenant Johnston went ashore with a small reconnaissance party, led by a native guide, to reconnoiter the area.[1]

While Johnston scouted the Birumbiru River area, Major Bigger took the First Platoon northwest up the coast to search the shore for signs of enemy troops. If they sighted the Japanese, they would land northwest of them, turn back along the jungle coast, and engage them by land. They passed Nukiki, all the while scanning the shoreline for Japanese barges or lookout posts. Because he was unable to locate enemy troops, Major Bigger decided to land half a mile to the northwest. With a half-squad rear guard left behind to watch the LCPR, the Marines went ashore and moved back along the coastal trail to Nukiki. The natives reported that the Japanese often used Nukiki as a barge stop, but this day the village was deserted. Although the natives were usually right, that did not mean the Marines should throw caution to the wind. They could be walking into an ambush. They fanned out and approached the deserted huts with caution.

Private Allman searched the trees for signs of enemy snipers. He held his folding stock carbine aimed to fire as he moved, but he did not see any Japanese. Allman was glad, too, because he did not know if he could hit anything with the ridiculous little weapon. He had trained for the past six months with a Johnson rifle, which he thought was without a doubt the best weapon he had ever fired. It was superior to both the Garand and the accurate Springfield .03. Just before the Choiseul operation, however, the brass had taken his Johnson rifle and handed him the inferior carbine. He still seethed at the stupidity of taking a man's trusted weapon from him the day before sending him into battle.

Private Wurzburger had been staying in contact with Lieutenant Johnston's patrol since they had been dropped off at the Birumbiru River. He, too, carried what he considered an inferior weapon: a folding stock Reising submachine gun. It had great stopping power, with its .45 slugs, and it was automatic, but it had a critical flaw—it jammed. Like Allman, Wurzburger was sorry he was not carrying a Johnson weapon.

Led by Major Bigger and Lieutenant Justice, the First Platoon checked the surrounding jungle and moved through Nukiki. This village was no different from Voza, Vagara, or Sangigai—several thatched-roof huts on stilts off the beach in an open area about one hundred yards from the jungle. It appeared to be deserted, but to make sure, Major Bigger sent scouts in a wide, extended radius around Nukiki. They reported no Japanese in the vicinity. Once again, the natives were right.

Mountain Camp

In the weapons platoon bivouac, well inside the battalion perimeter, Pfc. Harry Milkert was resting in his hammock. Three Marines were talking nearby, which was normal enough, but the language they spoke interested Milkert. These three men were Native Americans and they were each from different companies. One was in Sgt. Anthony J. Skotnicki's machine-gun section in Milkert's weapons platoon, not the mortars where Milkert's buddies were. The two others were from different companies and had probably just come to talk. Milkert listened, but he had no idea what they were saying.

On E Company's perimeter, Pfc. John Geddings was sitting with his buddies; as usual, he was cleaning his weapon. He carried a Thompson submachine gun that he affectionately named "Mary Jane" after his girlfriend. Geddings loved the weapon almost as much as he did his girlfriend. He told the others that Mary Jane would never let him down—even though he occasionally put the sear pin in backward, rendering the weapon useless. The sear pin was the only problem with the Thompson. It fit both correctly and backward; the only way to find out if it had been put in right was to fire it. Because they were on an enemy island, Geddings could not do that, so he was as careful as he could be when he put Mary Jane back together.

Also in E Company, Pfc. Hugh Greely had been relaxing in his hammock when he heard something that made his blood turn cold. "Leo Gruidl was killed in action yesterday." Greely and Gruidl had both been injured in chute school and met in a replacement battalion. They became best friends, but for some reason, Greely was put in E Company and Gruidl in F Company. Even though they were separated, they remained close friends, and one of them was always at the other's tent. Greely was devastated. He went to F Company's perimeter to talk with the men in Gruidl's squad.

Most of the Marines at the battalion's mountain camp, with the exception of those on patrol or guard duty, tried to catch up on their sleep, but that was easier said than done. As exhausted as most of them were, the heat was so unrelenting that many of the men were forced to go sit in the mountain stream to cool off. Pfc. Bruce "Red" McClure was bathing and relaxing in the cool water near the F Company bivouac when he heard the unmistakable sound of Washing Machine Charlie coming over the mountains.[2] When Charlie approached from the ocean they could hear him coming from a great distance. They had time to take cover. But when Charlie came at them from the opposite side of the mountains, they had very little time to hide.

Red immediately leaped out of the water and into the jungle as every man in the area started yelling at him at once. "Red, get out of the stream! They'll see you!" He was already out of the water and crouching next to one of his buddies under a tree when his friend finished his warning: "Take cover, Red. Jap plane."

1700—Major Bigger's Force

Private Allman was waiting for the order to move out when he heard a sound that almost made him hit the deck. For a second he thought it was a rifle shot. Whack, whack. Allman turned to see Major Bigger using a machete to open a coconut to get to the milk inside. It seemed to Allman that he was making an awful lot of noise doing it, however; that noise resounded through the village. Sgt. Edmond Harper must have shared Allman's thoughts because he quickly moved over to Bigger.

"Knock off that goddamn racket, major," said Harper. "There might be Japs around."

Major Bigger stopped chopping on the coconut and promptly ordered the unit to move out. They still had to patrol northwest to the Warrior River and they were running out of daylight. Eventually, they turned back to the southeast and picked up Lieutenant Johnston's patrol along the shore between Birumbiru and Nukiki. They arrived back at Voza at 1700.

2050—Battalion Camp

To assist the deception that a U.S. Marine Corps division had landed and begun offensive operations on Choiseul, it was important to make another attack soon after the one at Sangigai. This time the attack would be to the northwest, on November 1. This had been planned as far back as October 19 when Colonel Krulak reported to IMAC headquarters on Guadalcanal. Major Bigger would lead the raid; he would take G Company (minus the First Platoon) and land at the mouth of the Warrior River by LCPR. With an extra TBX team and some intelligence personnel attached, Bigger would travel inland on foot to attack the enemy at Choiseul Bay.

At 2050 Major Bigger made his report to Colonel Krulak about the plan. The apparent lack of a Japanese presence southeast of the Warrior River and Nukiki area gave Major Bigger confidence that his raid would take the enemy by surprise.[3] While Bigger and G Company made their attack, the rest of the battalion would prepare for the enemy counterattack that was sure to come.

Colonel Krulak wanted to lead the attack himself and send a larger force, but the dangers of conducting future aggressive raids against the numerically superior enemy had increased exponentially after the Sangigai attack. The Japanese would counterattack, that was sure; the Marines just did not know when. If Krulak sent another large raiding force as he had on October 30, he would be leaving his base camp with all its ammunition, supplies, medical stores, food, and radio equipment defended by fewer than half his battalion. If the Japanese hit the camp while most of his men were away, they might find themselves cut off without food and ammunition. The Japanese could hunt them down piecemeal in the jungle.

That exact scenario had irreparably weakened a crack brigade of Japanese infantry on Guadalcanal more than a year before when the First Raider Battalion landed at Tasimboko and destroyed all their supplies. Out of food and ammunition, the Japanese brigade was wiped out almost to a man. Because of this danger, Colonel Krulak had to keep the majority of his forces ready to defend his base. Besides, his orders were to raise hell, not to engage in battle. It was hard for his young warriors to understand this. Most of the young paratroopers wanted to load up with ammo and go fight.

Another key reason why Krulak could not lead the raid himself was his physical condition. He was ravaged by malaria, which was sapping his strength. He was also suffering from the bullets he had taken in the fire-fight: one bullet had passed through his arm, and others had left multiple shrapnel wounds in his face. Dr. Richard Lawrence had been unable to remove all of the steel fragments; one was still lodged below Krulak's eye. But it was Krulak's back that was taking the most out of him. He had injured it on a parachute jump on New Caledonia, causing permanent damage to his sciatic nerve. The muscle in his left leg had atrophied to the point where it had shrunk a full inch. Every day Krulak lived with constant lower back pain, but he tried not to let any of his men know it.

Lookout Post

Pvt. Richard Reneau and the other Marines of his squad were deployed in ambush position along the stream that led to Voza from the southeast. Like their opposite number on the Baregosonga River to the northwest, they were to guard the battalion flank against any Japanese probes. They would let the others know whether the enemy was approaching from the south-east. The stream they were deployed along afforded them the best defensive position in their area. They had been told to hold the enemy until reinforcements could arrive, and they waited for the coming night. Unlike the Baregosonga, which was a river large enough to accommodate an LCPR, this stream was only about fifteen yards across. A man could wade through it up to his chest. If the Japanese came at them in large numbers, their position could be overrun. With minimal effort, a force moving through the jungle well inland could outflank it.

Battalion Camp

Private Clark and Pfc. Raymond Hoskins were sleeping peacefully until Pfc. Earl F. Nevins woke them up to take their turn on guard duty. It was pitch dark when they followed Nevins out of the F Company perimeter to the listening post. They set up, and the other two Marines returned to their hammocks. Sitting beside each other in the darkness, neither Clark nor Hoskins spoke for the duration of their watch. Clark wanted to talk about the firefight, but he knew better; he did not want to die.

An hour later, when their shift was up, Clark took one of the phosphorescent vines that the natives had shown them how to find and tied it to the end of a stick. He used it as though he were a blind man tapping a white cane. Clark returned to the camp following a rope vine and knew that without it he would have gotten lost. Even after four days on Choiseul, he was amazed how dark it was on this island. It reminded him of when, as a child, he would go down into his family's tornado shelter on a bright sunny day and close the door. When he reached the bivouac, Clark hesitated. Moving in camp at night, when everyone slept, was extremely dangerous. Every sound a sleeping Marine heard was a Japanese soldier sneaking up to kill him. The wrong move could get somebody stabbed. With deliberate caution, Clark followed the vine to his squad's area.

Cpl. William D. Cole had warned them about a close call he had had, almost slashing his relief in the dark. Clark hoped everyone had been listening to him. When he got to Pfc. Ralph Bagwell's hammock he stopped. Bagwell and Pfc. Thomas Preston were his relief. He gently prodded Bagwell with his stick and whispered, "Baggy, it's your watch." Bagwell had been sound asleep when he felt something prod him. His adrenaline struck like lightning and he lashed out with his Ka-Bar. The razor-sharp knife slashed through the mosquito netting, chopped off the stick Clark was holding (just inches from his fingers), and severed the rope that held Bagwell's own hammock. He dropped like a sack of potatoes, hitting the ground with a muffled "Ouff."

"It's me Baggy," Clark hissed quickly. He was worried they would alarm the whole camp and start a firefight. "It's your watch."

"Okay," whispered Bagwell as he got up sheepishly. "Sorry."

Clark marveled at guys like Bagwell, and there were not many of them. He was one of the most likable guys in the battalion. Everything just rolled off his back. Unlike everyone else, Bagwell never complained about having to pull guard duty and he never swore. He always kept his head up and never had a bad word to say about anyone. To top it all off, Bagwell had the voice of a professional singer and could hit any note.

Clark led Bagwell and Preston out toward Hoskins and their outpost. He was still holding the vine and felt his way with his shortened stick. As he neared the spot where Hoskins should have been, Clark was puzzled not to find him anywhere. Where could he have gone? Clark prodded with his stick and was preparing to take one more step when he heard an irritated, "Get that damn stick out of my face."

Japanese Seventeenth Army

With reports of New Zealand troops invading the Treasury Islands and U.S. Marines now on Choiseul, Gen. Haruyoshi Hyakutake was getting his first indication as to where the next enemy attacks were coming. Although he was not convinced that these were actual invasion sites, he could not ignore the threat. Hyakutake immediately issued orders to send reinforcements from neighboring islands to help his besieged forces on Choiseul. Many of those reinforcements were coming from nearby Bougainville.

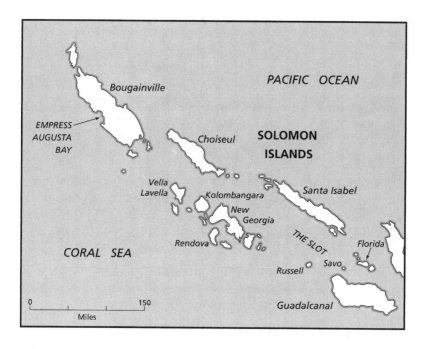

The Solomon Islands. On October 27, 1943, New Zealand troops landed on the Treasury Islands. On October 28, the Second Marine Parachute Battalion landed at Voza, Choiseul. On November 1, the Third Marine Division landed at Empress Augusta Bay Bougainville.

Chris Robinson

This drawing depicts the Marines' seven days of hit-and-run fighting
on Choiseul.

Howard "Barney" Baxter

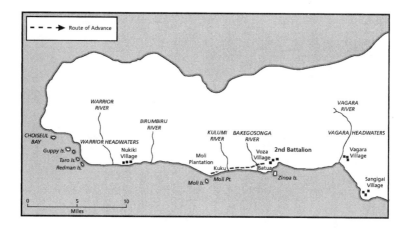

Choiseul Bay Attack. Lt. Gerald Averill's patrol moved northwest along the coast from Voza to Moli Point. The purpose of the mission was to see if troop movement in large numbers was possible. It was not; the jungle was nearly impenetrable.

Chris Robinson

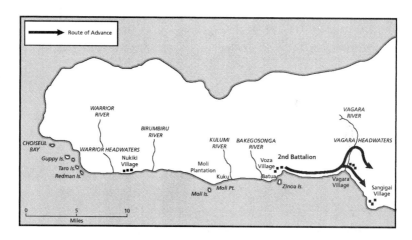

Sangigai Attack. Lt. Col. Victor Krulak's patrol left the battalion camp near Voza and followed the coastal trail southeast to the Vagara River. The patrol split up after crossing the river headwaters; a small party moved inland to reconnoiter northeast of Sangigai Village. Meanwhile, Krulak's main group moved back down the coast along the east bank of the river and followed the coast toward Sangigai.

Chris Robinson

John Conway poses with his Johnson light machine gun. Note his cut-off uniform. The heat was so intense that most Marines sliced off their sleeves and dungarees in an effort to stay cooler. Also note that none of the veterans interviewed for this book thought any other rifle was better than the Johnson.

Courtesy of James Ward

The Marine paratroopers also conducted extensive amphibious assault training. Pictured at the bottom, left to right, are: F Company members Charles Deason and Pfc. Carl J. Kuehne; middle, left to right, are Pfc. Bruce "Red" McClure and Pfc. Norman Dibbens. (This picture was actually taken when these men were in the Fifth Marine Division at Camp Tarawa, Hawaii.)

Courtesy of Norman Dibbens

John Holland, Pharmacist's Mate 1st Class

Courtesy of John Holland

Cpl. Benjamin F. "Cape" Caperton III of F Company (left) and
Cpl. William R. Zuegel of G Company (right)

Courtesy of Ben Capterton

Sgt. Edward "Tommy" Thomas

Courtesy of Howard "Barney" Baxter

Pfc. Robert Brutinel of E Company

Courtesy of Robert Brutinel

Pfc. J. N. Clark of F Company (left) and Pfc. Robert Nelson of G Company (right)

Courtesy of J. N. Clark

This cartoon of Victor H. Krulak, depicting "the Brute" when he was the lieutenant colonel in command of the Second Marine Parachute Battalion, hangs in his home office.

Courtesy of Gen. Victor Krulak

The artist's drawing of the island of Vella LaVella as seen from an LST.

Howard "Barney" Baxter

Chapter 7

BEST-LAID PLANS: NOVEMBER 1

He was one of us.

Pfc. Rudolph Engstrom, E Company, of Lt. Col. Victor H. Krulak

0600—Mountain Camp

It had been two days since the attack on the enemy barge station at Sangigai and there had been no response from the Japanese. With the intent to continue pressuring the enemy while making sure his outnumbered forces were in position to defend against a likely attack, at 0600 Lt. Col. Victor H. Krulak ordered Lt. Carl Bachman of Hq Company to take a patrol to the southeast toward Sangigai. The patrol was to make contact with Japanese forces in that area, determine their numbers, and test their response to the October 30 attack. Bachman led thirty-seven Marines, five native scouts, and Lt. (jg) Richard Keresey down to Voza where they followed' the well-worn coastal trail southeast toward the Vagara River. Bachman's patrol soon passed the Marine lookout post east of Voza and continued down to the village of Vagara and a very likely enemy contact.

0630—Voza

Maj. Warner T. Bigger and his northern task force boarded three LCPRs and headed northeast, paralleling the coast with the intention of landing in the mouth of the Warrior River. It was time to start the second phase of offensive operations on Choiseul. The force would land at the Warrior, move inland, and pass undetected through the dense jungle to strike the enemy from the interior at their main base in Choiseul Bay—well inland of their coastal lookouts. The northern task force consisted of two G Company infantry platoons (the Second and Third), and the weapons platoon with its machine-gun and mortar sections. Also attached were an additional TBX radio team and two men from Bn-3.

The force numbered eighty-seven men, with Major Bigger, the battalion executive officer, in overall command. Capt. William R. Day, the G Company commander, was second in command. Lt. Rae Duncan, Lt.

147

Samuel Johnston, and Lt. Douglas Morton were the platoon leaders accompanying the force. The Marine paratroopers moved northwest, paralleling the coast, past Kuku, Moli Island, the Birumbiru River, and Nukiki Village. They saw no sign of a Japanese presence.

Mountain Camp

Cpl. Benjamin F. "Cape" Caperton III was lying in his hammock when he heard, "Malaria control, malaria control. Atabrine speaking." It was Cpl. "Baron" Hoffman, Colonel Krulak's runner. Hoffman was moving through the E and F Company bivouacs reminding the men to take their malaria tablets. Hoffman was quite a character, one of those larger-than-life Marines capable of getting away with things others did not dare try. Cape had heard a rumor that Hoffman had a steel plate in his head from when he was partying with a few of his fellow paratroopers and some nurses back in San Diego. Apparently, in a drunken frenzy Hoffman had boasted that he was the greatest paratrooper that ever lived. H had grabbed a tablecloth for a parachute and leaped from the balcony of the bar shouting, "Geronimo!"

Hoffman was also famous because, unlike many of the other eighteen-year-olds, he could grow a beard within days. He called it "the beast," and it gave him the appearance of an old trapper. Colonel Krulak made Hoffman shave when the beard got out of control. At such times, he would report to the colonel, "The beast is dead." On November 1 on the island of Choiseul, however, the beast was very much alive and well; Hoffman looked more like a mountain man than a Marine. His dungarees were cut into shorts because of the heat and his sleeves were ripped off. As he moved through the hammocks running messages for Krulak, he would spout off advice to his comrades that he considered to be of profound relevance. It varied every time, but it always came across incredibly loud. It was not that he always yelled, he just had one of those voices that always seemed to carry.

Empress Augusta Bay

Two regiments of the Third Marine Division—the Third and the Ninth—along with the Second Raider Battalion were landing at Cape Torokina, Bougainville, while elements of the Third Raider Battalion assaulted nearby Puruata Island just offshore. Defending the area was one single company of Japanese infantry and one .75-mm cannon. Although vastly outnumbered, the enemy forces fought tenaciously and the lone artillery piece knocked out twelve Higgins Boats before being silenced by Sgt. Robert Owens, who single-handedly knocked out the enemy battery and posthumously received the Medal of Honor for his actions. The invasion did not go nearly as well as expected, however. Aside from the stiff enemy resistance, rough surf claimed an additional eighty-six landing craft. Nevertheless, the Marines swept away the enemy troops and were firmly on shore. The invasion was a success. As the Marines began to advance inland, expanding their perimeter, supplies, men, and ammunition poured ashore behind them. The real invasion had begun and only a few enemy troops had contested it.

Lieutenant Bachman's Patrol

As Bachman's patrol reached the northwest bank of the Vagara River, one of the native guides on point saw something and hissed a warning to the others. The column dropped along the trail while Bachman and Keresey crawled up to find out what was happening. The native pointed to the muddy banks of the Vagara River where fresh split-toed footprints told them a Japanese patrol had recently passed.[1] The Marines stayed low, spreading out in the jungle along the coastal trail while the point men and guides scanned the opposite bank of the river.

They had waited merely a few moments when the guides saw something else. This time it was a Japanese soldier. The man was signaling to someone the Marines could not see. When he finished gesturing, he turned and disappeared into the jungle. Convinced that they had not been seen, Bachman ordered his patrol to move inland through the jungle along the Vagara River to the headwaters. There they could cross unseen behind the steep hill where F Company had forded two days before. They reached the headwaters and, sending a half squad across first to draw fire, the scouts checked the opposite bank for an ambush before waving the others across. Once everyone was across at the headwaters, they followed a small rivulet south toward the ocean until they were almost at Vagara Village. As they neared the huts, they spotted a Japanese pontoon boat on the beach more than two hundred yards away. The boat pulled out and headed back down the coast while the Marines moved on its former position. In the sand along the beach, more fresh split-toed footprints moved into the jungle. Bachman ordered his men to spread out and be ready.

Meanwhile, the native guides assisting the Marines studied the ground. One of them moved over to the lieutenant and told Bachman that a sixteen-man patrol had just landed. They were definitely still in the area. The Marines were deployed in the jungle along the beach near Vagara. Lieutenant Keresey stepped out to get a better look at the water to see if

PT boats could navigate the river here. He did not go much farther than a few feet, and he had only been exposed for about thirty seconds, when rifle and machine-gun fire opened up from the jungle across the clearing. It was from the southeast side of the village and forced everyone to ground. Keresey dove back into the jungle as the Marines returned fire. Lieutenant Bachman ordered six of his JLMGs deployed along the riverbank to cut loose. Heavy bursts from automatic rifles supplemented by antitank grenades launched into the Japanese positions considerably reduced the enemy rate of fire. The two opposing sides blasted back and forth, but the Marine firepower settled the argument. With suppressing fire from the six JLMGs eating up the jungle around the Japanese line and explosions from the anti-tank grenades bursting inside the tree line, the enemy fire stopped completely as the Japanese retreated to the southeast toward Sangigai. The Marine paratroopers moved cautiously through the former enemy positions and counted seven dead. The Marines went through the pockets and packs of the Japanese soldiers for anything that might prove valuable, but came up empty. Their mission had been a success, nonetheless. They had been told to make contact with the enemy, and had killed seven without taking any casualties. Bachman ordered his patrol back to Voza.

Major Bigger's Force

In the surf several hundred yards off shore from the mouth of the Warrior River, Pfc. Howard "Barney" Baxter watched from his landing craft as Lieutenant Johnston and three men waded ashore from two hundred yards out. The lieutenant was reconnoitering the company's landing site to make sure the others were not wading into an ambush.

Barney was a G Company Marine who thought Lieutenant Johnston was one of the bravest men he had ever known. In fact, in his humble opinion, Johnston and Duncan were two of the finest officers in the U.S. Marines Corps.

When Johnston's shore party signaled it was safe to come in, the LCPRs tried to move into the mouth of the river. They were still two hundred yards from shore when the boats promptly became stuck in the shallow coral. The coxswain reversed the engines and approached from a new angle, but he could not get in on the second attempt either.

Try as they might, with engines roaring, the coxswains were unable to get the boats in. Finally, Major Bigger ordered everyone out, to shore. Sgt. Thomas Siefke looked over the side of his Higgins Boat and saw shallow water. Siefke ordered his squad out of the boat and onto the coral. The water was up to their knees, but once they cleared the reef, they dropped into deep surf up to their chests. With their packs, ammunition, and equipment now thoroughly soaked, the Marines waded ashore with weapons held high over their heads. By 1130 the entire force had landed and was moving inland.

Pfc. George P. Adams stepped ashore carrying his big radio. He had held it over his head on the way in to keep it dry. Knowing enemy troops could be waiting in ambush, he also carried his Johnson rifle. As soon as Adams stepped ashore, his company commander, Captain Day, told him to raise battalion. He stepped to the edge of the jungle, set the cumbersome TBX on the ground, and started setting the frequency. Adams tried to raise battalion but could not. Since they had been on Choiseul, they had had nothing but problems with the TBXs. Adams had heard about the trouble E Company and F Company had during the Sangigai attack and hoped they would not have the same problems.

Major Bigger and Captain Day organized their men and gave the platoon leaders their instructions. As the column prepared to move out, Lieutenant Johnston moved over to Sergeant Siefke, one of his squad leaders. "Tom," he said, "we're going to keep a TBX crew here to keep contact with battalion. We're going to leave your squad here to protect them."

"Okay," replied Siefke, hiding his disappointment. Siefke told his squad they would miss the raid. While the others went into combat, they would babysit the TBX team.

The northern task force left the small group about one hundred yards from the mouth of the river and proceeded inland under the direction of Peta Kiri and Peta Nu. The column moved up toward the headwaters of the Warrior River where they could cross to the northwest side. More than one man, PM1 John Holland included, wondered why they had not landed on the northwest side to begin with.[2]

Back at the mouth of the Warrior, Siefke set his men in a defensive perimeter around the TBX crew. His squad was deployed in a circle, with their weapons facing out in all directions, while the TBX crew huddled in their midst. Siefke's squad—Cpl. Mike Vinich, and Pfcs. Raymond Pierce, Robert Neff, James Moe, Leo Henslick, Clarence Cameron, and Robert Poe—were heavily armed. The sergeant knew they would be outnumbered, but if the Japanese came at them, he felt confident his men would give a good account of themselves.

Angry and upset about missing the raid, some of the men complained in whispers. "Why did Sam pick us to stay here?"

"Because we're dependable," Siefke replied. "Now keep it down. There might be Nips around." Siefke knew they still might see all the action they could ever want, and he told his men so. They had the important job of holding a small corridor along the southeast bank of the Warrior for the others. Bigger's raiding party would need to cross later that afternoon and Siefke's squad would ensure they were not wading into an ambush. Also, the rest of the company had a lot of men to fight with. Their little patrol had fifteen men. If they encountered a large group of Japanese troops, his men would change their tune fast. They would be wishing they had never left the battalion hideout.

Mountain Camp

Pfc. Louis Komnenich, an E Company trooper from Chicago, Illinois, was sitting in the cool stream that ran through the battalion camp washing his socks. Everything needed to be washed, especially his dungarees, but he had to wash his socks, too. Trench foot and jungle rot were epidemic. He knew he needed to keep his feet clean, so he scrubbed his socks against a rock. Looking up, he was surprised to see Colonel Krulak in the stream not ten feet away doing the same thing. Komnenich thought Krulak was one of the finest officers he had ever known. So many officers would make some private do their laundry for them, but not Krulak. That was why his men would follow him anywhere. Komnenich noticed Krulak's face was bandaged—he had heard the Brute got shot—and also saw a bandage on the colonel's arm. Komnenich wondered if he took a bullet there, too.

"Hello," said Komnenich to Krulak.

"Hello, Louis," replied Krulak. They talked for a few minutes while the colonel finished washing his socks. Then he returned to his command post. Komnenich marveled at Krulak's amazing memory. There were almost 650 men in the battalion, yet the colonel seemed to know every one of them by first and last name.

Major Bigger's Force

Major Bigger led his force inland along the Warrior to the headwaters where it was shallow enough to ford the river without having to swim. For some reason Barney did not know, they had been let off on the wrong side of the Warrior and now had to cross it. The river appeared to be about forty yards wide, much narrower than the area where they had left the TBX team. There the river was as wide as one hundred yards in places. Lieutenant

Johnston, Peta Kiri, and two Marines went across first to draw fire. If they got shot up, Bigger and the others would know it was an ambush.

With every step they took, the others expected to see them shot down in the water, but they made it across and disappeared into the jungle to reconnoiter the area. After a few minutes, Johnston reappeared and gave the all-clear signal. Soon Peta Nu and Peta Kiri were leading the company through the thick jungle in a northwesterly direction. Pharmacist's Mate Holland noted that Peta Nu did not seem to be suffering from his broken hand. Holland had bandaged it only five days prior, but he realized he should not be surprised. Even right after the accident Peta Nu had not shown any sign of pain.

Sergeant Siefke's Squad

As they waited throughout the day, taking turns on guard, Siefke watched the TBX team fiddle with their radio from time to time. They kept trying to raise battalion or Bigger's force, but they never had any luck.

1500—Major Bigger's Force

Major Bigger's paratroopers had been moving slowly through the dense jungle for almost two hours and there was growing concern that the unit was falling behind schedule. They were traveling in dense swampland with great difficulty, and their pace had slowed considerably.

It was hot and humid. Besides their own weapons and ammunition, each man carried an additional 60-mm mortar round and the mortar crews carried two or three.

Private Baxter was sweating profusely in the tropical heat and he had already drained half his canteen. His equipment, weapons, and ammunition were weighing him down. As assistant JLMG man to Pfc. Frank Fagoni, he carried ammo for Fagoni, too.

The company snaked through the jungle and as they moved deeper into enemy territory, many of the men became aware of what a small force they actually were. They had started with eighty-seven men, but they had left the five-man TBX team along the Warrior with Siefke's ten-man squad for protection. That left seventy-two men—not many if they ran into Japanese forces moving down to engage the invaders.

As they trudged through the swamp pushing to keep to their schedule, it seemed to Pharmacist's Mate Holland that they were going in circles. They still had to reach the coast, mortar the enemy positions, and return to the Warrior before sundown to get picked up by the boats. Holland was not the only man to worry. The next thing he knew, the column had stopped.

Major Bigger called a halt and conferred with his officers and the two native scouts. Peta Kiri and Peta Nu explained that that part of the island was another tribe's territory, and neither man had actually been here before. Worse, they admitted they were lost. The tribe whose territory they were now lost in had sided with the Japanese. At that point, Major Bigger decided to simply head for the coast. Pulling out his compass, with Captain Day double-checking, he set an azimuth in a west-southwest direction. Once they hit the ocean, they would align themselves again. Right now it was important to get back on track.

Pfc. William O'Gieglo, from Tennessee, was the number two gunner in Sgt. Gordon Jackson's mortar team. His best friend, Cpl. Edward "Jimmy" Schnell, was standing beside him. Jimmy carried a St. Christopher medallion around his neck that he was always fingering. St. Christopher was the patron saint of travelers and O'Gieglo knew they were lost. "Maybe you should give your St. Christopher medallion to Bigger," suggested O'Gieglo.

Pfc. Ned Russell heard grumbling from the men in his machine-gun section. Apparently, they were lost. Russell thought sarcastically that any minute they would probably send for him to become their next scout. Since he was a Native American, everyone always figured he could track. A few months back, on New Caledonia, they were practicing rubber boat training when a captain turned to him and said, "Russell, you're an Indian. I want you as helmsman." He did as he was ordered, but when they began their practice assault on the beach, their boat started going in circles. The captain was apoplectic. Some brass was watching the beach assault, and he was in Russell's boat.

"What the hell is wrong with you, Russell?" raged the captain. "You're supposed to be an Indian, for Christ's sake."

"I'm an Apache," Russell replied defensively. "There's no water in Arizona." He figured the captain must have read *The Last of the Mohicans* and thought all Native Americans could steer canoes, but Russell had never even seen one.

The northern task force continued on, but the traveling was so slow they were hopelessly behind schedule. Sloshing through thick jungle swamp, any speed above a crawl was impossible. After another hour, at roughly 1500, Bigger and his officers conferred again and decided that the company would spend the night in the swamp. They would make the raid the following day, November 2. Ordering the seventy-two-man force to form a perimeter, Bigger again tried to raise both battalion and the TBX team along the Warrior by radio. Still no luck. The major then decided to send word back to Siefke's squad at the Warrior. Via their TBX, they would inform battalion of the change in plans and move the LCPRs back to the protection of Voza for the night. The next decision for Major Bigger to make was selecting who would go back. He conferred with Captain Day and Lieutenants Johnston, Duncan, and Morton, and they decided that Duncan would head back with one squad of men for protection. Duncan would take Sgt. Wilburn Lipscomb's squad back to the Warrior, contact Siefke and the TBX team, and through them inform Colonel Krulak of their new plans. They were also to let the Brute know about their radio trouble.

At just after 1500 Duncan and his ten-man patrol departed for the Warrior. Bigger's force now numbered sixty-one men. The remaining Marines had no recourse but to bivouac in the swamp for the night. Inside the G Company perimeter, Holland was trying to find a spot in their swampy campsite where he might spend the night without lying in water. Holland's buddy Sgt. Frank Muller turned to Major Bigger. "Hey, major," he said, "this is our number one corpsman. We'd better take care of him."

"What the hell?" thought Holland. "Where did that come from?" Holland did not say anything aloud, but Muller's comment worried him. For Muller—the best Marine Holland had ever seen—to say that meant they were going to get hit—tonight. Major Bigger agreed, and told Holland to go over to Lieutenant Morton's machine-gun section. Holland did so, but he suddenly did not feel too good. He knew his friend well. Muller must have sensed something the others did not.

The raiding force of barely two platoons of paratroopers spread out in a circular defensive perimeter and waited out the darkness. It was an uncomfortable night in the humid, mosquito-infested swamp. This was to have been a one-day raid, so each man had left his hammock back at the mountain hideout. Everyone was miserable, hot, thirsty, and eaten by the swarms of insects that had descended. They had to fill their canteens with swamp water and put Halizone tablets in before drinking.[3]

Pfc. Gonzalo Torres was another of the sixty-one Marines in the G Company perimeter. He grew up in a Texas orphanage, where since age seven, he had known Pfc. Billy Joe Cagle and Pfc. Hardy Brown. When they turned eighteen, the three of them joined the Marines and went to boot camp in an all-Texas platoon. They did everything together and decided to sign up for the paratroopers. They were placed in the Second Battalion, but when their small class was divided into thirds alphabetically, Cagle and

Brown went to E Company and Torres went to G Company. Now he was lost in a swamp on a Japanese island twenty miles from the rest of his unit.

Battalion Camp

The Marines were constantly hungry; many were losing weight. The only food the leathernecks had to eat on Choiseul was one D-bar and one K-ration a day. Unless they could scrounge other food from the jungle, they would go hungry.

Pfc. Robert Dubson had paid attention when the natives had showed them how to find food in the rain forest. Besides the occasional coconuts that were now depleted in the area of the mountain bivouac where the Marines foraged, Dubson learned that they could cut out the top of a certain type of palm tree that grew in abundance on Choiseul because its center tasted like cabbage. Using his Ka-Bar, Dubson diced the cabbage-like vegetable into his canteen cup and mixed it with his K-ration. It almost made his food taste good.

Dubson was eating his ration when four of Seton's natives, who were acting as stretcher bearers, moved over to where the wounded were being held. They stopped by Pfc. Kurt Garbuschewski's stretcher, prompting him to cry out in feigned terror, "They're going to put me in a pot and cook me. Don't let 'em take me!" Everyone laughed because the natives did look like Hollywood's version of headhunters.

Garbuschewski, Pfc. Milton O'Neal, Pfc. Roger Kirkpatrick, and the other seriously wounded were to be moved down to the beach for evacuation by a PBY. Because the plane had limited room, however, not all of the wounded could be taken off at once. Pfc. John Erotas was still unconscious from the grenade blast that had lodged a piece of shrapnel in his head, but his vital signs were strong, so it was decided he would stay.

Pfc. Orrin Hall and his buddies Pfc. Kenneth Twigg, Pfc. James Gibson, and Sgt. George Gerarden sat in the cool stream nearby talking about the firefight as each remembered it. They retold their experiences but the only thing they all seemed to remember in common was PM1 Clay Dunigan's hysterical "Tojo eat shit."

Farther down the line, Pfc. J. N. Clark was sitting next to his buddy and assistant JLMG man, Pfc. Raymond Hoskins. As usual, they were arguing about something. Clark thought Hoskins was quite a character, capable of almost anything. Clark remembered one incident on Vella LaVella just before they had come to Choiseul. Lt. William King had been walking past them on his way to Colonel Krulak's CP when he said to Hoskins, "You need a shave, Marine."

"Yes, sir," answered Hoskins, "an' a fuckin' haircut, too."

Lieutenant King did a double take but did not say anything. "How do you get away with it?" asked Clark, constantly amazed at his buddy's ability to pull off unrivaled feats of insubordination without getting into trouble. Before Hoskins could answer, Capt. Spencer Pratt walked up.

"How's it going, Hoskins?" asked Pratt.

"When it gets too fuckin' rough for the officers," replied Hoskins, "it'll be just right for me, cap'n." Pratt laughed out loud and moved past them in the same direction as King.

Japanese Seventeenth Army

Reports of New Zealanders on the Treasury Islands and U.S. Marines landings at both Choiseul and Bougainville seemed to confuse the Japanese command. How did the Allies have the manpower and matériel to launch three separate invasions? Gen. Haruyoshi Hyakutake had suffered utter defeat and catastrophe on Guadalcanal and now, in the fog of war, he had to decide which of these landings were actual invasions and which were diversions. Hesitant to make a decision, just as Adm. William F. Halsey had hoped, Hyakutake dispatched reinforcements to Choiseul from Bougainville, after the Marine landings at Empress Augusta Bay.

Lieutenant Duncan's Patrol

Duncan and Lipscomb's squad moved back in a southeast direction toward the Warrior River to link up with the TBX team. Their orders were to get word to Colonel Krulak that the mission was now a two-day operation and inform him of the radio trouble. It was difficult traveling for Duncan and his men. They had to move quickly to make it to the river before dark, but at the same time, they had to move carefully because they were in enemy territory. The dense jungle swamp made it difficult to move quickly and stay oriented. Duncan stopped from time to time to check his compass before moving on. Once everyone had crossed the Warrior River they moved toward the mouth in search of the TBX team.

They were almost to the area where they believed Siefke's squad was when point man Duncan heard unnatural noises in the jungle ahead. Cautiously, Duncan crept ahead and peered through the dense brush in front of him. Not fifteen yards away in the jungle was a small Japanese camp. Staying carefully concealed, Duncan began to count the enemy infantry. There were ten of them—and there were only eleven in his patrol.

Duncan wanted to hit them. He hated to let their enemy, so ripe for ambush, go unpunished, especially because they could probably wipe out the lot of them in their first volley. His orders, however, were to remain undetected. They needed to get word back to the boats to get away and come back the next day. A firefight might jeopardize everyone because it was highly doubtful this was a lone squad in the jungle. More likely, it was part of a larger Japanese force—probably a platoon or a company bivouacked in the area. If the enemy force were that size, he and his ten Marines would be hurt if they got into a firefight.

Moving back to his men, Duncan knelt down and told them of the enemy troops less than fifty feet away. He whispered to his men to keep it quiet. They would flank the Japanese camp. Once around them and back to the river, they would continue toward the ocean to look for the TBX team. Motioning his men to follow him, Duncan started out in a wide arc around the enemy position.

1600—Mountain Camp

At 1600 hours, twenty-seven Marines under the command of Lt. John Richards left the mountain hideout to set up an ambush position along the Vagara River. The battalion periodically sent feeler patrols out to stay informed of enemy troop movements; the First Platoon of E Company now had the duty. This patrol was in the opposite direction of where Major Bigger's party was raiding and on the Marine side of the Vagara River. The Sangigai attack had happened two days ago, and Lieutenant Bachman's patrol had hit the Japanese at Vagara Village earlier that day. The enemy would undoubtedly be sending out patrols of their own to find out exactly where the Marines were and what their strength was. Bachman's patrol had sent them fleeing back to Sangigai; Richards's patrol would lie in wait for them to return.

Sergeant Siefke's Squad

Assistant squad leader Vinich was in ambush position behind a fallen log when he and Private Cameron heard the sound of approaching men in the jungle brush. Cameron already had his JLMG prepared to fire. They expected the rest of the company to arrive before dark, but that did not mean these were not Japanese approaching. Vinich motioned to alert the others and got ready with his own Johnson rifle. The noise was getting closer when Vinich leaned over to Cameron. "Make sure they're Japs before you fire," he whispered. "They might be a friendly." Just then, through the jungle about ten yards away, he thought he recognized Lieutenant Duncan.

"I think it's Duncan," whispered Vinich quickly. They had almost fired on him. They had made visual recognition, so they did not bother to challenge. Duncan quickly signaled for silence and his squad approached. Vinich wondered where the rest of the company was. He had expected a long line of troops, but only eleven men walked in. "We ran into some Nips," whispered Duncan. "They're close. At least ten of them about fifty yards or so from here." Duncan told them what had happened and that the rest of the company would not be coming until the next day. "We're going to move farther away," Duncan told Siefke and the TBX team. "I want you to raise the Brute and . . ."

"Lieutenant," interrupted Siefke, "the radio hasn't worked all day."

Duncan was forced to make a decision on the spot. "All right," he instructed Siefke, Lipscomb, and the other NCOs, "this is what we're going to do. Tom [Siefke], take your squad and get back to Nukiki. It's too dangerous to stay here with at least one enemy patrol so close by. The rendezvous point is Nukiki Village. It should be safe there. Major Bigger found the village empty yesterday. The main thing is to make it back and alert Colonel Krulak of our radio trouble and the battalion's new extraction time for tomorrow. Sergeant Lipscomb's squad and the TBX team will wait with me at the river mouth for the LCPRs."

They were separating because there were too many variables. What if the boats did not come? What if the boats were at Nukiki? They could have been shot up from the air. By splitting up, if either group got hit, the other would get word to the colonel. Of course, they hoped they would not both be hit.

With that, the two patrols departed. Siefke's squad moved off in the direction of Nukiki. Private Neff and squad leader Sergeant Siefke were up front; Private Pierce and assistant squad leader Corporal Vinich brought up the rear. They were only a few hundred yards from the mouth of the Warrior and the boats that should be arriving before dark. The Marines could just imagine how surprised they would be when sixteen men, instead of the entire eighty-seven man northern task force, waded out to be picked up.

Channel between Zinoa Island and Voza

When IMAC was informed of the captured hydrographic charts showing the waters around Bougainville, they immediately dispatched a navy PBY

to land in the channel between Zinoa Island and Voza Beach and pick up
the documents. That same Catalina would evacuate some of the wounded.
PM2 Chester "Chet" Finnegan was tending one of those wounded, Private
O'Neal, who had lost a lot of blood from his multiple gunshot wounds and
had gone through bottle after bottle of plasma. He was white as a sheet
from blood loss, and since the battle two days prior, Dr. H. E. Hinman and
Dr. Richard Lawrence were trying desperately to keep him alive. Neither
of the doctors was present at that time, and it was Finnegan's job to get the
wounded man into the PBY. Finnegan tried to put more plasma in O'Neal,
but the man's vein was dried up. The pharmacist's mate searched frantically for a healthy vein to stick. Adding to Finnegan's stress was the reality
that every second the PBY was exposed in the channel increased the like-
lihood of enemy fighters seeing it. If that happened, all the wounded men
and the PBY crew would die.

Finnegan kept sticking O'Neal's arm, but he could not find a vein. He
stuck O'Neal's foot, his big toe, and his hands. Nothing. Finally, he knew if
he did not give him a cut down, the wounded Marine would die. Using
a scalpel, Finnegan cut a flap of skin on the arch of O'Neal's foot and
peeled it back to expose a vein. O'Neal hardly even bled. How could he?
He did not have any blood left in his body. Pushing the flesh back,
Finnegan put a hemostat on the vein, and almost as if he were threading
a needle, stuck the dry vein. Finnegan then released the hemostat and,
once more, O'Neal had a chance.

Finnegan and the others ran him onto the waiting LCPR that was carrying the maps and the other wounded. The boat quickly moved out to
the floatplane. Just before they were able to get O'Neal on board, the
wounded leatherneck passed away. He had simply lost too much blood.
Finnegan could only shake his head in frustration as his patient died. The
boat reached the plane where O'Neal, Kirkpatrick, Garbuschewski, and
others, along with the documents, were quickly transferred. The Higgins
Boat moved away and the PBY started up its engines. Within minutes, it
had lifted into the air.

Lieutenant Richards's Patrol

The First Platoon of E Company was moving down a trail toward the Vagara
River on an ambush patrol. Pfc. Hugh Greely was one of those Marines,
and he was still suffering from amoebic dysentery. He had traded his K-
rations for his buddies' D-bars because the D-bars were the only thing his
body would take. Greely was in the machine-gun section toward the rear

of the column. Private Brown, their gunner, was behind Greely; ammunition bearers Pfc. Harold Frackelton and Cpl. Samuel C. Walker were behind him.

Up ahead of Greely's section trudged the second squad, and still farther up, Sgt. Philip Romero's squad was walking point. They had just reached a small stream maybe fifteen yards wide and were preparing to cross it when Lieutenant Richards told them to hold up. A river or stream crossing was always the worst part of a patrol. The Marines set most of their ambushes along bodies of water, so it was safe to assume the Japanese did the same. The best spot to hit the enemy was when they waded into open water, when they were completely exposed, with no cover anywhere. Knowing this, the Marines were understandably wary when crossing streams, rivers, or hitting a beach.

Romero's first squad was crossing to spread out on the opposite bank to cover the second and third squads. Meanwhile, the point men—Pfc. William Provost and Pfc. Donald "Hink" Hinkle—continued down the trail, Hink walking about ten feet behind Provost. Provost was a replacement; Hink, a battalion scout, could tell he was a gung ho kid. In the lead, he was not moving with the caution that Hink saw in veterans. Hink noticed a complete lack of birds flying out of the trees ahead of them. They could not walk through the jungle without seeing and hearing hundreds of birds, but these trees were still. Suddenly a .25-caliber bullet struck Provost in the head, sending Hink diving for cover. More rifle fire exploded from the jungle ahead, and a Nambu machine gun stitched the trees along the stream. Hink was hiding behind a large root and could not return fire; he was trying to stay low and alive. But he had seen that the shot that had killed Provost came from a big tree just ahead of them.

Pfc. Frank Dudek was chest deep in the middle of the water with his rifle over his head when the firing broke out. His first instinct was to go prone, so he inadvertently dunked himself. He came up instantly and brought his rifle down as he searched for targets ahead, but water running in streams down his helmet blocked his vision. Suddenly, in a tree about twenty yards away, Dudek saw what he thought was a Japanese sniper's helmeted head. He fired and made a direct hit. The "helmet" exploded. It was not a helmet, though; it was a coconut.

On the Marine side of the river, Greely had not yet reached the stream when the shots broke out, sending everyone diving for cover. Greely and Pfc. Burt Bueller both dove and happened to get behind the same small tree. A bullet struck the slender trunk between the two and they exchanged quick glances before crawling for better cover. Gunfire was exploding everywhere as Americans and Japanese blasted at each other through the jungle. The bullets ripped the trees to shreds, and leaves fell around them like rain. Greely emptied his carbine at muzzle flashes across the stream while next to him Brown blasted away with bursts from his A-4 machine gun. Everybody went through a number of magazines or belts, firing in lanes between the Marines on the opposite bank.

The patrol had walked into a Japanese ambush. An enemy sniper had prematurely sprung the trap by shooting Provost, and firing broke out. If the parachutists had not stopped at the river to fan out to protect the men crossing behind them, a lot more Marines would be lying dead on the trail.

But what were the Japanese doing here? The Marines had underestimated the speed with which their enemy would respond to Bachman's attack only hours earlier. They planned to set a trap along the Vagara River, but the Japanese were already two miles north of their proposed ambush site, ambushing them.

Most of Sergeant Romero's squad was on the Japanese side of the river and they began to return fire. "Lame duck up front," shouted Pfc. Richard Lipe back over his shoulder. This was to tell the others they had a wounded man. Lipe did not know Provost had been killed.

"He's dead," Hink shouted back.

Pfc. W. Garth Bonner took cover behind a log and saw bullets kicking up all around his squad leader, Romero. Bonner could not see the sniper but he could hear where the shots were coming from—a tree about fifteen yards away. Bonner was sure Romero was going to get hit any second. "Caesar, get down," he shouted. "There's a sniper shooting at you. He's up in the tree to your left."

"Well, shoot the son of a bitch!" roared Romero. "Don't tell me about him!"

Bonner brought up his Johnson rifle and pumped three shots into the area of branches where he thought the sniper was, and a Japanese soldier fell out of the tree. Before the man could hit the ground the rope tying him to the branch caught, snapping his body to a halt five feet off the jungle floor.

At that same moment, Hink saw muzzle flashes from a tree ahead and lifted his rifle up to shoot. Just as he aimed to fire, the sniper was hit and fell out of the tree. The lifeless Japanese soldier was hanging upside down, swinging like a pendulum over the trail, suspended by a rope. Hink was the closest Marine to the Japanese line, so he crawled back toward the river.

Only seconds had passed since the firefight began, but the jungle was being blown apart by rifle and machine-gun fire. Private Dudek was still in the middle of the stream with water kicking up around him where bullets struck. All he could think about was that if anyone had seen him kill that coconut he would never hear the end of it. If his buddies found out he was a fruit shooter they would rib him forever. Just then, a bullet kicked up a little too close for comfort and brought him back to reality. If he stayed where he was, he would die. He had two choices—forward or back—and he went back. Dudek strove against the water back to the northwest side of the stream; it seemed like he had never moved so slowly in his life. Bullets kicked up around him and it was as if the stream was alive and fighting to keep him from gaining the bank. Just as he climbed out of the water, Dudek felt a sharp burning pain in his groin. "Oh my God," he said, "I'm hit."

The pain was intense, but Dudek was not behind cover yet. Crawling to the side, he reached the relative safety of cover and got behind it. Dudek instantly dropped his dungarees and checked himself for a gunshot wound. He could not see any blood, and there was no visible injury, so he pulled his pants back up. His groin still burned like fire, but he had not been shot. "Great," he thought, "now I have some incurable genital jungle disease from the river." Dudek aimed his rifle across the stream but did not see any enemy troops to fire at. Since he did not want to provide an enemy soldier a muzzle flash to shoot at, he sat and waited. Dudek watched for an enemy rush but could see only the jump boots of prone Marines. Dudek heard explosion after explosion amidst the staccato of machine-gun and rifle fire and he knew someone was throwing grenades.

Back across the river the Marines had engaged many Japanese troops and were holding their own because of the superior firepower of their Johnson weapons. Lipe's element crawled back to Pfc. John Geddings's element. Sergeant Romero's squad was now working to pump suppressing fire at the enemy. "Where's Provost?" asked Bonner.

"He's dead," replied Lipe. Bonner did not have time to take in the fact that his buddy was dead. Geddings snapped an order at him and the others nearby.

"There are some Nips on the other side of this big log. I'm going to toss this over," he said, motioning with a grenade in his hand. "After it explodes, I'll jump over the log and let them have it with Mary Jane. You guys go around the side."

They all checked their weapons and got ready. With all eyes on Geddings, they watched him release the pin. The spoon flew off with a ping, and Geddings waited three seconds before lobbing it over the huge root. The grenade exploded with a muffled roar, sending bark, leaves, and sticks flying.

Instantly everybody was up and firing like hell. Everyone that is, except Geddings. Geddings jumped up and pulled the trigger, but Mary Jane would not fire. He had accidentally put the sear pin in backwards. Now she was useless except as a club. Geddings found himself face to face with three enemy soldiers. The grenade had killed one of them, but had merely stunned the other two. There was no time to think, only to react. Geddings flashed out his Ka-Bar and leaped over the log, stabbing and slashing, and killed both men. Meanwhile, the other men in his squad blasted the Japanese line with everything they had. The opposing sides fired back and forth through the jungle, and then everything went silent.

On the Marine side of the stream, Greely and Dudek waited for something to happen. The firing had died down on the Japanese side and the Marines could not see anything over there. Nobody knew what had happened, but after a few moments the point squad slowly crawled backward into sight. Hink, Bonner, Romero and the others moved down into the water and waded back across under the protective guns of Brown, Greely, Dudek, and the others. During their withdrawal, the Japanese never fired a shot. Once all the Marines were on the northwest side of the stream, they held their positions, waiting for the enemy to attack.

After about twenty minutes with still no sign of the enemy, Lieutenant Richards ordered his squad leaders together. "There's no reason to keep going to the Vagara when the Japs are already here," Richards told his men. "Our orders are hit and run." They had lost one man, Private Provost, but they were not about to lose another by sending him to get the body. They left Provost where he had fallen along the trail.

The patrol prepared to move back, but there was one problem. It would be dark soon. Movement at night was deadly business, especially when they had to approach a battalion lookout post. The guards there would undoubtedly be jumpy from all the gunfire they had heard. Richards decided to send a few of his men ahead of the rest. Richards grabbed one of his men. "It's almost dark. I want you to return as fast as you can and tell our outpost we'll be coming through in the dark."

The runner left immediately, with a few men trailing him; he sprinted back down the path to reach the lookout post before nightfall. Dusk was literally minutes away. Once they reached the outpost, they would tell the Marines there not to fire at the first twig that broke ahead of them in the night. The rest of Richards's platoon made an organized withdrawal back toward Voza.

Lieutenant Duncan's Patrol

Duncan, the TBX team, and Sergeant Lipscomb's squad were waiting at the mouth of the Warrior when the LCPRs arrived to extract Major Bigger's northern task force. Wading out to the boats, the parachutists boarded and told the naval officer and coxswain to head back to Voza. If Siefke's squad were already at Nukiki, they would pick them up. If not, they would return for them in the morning. They could not wait around. It was absolutely essential to get the boats to protection and let the colonel know what was happening. They made the quick trip to Nukiki but found the area deserted. Siefke's squad was probably still working their way through the jungle. Duncan ordered the LCPRs to return to Voza.

1800—Sergeant Siefke's Squad

Siefke's squad had split from Lieutenant Duncan with orders to make it to Nukiki. If the boats were there, they were to get to Voza and inform the colonel of their radio trouble and move the boats to safety. Duncan had gone down to the ocean to wait for the boats with the same mission. Between the two groups, someone should be able to find the LCPRs and make it back to get word to Colonel Krulak.

It was around 1800 and Siefke's squad was making good time. They were almost to Nukiki Village when four dogs came scurrying down the trail toward them. The dogs did not stop or dart into the jungle but slunk past the Marines in fear, their tails low. "What the hell?" thought Siefke. That was definitely not normal canine behavior. The dogs did not even bark. "We need to get off this trail," said Siefke.

It was almost dark and Siefke was not going to gamble that it was Duncan or any other Marines that had sent the dogs running in fear out of Nukiki. If there were Marines in the village, they would be just as likely to hurl grenades at movement in the dark as the Japanese would. They could wait until morning to find out whether the village was empty or occupied by friend or foe. Siefke's squad moved off the coastal trail in the last of the fading light, through the narrow strip of jungle, and down onto the sandy beach where a long coral outcropping extended out into the surf from the beach.

"Let's make a circular perimeter defense," said Siefke to his men. "We'll touch our heels and dig in." Siefke was about to tell his men to dig deep holes in the sand when his assistant squad leader Vinich spoke up.

"Tom, let's not stay here. Let's get up in these coral rocks. If anyone comes through here, nobody's going to climb on the coral." Siefke thought about it for a moment, weighing the pros and cons. If they got up on the rocks, they could not dig in and it would be uncomfortable, but the enemy was not likely to crawl aimlessly on the rocks, whereas they might patrol the beach. It was a natural jetty that did offer some concealment.

"You're right, Mike. Good idea."

"Hell, we do that in Wyoming," said Vinich. "We get up in the rocks."

Siefke moved his men into the coral formation, making a perimeter defense with heels touching. They could not dig in, but it felt safe. They could not see their surroundings without lifting their heads, so they were confident they were hidden. Also, they appeared to be on a deserted stretch of beach. Surrounded by beach on two sides, with jungle in front and ocean behind them, they settled in for the night.

Battalion Southeast Listening Post

Five Marines ran flat out back down the trail to reach the battalion southeast lookout post before dark. Their orders were to tell the guards that the rest of their patrol would be following and not to shoot at the first noise they heard.

Dudek was one of those five men, but he had not been told why they were running. He had just seen men take off, his buddy Pfc. Ralph Beneke being one of them, and thought the whole platoon was retreating. It was a mad dash down the trail, and Dudek figured the others were right behind him. Dudek was trying not to laugh thinking about how ignoble this must look. He knew there had to be more than a company of Japanese attacking them to make Richards order the platoon to retreat like this, and that was a sobering thought. As he ran, his groin still burned. He would go immediately to Dr. Lawrence once they got back.

When they arrived at the lookout post it was seconds before dark fell, and Dudek heard them give the password and countersign. Strangely, the rest of the platoon was not behind them. They told the G Company paratroopers on lookout why they had run back down the trail and that the rest of the patrol would be coming along soon in a single-file line.

"Ohhhh." What a complete mess this afternoon had been. Dudek's only contribution to the firefight had been to shoot a coconut, and he had thought they were in a full-blown panicked retreat. He was glad to find out he was wrong, and walked to the stream to wash his aching genitals. By now, the burning sensation in his groin was unbearable. Dropping his dungarees again, he saw that the citronella mosquito repellant in his pocket had leaked, and that was what had caused the burning. He breathed a sigh of relief that he did not have some disease, and moved into the stream to wash himself. The others had already spread out and were slaking their thirst.

"Dudek!" spat a disgusted Marine filling his canteen not far away. "Goddammit! We have to drink that water."

"But I'm downstream from you. Whadya care?"

"But what about the guys further downstream from you?"

"What they don't know won't hurt 'em."

After he cleaned off he joined the others to wait for the rest of the platoon. In whispers, they talked about the firefight. Someone dubbed Geddings the "Pineapple Kid" because he threw so many hand grenades. "So he was the one responsible for all those explosions," thought Dudek. The others laughed, knowing they had found a nickname that would stick. Dudek never told anyone about what happened to him during the firefight. He could just imagine what his name would be if anyone knew he had shot a coconut.

Major Bigger's Force

The Marines were trying to make it through an uneasy night in the swamp. There was no real sleep for any of them. No one could find a dry spot, and the mosquitoes were ravenous. Holland sat beside his buddy Muller talking about home and better times. Suddenly Muller turned and said, "If either of us gets hit, the survivor should go tell the other's family. It would be hard for them not to know."

Holland, a married man, agreed. "Sure, Frank."

"Shake on it," said Muller, extending his hand.

"Sure," said Holland again, shaking his buddy's hand.

Not far away, Barney and Fagoni sat in a forward guard post. Barney swore he could just faintly hear dogs barking in the distance. He assumed the Japanese were out looking for them and figured the dogs could smell the American presence, although they probably could not track them in the brackish water. Barney knew they had sent his platoon lieutenant back to get a message to the TBX team along the river because they had not been able to make radio contact yet. Feeling uneasy about having the battalion's best officer gone, he wished it had been his squad that had gone with Lieutenant Duncan. Actually, Barney thought his best scenario would have been for Major Bigger to take the patrol back.

Barney was a rare type in the Marine Corps: he did not smoke, drink, curse, or womanize. Still, he was well liked. "You don't like to curse, do you?" Pfc. Bill Cougar had asked him once. Barney had never really thought about it because his mother had raised him and his brothers to keep their language clean; cursing was unacceptable in their household.

"No, I don't," he answered. Barney never made derogatory remarks about women either, something that was also rare. His mother had explained a simple fact that Barney never forgot. "The young ladies you meet will be the future mothers of our nation. Treat them with respect."

He sat in the warm brown water and tried to keep his rifle clear of the swamp. He was not worried about it jamming. It was a Johnson rifle and he had never had one jam on him or heard of one jamming, but he did not want to tempt fate. It was just good practice to keep your weapon clean and dry. Barney remembered the day he landed on Guadalcanal carrying the Johnson. It was a coveted weapon among the combat veterans already there, all of whom wanted to trade for them. A grizzled old sergeant carrying an M-1 Garand had sauntered over to him.

"I'm going to show you how good your Johnson rifles are compared to our Garands," he said. He put a round in his M-1 and, to everyone's surprise, he buried it in the sand. He looked out into the water and pointed to a coconut bobbing in the surf about a hundred yards out. The sergeant asked, "See that coconut? Watch this." He reached down, pulled the M-1 out of the sand, aimed, and pulled the trigger. Nothing. The rifle jammed. No surprise. How could he expect it to fire? He grabbed Barney's rifle and, before Barney could protest, he buried it in the sand. "Now watch that coconut," said the tough old sergeant pointing out into the water again. He waited just a moment, pulled the Johnson out of the sand, aimed, and fired. The coconut exploded in the water. "This is the best weapon you will ever carry," said the sergeant. "It will fire *every* time."

Battalion Southeast Listening Post

Lieutenant Richards's patrol moved in complete darkness in a single file back along the trail they had come down an hour earlier. The Marines were connected hand on shoulder as they moved slowly through the night. They had been traveling blindly in the dark for a while and figured they were getting close to the battalion lookout post. As they neared the flowing stream where the Marine outpost was waiting in ambush, they heard a challenge in the darkness.

"Halt. Who's there?"

"One-Ball Riley," answered Garth Bonner. "Who wants to know?"

"Old Riley's daughter. Is that you, Bonner?"

"Yeah, who are you?"

"Bill Bowman, G Company."

"Be sure to challenge each one of us. The Nips might have infiltrated our column."

Sergeant Siefke's Squad

All night long Siefke's squad heard voices and movement from around their position. Vinich was glad they had moved onto the coral when they did. From the sound of it, they were very fortunate to have gotten off the trail because the only place the noise did not come from was the ocean. They were surrounded.

The Marines listened, but they could not tell if the voices were English or Japanese. They were too faint and the sound of the surf drowned them out.

Battalion Northwest Lookout Post

Cpl. William D. Cole and his squad were sitting guard at the battalion lookout post along the Baregosonga River. They were guarding the coastal trail that led to Voza and the battalion flank from the northwest. Any Japanese moving from the northern part of the island had only one approach from that direction—the narrow strip of ground between the steep mountain and the ocean at the Baregosonga. Their ambush position gave them an excellent defensive position and provided deadly enfilading fire at anyone coming at them across the wide river. Their squad could easily wipe out a platoon of Japanese if they tried to cross here.

Clark was in Cole's squad. He knew G Company had made a raid to the north and were supposed to have returned after they had raised enough hell. They should have been back by now. Rumor had it they had been ambushed, and as of yet, nobody had made it back.

Clark was sitting close to Hoskins. "The jungle is a strange place," thought Clark. The sounds were loud, eerie, and menacing. Birds screamed like women, bugs tormented them every second, and animals moved and slithered making them think there was someone next to them in the darkness. Those sounds could disappear completely without a warning, however, or they could hear men whispering from twenty yards away, like at that moment. Their whispers carried to Clark and Hoskins who could not help but eavesdrop.

"We've got real problems," said one of the voices with a thick Chicago accent. "There are three thousand Nips between us and G Company, and G Company's coming this way. They missed their boats and are walking out. They're in deep shit."

"Deep shit is right," thought Clark, "for us. There are only ten of us, and three thousand Nips. Damn right we've got real problems."

Clark was crouched behind a banyan root for cover, and he searched the darkness of the opposite bank for Japanese troops. He remembered the frenzied *banzai* from the day before. It had been daylight during that fight, but now it was pitch black. He also realized there had been many Marines helping beat back that charge. Now there would be but ten, and that *banzai* had come at them incredibly fast.

Empress Augusta Bay

By the waning minutes of November 1, the Third Marine Division had fourteen thousand men on shore on Bougainville with the supplies and munitions to sustain them for weeks to come. The Marines dug in and prepared for an enemy counterattack. They had had two hundred casualties during the day's vicious fighting, and they had lost dozens and dozens of Higgins Boats. Nevertheless, the landing was definitely a success. The Japanese seemed hesitant to counterattack and General Hyakutake withheld his reserves to see if this was yet another American feint.

Chapter 8

WARRIOR RIVER: NOVEMBER 2

God came down and protected us. That's the truth.

Pfc. Henry Blum, G Company, on the rainsquall
that shielded them from the Japanese at the mouth
of the Warrior River on November 2, 1943

0500—Sergeant Siefke's Squad

Dawn, in its magnificence, was breaking. In the early morning light, Sgt. Thomas Siefke stood up to urinate and get a look at his surroundings when the magnitude of their danger was revealed to him. Quickly dropping to his belly, he hissed a warning to his squad. "Stay down. Stay quiet."

Peeking over the coral Siefke saw his squad surrounded by Japanese troops on three sides. Only blind luck or the grace of God had saved them from disaster. If they had slept off the trail in the jungle, at least a platoon of Japanese soldiers would have stumbled on them at some point during the night. If they had stayed on the beach, they would now be visible to the enemy troops on their flank. Siefke remembered the dogs. "Thank God they came down when they did." Those dogs had told him something was wrong in the village.

With a platoon of enemy troops 50 yards on one side and at least a company not 150 yards on the other, Siefke racked his brain for a way out. The Japanese were relaxed, waking up, cooking, and cleaning their rifles. They seemed to be completely unaware that a squad of U.S. Marines paratroopers was in their midst.

The roar of the surf drowned out all noises as Siefke and his men spoke in hushed whispers about what possible options they might have—if any. They all knew that unless the Japanese left the area, there was no way they were going to get out of there by land. It was possible the boats might come by, but what if they did not? And if they did, how could the boats get in to pick them up without taking fire from two hundred Japanese troops? It was enough to make the most battle-hardened Marine nervous. Already sweating in the morning heat, the Marines could do nothing but wait.

171

0530—Major Bigger's Force

At first light, Maj. Warner T. Bigger ordered his men to continue their mission. No one had really slept that night, and they were all hungry, tired, and thirsty. They had been eaten alive by mosquitoes and were soaking wet from the swamp water. Everyone worried about jungle rot—they all had some form of painful itching and chaffing from the heat and moisture.

Major Bigger assembled the officers and had a quick briefing. When they finished, he and Capt. William R. Day each made a separate azimuth west-southwest with their compasses, conferred, and headed off in that direction. The column followed in single file through the swamp. Everyone hoped they were finally moving toward the coast.

0600—Sergeant Siefke's Squad

For more than an hour Sergeant Siefke and his squad hugged the coral out-cropping where they hid and prayed that the Japanese would break camp and leave the area. They did not care where they went; they just wanted them to leave Nukiki. They were worried that a Japanese soldier would go for a stroll along the beach or move into the surf to bath and see them. One thing was certain—if they got into a firefight here, there was no way they would make it out alive. There were too many enemy troops. Once the Japanese sighted in their mortars, it would be over. But if it came to that, Siefke knew they would take a lot of Japanese with them because unlike the Japanese, his squad had coral rock cover and they were ready. "A boat," hissed Pfc. Leo Henslick pointing to the southeast. They all looked out; sure enough, they could see three boats moving up the coast toward them. They were paralleling the shore in a northwest direction moving toward the Warrior River.

"I wonder if they're ours," said Cpl. Mike Vinich. "[Lt. Rae] Duncan said he'd pick us up at Nukiki."

"They gotta be," said Siefke. "Mike, you know sign language, right?" "Yeah," replied Vinich.

"Go out and see if they're our boats. If they are, signal them in." "Okay."

"We'll cover you," said Siefke.

As Vinich crawled on his belly down the coral rocks toward the ocean, Siefke told his men to be ready to fire on his command. Because they were already spread out in a semicircle facing the Japanese, they just waited.

Vinich knew semaphore and would try to signal the boats—if they were the navy LCPRs. Vinich followed the small outcropping out as far as he could. About fifty yards from the rest of the squad he was still only a hundred yards from the closest enemy soldiers. He moved out onto the coral in the breaking surf and stopped. He could not go any farther without entering the water. He feared he was now visible to the Japanese platoon on their flank anyway. As we watched the boats getting closer, he was able to make out the unmistakable shape of Higgins Boats. Convinced they were friendly and not Japanese barges, Vinich stood straight up. "Come in, urgent," he signaled in big, deliberate motions.

0630—Lieutenant Duncan's LCPR

Lieutenant Duncan was scanning the beach with his binoculars. The night before, he had told Sergeant Siefke's squad to make it to Nukiki and that was where he was looking for them. The navy officers and coxswains on the three boats were looking, too. One of them saw movement and shouted aloud. Duncan warned his gunners to get ready because someone was moving on the coral rocks in the distance ahead. Now they could see the unmistakable signal the man was making over and over. "Come in, urgent; come in, urgent; come in, urgent."

Duncan and the navy officer on board looked through their binoculars and saw a man in Marine uniform signaling them from a coral jetty. If Vinich had not known semaphore, the gunner on the LCPRs could easily have mistaken him for a Japanese soldier. Lieutenant Duncan had expected to find Siefke's squad right where they were. What he had not expected was for the area to be a bivouac for two companies of enemy infantry. They began to take fire.

Sergeant Siefke's Squad

Siefke and the rest of his squad had sighted in on the Japanese when Vinich crawled out. Siefke told his men to keep their rifles aimed in their designated areas. They were in a semicircle and if everyone turned to shoot in the same direction they would leave a blind spot. "Stay in your positions," he ordered.

Siefke was surprised that the Japanese had not become alarmed by the approaching boats. Maybe they thought they were Japanese barges. Watching Vinich out of the corner of his eye, Siefke saw him stand straight up and make the signals, but he never stopped watching the Japanese. It seemed impossible, but maybe they would not even see Vinich. None of them seemed to have noticed him yet. Siefke soon found how unrealistic that hope was.

It took a few seconds, but at last one of the Japanese soldiers noticed the movement. He seemed not to understand at first, but it must have hit him like a punch. A U.S. Marine was standing straight up on the coral rocks not one hundred yards away. He pointed and shouted to the others. At first, the Japanese platoon reacted slowly, as if not understanding. Sergeant Siefke opened fire.

Siefke went through a magazine in seconds and slapped another one in while Pfc. James Moe cut loose with his JLMG, spraying the enemy troops with automatic fire. It was a bloodletting at only fifty yards. The Japanese were caught completely by surprise and dropped or ran in chaos. All the Marines were firing now, and the Japanese soldiers who were not shot in the first few seconds fled toward the jungle.

Vinich was still standing straight up signaling in expansive motions, "Come in, urgent." He had already made the signal half a dozen times and saw the boats turning in toward them. He heard his squad firing on the beach behind him and saw the LCPRs open up with their heavy machine guns. Tracer fire stabbed into the tree line where the Japanese had fled. Vinich leaped into the surf and waded out to the boats.

Back on the coral outcropping, Siefke looked back over his shoulder and saw the boats coming in. With the exception of Moe, whose automatic rifle he needed, Seifke ordered his men to fall back to the LCPRs. He and Moe would lay down covering fire while the others escaped. The men leaped up and raced down the coral toward the ocean.

Vinich reached an LCPR and climbed on board. The first person he saw was Lieutenant Duncan. The LCPR's machine guns were returning fire at the jungle edge on Siefke's right, but Vinich corrected them. "Concentrate your fire there," he shouted, pointing at the cove on Siefke's left where the company of enemy infantry had been. The crew had old World War I Lewis guns and they blasted away, forcing the Japanese to fall back into the jungle.

Back on the rocks Siefke and Moe fired until they saw their squad had cleared the coral and were now wading in the surf. Siefke was worried that the enemy would start lobbing mortar rounds in on them, and he told Moe to get moving. They leaped up and, staying low, sprinted back together down the jetty, jumped into the surf, and waded out to the boats as fast as they could. The closest LCPR was about two hundred yards from shore and maybe 250 yards from the Japanese troops, who were now inside the jungle. The Marines were taking sporadic fire, but it was relatively inaccurate because the antiaircraft machine guns on the LCPRs forced the Japanese to stay hidden. Under the protective guns of the three LCPRs, the paratroopers gained the boats, with Siefke and Moe the last on board. The LCPRs turned southeast and headed back for Voza, moving about a thousand yards off the beach. They had not gone more than a mile when they saw a Japanese Daihatsu barge beached along the shore southeast of Nukiki, and then another and another—eight Japanese barges in all along the shore between Nukiki and Moli Plantation. Each barge carried a platoon, so the Japanese had to have landed with at least two reinforced companies. Were those some of the troops they saw at Nukiki or were they additional troops? If so, the Japanese could have an entire battalion between Nukiki and Moli Plantation alone. Either way, the ruse was working. Siefke and the others saw firsthand how the Japanese were rushing troops from the other islands to stop the Marine invasion of Choiseul.

The LCPRs arrived back at Voza and Siefke double-timed it up to Lt. Col. Victor H. Krulak's CP to give his report while the rest of his squad worked their way up to the battalion camp.

0800—Mountain Camp

The area to the southeast of the battalion hideout was proving, as suspected, to be a hotbed for enemy activity. On October 29, Colonel Krulak had ambushed and destroyed a Japanese barge between the village of Vagara and Sangigai, killing seven enemy soldiers. Later that day, Sgt. Norman Law's squad killed seven more when they ambushed a Japanese patrol three-fourths of a mile from Voza. On October 30, the battalion had attacked and destroyed the enemy barge station at Sangigai, killing seventy-two enemy soldiers and sending more than three hundred fleeing into the jungle. They had also destroyed a great deal of the enemy's stores of ammunition, supplies, and another barge. On November 1, Lt. Carl Bachman had led a patrol in that direction and kicked up a firefight at Vagara Village, killing seven enemy soldiers. Most recently, the previous night, Lt. John Richards's First Platoon had been ambushed between the battalion listening post and Vagara. All the action seemed to be to the southeast, and now Lt. Donald Justice was taking a patrol consisting mainly of the First Platoon, G Company, to Sangigai. Their orders were to make contact with any

Japanese forces northwest of Sangigai. The battalion needed to know if the Japanese had reinforced the barge station. If it had, Justice's patrol was to hit them and get word back to battalion. A few E Company troopers would accompany the patrol to recover the body of Pfc. William J. Provost, the Marine who had been killed the day before when Lieutenant Richards's patrol tripped a Japanese ambush northwest of Vagara.

Accompanying that thirty-man patrol were Sgt. Frank Banner, Pfc. Charles Allman, Pfc. Jack Carns, and Pfc. Billy Dale Bowman of the First Platoon, G Company; Pfc. Jim Ward from Hq Company; and Pfc. Donald "Hink" Hinkle and Pfc. Robert Brutinel of E Company. Told to make contact with the Japanese as far down as Sangigai, many of the paratroopers wondered if they would make it much farther than the battalion lookout post. The Japanese were obviously in the area. Bowman had been at the lookout post the night before when Lieutenant Richards's platoon came back. That patrol had been hit almost two miles from Voza, some eight miles from Sangigai.

0930—Colonel Krulak's CP

It was 0930 when Sergeant Siefke arrived at Colonel Krulak's command post. It was blisteringly hot already, and Siefke was sweating profusely when he entered. The colonel was sitting down with a damp cloth between his knees, trying to keep cool in the insufferable heat. Siefke informed the Brute of the situation while he tried to catch his breath. "Colonel, there are at least two companies of Japanese at Nukiki Village," began Siefke. "We counted an additional eight enemy barges between Nukiki and Moli Point. We just barely got away."

Krulak listened and calmly turned to his radio operator. "Get hold of the PT boat base at Lambu Lambu," said Krulak to Pfc. Norman Wurzburger. "We're likely to see some action tonight."

Siefke noticed that Lieutenant Duncan was there, too. He must have double-timed it to the camp just as he had done. Duncan and Krulak conferred about the boats, and Siefke heard them talking about the raiding party under Major Bigger. Krulak dismissed Siefke, and he left the CP without knowing what they had said. He figured the LCPRs would be heading out to pick up the northern task force later in the afternoon. From what Duncan had told him, there was no use going to get them now. They had not even made their attack yet. The northern task force would not be at the Warrior River until 1700.

1130—Major Bigger's Force

The northern task force had been moving slowly and painfully through the jungle swamps when Major Bigger called a temporary halt to recheck his azimuth. When he did, Capt. William R. Day turned to PM1 John Holland standing beside him.

"John, you've got good hearing. What's that noise?"

Holland cocked his head to the side to listen. After a few seconds he said, "Sounds like surf to me."

"I thought so," replied Day. "Good. Now we finally know where we are."

At 1130, the northern task force reached the ocean between the Warrior River and their destination, Choiseul Bay. Once again Pfc. George P. Adams was told to try to raise the Warrior River TBX team or battalion, but just like every other time he had tried over the past twenty-four hours, he could not reach anyone "Captain," said Adams, "I've tried the radio so many times the batteries are shot."

"Destroy it," instructed Day. "It's too heavy to lug around if it doesn't work." Only too willing to oblige, Adams smashed the radio and threw it into the ocean.

Without a radio, Adams was now an extra runner for Captain Day. His first assignment was to accompany a five-man patrol back to the Warrior River. Major Bigger and Captain Day assembled the five-man detachment and briefed them. "Get back to the Warrior and locate the TBX team," Bigger said to Sgt. Rahland Wilson, the ranking man on the patrol. "Get a message off to Colonel Krulak. Tell him what's going on and request that the LCPRs pick up the rest of us at the mouth of Warrior at 1500. Got it? 1500."

"Got it," replied Wilson.

The other members of the patrol were Adams, Pfc. Roy J. Gallagher, Pfc. Paul J. Hamilton, and PM3 Richard Walker. The five men handed over the mortar shells they helped carry and the remaining men distributed them among themselves. The Marines were never happy when more men split from the main group, because their loads increased. Sergeant Wilson led his small party of four men to the southeast along the coast trail headed for the Warrior.[1]

Major Bigger and the main group, now numbering fifty-six men, moved off in the opposite direction, to the northwest, paralleling the coast. As their numbers shrank from eighty-seven to fifty-six, more than one man in the main raiding party thought of George Custer splitting his command.

Instead of Benteen and Reno it was Siefke and Duncan. Now another TBX team under Sergeant Wilson was splitting from them with five more men. Both groups were moving in unfamiliar territory, approaching an unknown number of enemy troops. It was disconcerting.

Lambu Lambu Cove—Vella LaVella

A message marked urgent arrived at the PT boat base at Lambu Lambu. It said that a patrol of Marine paratroopers were cut off and trapped on the neighboring island of Choiseul by a battalion of Japanese somewhere near the mouth of the Warrior River. The commanding officer of the parachute battalion was requesting PT boat assistance for the stranded patrol. Lt. Arthur H. Berndston took the message and ran to the operations bunker down near the docks. Of the five boats in his command, one was useless (up on dry dock), and two had already been sent out on a mission and were gone for the night. That left two boats, one of which was refueling. It was number 59, and its skipper, Lt. John F. Kennedy, was standing on the dock helping his crew manhandle a barrel of oil to the boat. Berndston ran up to Kennedy and showed him the message, asking him how much fuel he had. Kennedy read it quickly and asked his men the same question. "Seven hundred gallons," came the reply. The message said the Marines were trapped at the Warrior River on Choiseul. Seven hundred gallons would be enough to get them over, but both officers knew it would not be enough to get them back. The other boat was fully fueled. The officers discussed it quickly and decided that both boats would go, and when the 59 ran out of fuel, the other would tow it. Kennedy told his men to "Wind 'er up." They were going to pick up some Marines who were in trouble.

Lieutenant Justice's Patrol

Private Allman snaked along the jungle trail into the area where Private Provost had been killed. They had just crossed the small stream where Pfc. Frank Dudek shot a coconut the day before and were moving cautiously, vigilant for signs of an enemy ambush. Allman was not at point, but he was not more than a few men behind when the native guide suddenly darted to the side and disappeared in the jungle. The Marines immediately took cover and waited. Allman had his carbine aimed down the trail, expecting a Japanese patrol to walk into them any second. When the Japanese patrol did not appear, he realized the native had sensed an ambush and saved them all. Suddenly, an overpowering stench came to Allman's nostrils, so bad it made the hair on the back of his neck stand on end. It was the smell of death. Nothing happened for another ten minutes. Lieutenant Justice ordered a scout ahead. Because the man's sole job was to see if he drew fire, when no shots greeted his movement another element moved forward until the entire platoon moved into the area.

It was not hard to find Provost's body. He was right where the E Company guys said he would be, lying facedown just beyond the rivulet. There were a number of Japanese bodies, too, which surprised Allman because he had heard that the Marines were the ones who had been ambushed. Eight enemy dead were nearby and along the trail. The guide had not come back yet and that worried them, but after a while they figured he must have been spooked by the smell of the dead man and taken off.

Private Hinkle, Easy Company, took the dead man's dog tags for registration. Sgt. Vernon Hammond found a board from a packing crate and used his Ka-Bar to etch Provost's epitaph. Once he finished carving, he tied the board to a stick that would be the vertical part for a cross.

Meanwhile, Brutinel dug a shallow hole just off the beach, where Provost was laid to rest. Brutinel was a Catholic and probably one of the only men in the battalion to carry one of the small prayer books issued by the Marine Corps. He said last rites over the fallen Marine.[2] Private Ward watched them bury the fallen Marine beside a small stream of water along the beach. It looked like a very lonely place for a grave. They covered Provost with earth. The eighteen-year-old Provost's epitaph, scribbled on a makeshift cross, read: "Here lies a good Marine, whose time in hell on Earth hath seen. Pfc. William J. Provost, USMC."

Without the native scouts to guide them, the patrol continued cautiously down to the Vagara River, their sole purpose to make contact with the Japanese.

1100—Mountain Camp

Up to that point, all of the combat seen by the paratroopers had come from the southeast in the direction of Sangigai. Early on this particular morning, however, Lieutenant Duncan had sighted eight enemy barges between Moli Point and Moli Plantation. Sergeant Siefke had made contact with two companies of enemy infantry at Nukiki and there were possibly two more in the vicinity capable of hitting the battalion within the hour. Intelligence reports from the natives were also filtering in and indicated enemy troops now active on both sides of the battalion and closing in. It appeared that at least a battalion of enemy troops was between Moli Point and Major Bigger's raiding party.

Consequently, there was nothing they could do for Bigger. Lt. Donald Castle and twenty-seven men moved to the west flank listening post at the Baregosonga River to provide a little insurance on the battalion's northwest flank. Their mission was to mine the northwest approaches to the Baregosonga. Expecting his Marines to be hit from both flanks, Colonel Krulak ordered the security teams to be beefed up from a squad to a platoon level at both outposts.

At 1100, an ammunition airdrop from IMAC delivered crates of grenades and ammunition to the Second Battalion. The Marines had gone through a lot of ammo during the Sangigai attack and Krulak had requested additional supply via air.

Sitting with his squad on guard duty down at Voza, Pfc. Robert Adams and Pfc. Glenn Barbee watched a DC-3 come in low over Voza Beach. The DC-3 was almost directly over them, with its side door open. Adams recognized the man shoving the supplies out. "Hey," said Adams looking up at the plane as the man in the door shoved supplies out, "I've seen that guy on Vella."

"Yeah," said Barbee, "I recognize him, too, but I don't know his name."

More supplies dropped out of the plane, followed quickly by something else. Two parachutes opened up and slowly descended over the squad of Marines below. Unlike the other drops, which were crates, one parachute was tied to a pack. When the cargo hit the ground, the curious Marines moved over to see what it was. Adams opened the pack and to his great surprise and immeasurable delight he found bottles of Coca-Cola. They had been placed in a protective burlap wrap so they would not break. Laughing at this unbelievable stroke of fortune, the cheering Marines popped open the cokes and savored the taste. To get a Coca-Cola after almost a week on an enemy island was better than an early Christmas. Adams could not believe the kindness of that navy crew. "What good men they must be," he thought. They had used their parachutes to give strangers they would never see or know a simple gift.

1200—Major Bigger's Force

At about noon, the northern task force under Major Bigger was almost halfway to their destination of Choiseul Bay, with at least two miles to go. Each man was heavily laden with ammunition and carried two or three mortar rounds. In addition to the weight, it was miserably hot and humid.

As the force paralleled Taro and Redman Islands, Cpl. William R. Zuegel and Lt. Samuel Johnston were leading Pfc. Gene Bay's squad at the head of the column when they encountered a Japanese army lookout post along the ocean. It was a small five-man camp, and point man Zuegel walked right into it. Like an old west gunfight, everyone went for his weapon; but unlike the Japanese, whose weapons were stacked in a teepee-like pile, Zuegel brought his up from the hip. He fired again and again, and a JLMG opened up with a quick fusillade. Soon, everything was quiet again.

Everyone went to ground at the sound of the shots, but in a few minutes an all clear signal got the column up and moving again. Private Bay, of Casper, Wyoming, entered the former enemy post to see five dead Japanese scattered around the camp. "Damn, Zuegel," he commented, "you're a hell of a shot."

Bay saw that the Japanese had been caught completely unaware and had not fired a round. Their untouched rifles were still leaning in a teepee configuration near the fire. Two of the enemy had been swimming and their blood stained the surf, pushed up onto the beach by the lapping waves. The others were lying around the camp. One had fallen over a log they probably used as a bench. It was clear the Japanese never had a chance. "Collect their rifles," ordered Captain Day. "Throw them into the surf."

Zuegel and Johnston passed through the enemy lookout post while the others searched for anything that might be of military value. They also looked for souvenirs. The Marines immediately noticed something about the camp—something nonmilitary but far more important to them than the captured Sangigai documents. A large pot of rice was cooking over the fire, and the fragrance of fresh food almost started a stampede. Since the afternoon of October 27, all that the Marine paratroopers had eaten was one small can of food and an ersatz chocolate bar every day. As the column of Marines passed through the camp, each man greedily scooped up a canteen cup full of rice from the big pot. There was enough rice to feed at least a platoon, maybe more. Bay gobbled up his delicious cupful in seconds. He was starving and had been for the past six days.

But the quantity of rice raised the question, why would five men be cooking so much food? It was obvious—there had to be many more Japanese in the area. Major Bigger and Captain Day ordered the squad leaders to keep their men ready for an enemy attack, and held a quick briefing. They were concerned that the short firefight had alerted other Japanese in the area, so they decided to switch from their primary target of Choiseul Bay to their secondary target of Guppy Island, with its large fuel dump. But even with their new target they still had a little way to go before they were in a position to attack.

PM3 Paul Salfrank saw the dead men and immediately looked for Japanese blankets. The Marines prized the blankets for their comfort and texture. Unfortunately, it looked like the camp had already been picked clean. The Marines took everything of value from the enemy dead.

When Pfc. Henry Blum of upstate Pennsylvania moved through the camp he saw an empty cooking pot that had been kicked into a smoldering fire. Blum and the men behind him did not even know about the rice they had missed out on. It was a good thing, too, because as hungry as they all were, it might have started some fistfights.

Pfc. Ned Russell was walking with Sgt. Anthony J. Skotnicki's weapons platoon. When Russell passed through, he thought the dead enemy soldiers looked like little boys. They had all heard about how tall the Japanese Marines were—that was all the E and F Company guys talked about after their Sangigai battle—but these Japanese obviously were not in the same outfit. Russell took a closer look at the dead men and noted how much more his skin color resembled these Japanese than his white countrymen. The column filed past the camp, but he could not get it out of his head that the enemy troops looked like children, they were so small.

Sergeant Wilson's Patrol

Sergeant Wilson and his squad reached the northwest bank of the Warrior River and looked across for any sign of the TBX team. Wilson and his four men were to make contact with the Marines in the area and tell them the new extraction time that Major Bigger requested.

Even though Private G. Adams had landed at the Warrior River the day before, he was shocked at how wide the river was. He stood at the mouth on the northwest side, opposite where they had landed the day before, and wondered how they would cross. The day before, up at the headwaters, they had been able to wade across. Now they would have to swim to reach the other side, or move the mile or so up to the headwaters again. They assumed it was reasonably safe, because they knew that Siefke's squad and the TBX team were directly across the river from them. Also, Lieutenant Duncan and Sgt. Wilburn Lipscomb's squad had gone back the day before to inform battalion that the main group was lost and that the TBX was not working. That put twenty-six Marines on the southeast side of the river holding open a corridor. They should be safe.

They *should* be safe, but they might not be. Sergeant Wilson did not like the idea of ordering anybody across, so he suggested they draw straws to decide who would go. They did not have any straws, so they broke small twigs into two sizes: four long and one short. Each man took his turn. Adams drew one of the straws that Wilson held in his hand, and gave an imperceptible sigh of relief when he saw it would not be him. Everyone drew, and Pfc. Robert Gallaher held the short straw. He would be the one to swim the river. Gallaher stripped off his dungarees and shirt and waded into the water, leaving his rifle and ammunition with the others. The four Marines watched and waited as Gallaher swam across the broad river mouth. It was a long way across and it took him a while; finally, the others watched him gain the bank on the opposite side. Just as Gallaher climbed out of the water, four Japanese soldiers sprang out of the jungle, grabbed him, and disappeared with him into the jungle. "Oh my God," gulped Adams.

The others were muttering in frustration and fear, too. Nobody dared fire. They did not have targets and they might hit Gallaher. Also, they did not know how many Japanese were in the area and there were only four Marines now. There had been at least that many Japanese on the opposite bank and there might be more on both sides of the river. If they got in a firefight and there were greater enemy numbers, they would be over-whelmed. They needed to stay hidden. Wilson motioned "assemble on me," and in the cover of the jungle, they discussed their options. It was obvious they could not cross the river here. They also could not go back to try to find the others because the entire company might get ambushed. The only reason they had been sent back in the first place was to get the LCPRs for the others. The four Americans knew their only option was to get across the Warrior River and get word back to battalion. They would do that by moving up to the headwaters where they had crossed the day before. Once across, they could continue back down to find the TBX team or Duncan's squad, if they were still alive. They knew the only safety for the rest of the company lay in contacting the LCPRs or getting word back to Voza via TBX.

They paralleled the river inland to the north, moving cautiously. Walker was a corpsman and had previously only carried a .45 pistol. Now he carried Gallaher's Johnson rifle and ammunition.

1420—Mountain Camp

At 1420 the Second Marine Parachute Battalion sent a message to IMAC. Colonel Krulak informed his superiors of the attacks his Marines were conducting and repeated that his battalion could continue their mission successfully for the remaining week. They were scheduled to be on Choiseul for fourteen days and would do so, even though increased enemy activity due to Marine attacks up and down the coast would undoubtedly hamper future operations.

Major Bigger's Force

Major Bigger's raiding party reached the area southeast and across the channel from Guppy Island. Bigger told his men to spread out. He had been worried that the earlier firing had alerted any Japanese in the area, so he decided to switch from their primary target of the enemy installations at Choiseul Bay to their alternate target of the fuel dump on Guppy Island. Choiseul Bay was still two miles up the coast, a very ambitious endeavor to attempt with little more than fifty men, especially because their presence might have been announced when they fired up that look-out post. There was an entire regiment of enemy troops in the vicinity they were now raiding, and if they had been detected, they would need to get out of there in a hurry.

They were now in a position to strike their secondary target. The Marines deployed in a defensive perimeter, and Lieutenant Johnston told Sgt. Robert Cavin's squad to set up facing the jungle to watch their backs. Cavin, Bay, and the others got behind fallen logs and roots with weapons facing inland. Bay watched the mortar section pass through them, moving up to the beach, and disappear from sight. The jungle was too dense where they were. Bay and the others were disappointed they would not be able to see what was happening.

Along the jungle edge, Lt. Douglas Morton ordered Sgt. Gordon Jackson, to set up his team so they could begin firing on the little island. Jackson, the mortar section leader, began looking for a spot to place their weapons, but it soon became apparent that the canopy of trees overhead would make it impossible to fire from the shore. To remedy that problem Morton had the mortar crew wade out into the shallow surf carrying their weapons. When they got just far enough out so that the overhanging trees would not interfere with firing, they set up. The barrels of their mortars just cleared the surface of the water. They were lucky, too, because if there had been high surf they would not have been able to do it.

Only one mortar was set up. Its crew was Cpl. Edward "Jimmy" Schnell, Pfc. William O'Gieglo, and Pfc. Barney Bigby, with ammunition bearers Pfc. Larry Smith and Pfc. Ray Huffer. Smith and Huffer were gathering ammunition from everyone and stacking it on the trail. "Fire for range twelve hundred yards," instructed Sergeant Jackson.

Number two gunner O'Gieglo adjusted the increments on the shell before handing it to number one gunner Jimmy Schnell, who had already set the angle of the mortar. He simply dropped the 60-mm round down the tube. With a muffled plunk, the explosive arced its way across the channel. Major Bigger, Captain Day, Lieutenants Johnston and Morton, and the mortar crews all watched the island across the channel hoping to see an explosion. Anxious seconds passed before the round exploded in the water, well short of the beach. Everyone suddenly had the same thought—they would not have the range to hit the island.

"Raise to fifteen hundred yards," instructed Jackson, knowing this was the maximum range for their little 60-mm mortars. If this did not work, it was a wasted trip, or they would have to make the decision to continue their dangerous trek to Choiseul Bay. Schnell adjusted the mortar tube angle, this time to its maximum range, and O'Gieglo added the maximum increments. With the same muffled plunk, Jimmy sent it on its way. Watching a mortar round going up is very easy for the men who fire it. It is watching it go down that is difficult. They lost sight of it as it arced across the channel, so they all watched Guppy Island, anxious for the burst. They were rewarded with an explosion just inside the tree line.

"Thank God, we're in business," murmured the men.

"Fire for effect," ordered Lieutenant Morton. "Fire for effect," repeated Sergeant Jackson.

They began to lob rounds across the channel while Smith and Huffer carried shells out from the stacks onshore to the water. They handed them to Bigby and returned to grab more. Bigby handed each shell to O'Gieglo, who adjusted the increments and gave it to Jimmy. Jimmy leaned to the side and dropped one shell after the other down the tube. After about the tenth shell, the Marines were rewarded yet again when roaring flames shot up and a giant billowing plume of smoke rose above the tree line. The paratroopers were elated. Their muffled shouts of approval told the men in the jungle, like Bay, that the mortar crew was having success. "Keep it down," warned Captain Day to his jubilant Marines. "There might be Nips around."

Barney and Pfc. Frank Fagoni were two of the lucky men deployed along the coastal trail. Unlike most of the Marines who were in the jungle to defend against a Japanese attack from their rear, Barney only had to look over his shoulder to see the mortar team firing.

As Barney watched, black smoke rose up in clouds from Guppy Island. The vegetation on the little island looked just as intense as it was on Choiseul, so Barney could not see what they hit, but it was obviously flammable. He could see tracers firing out from the jungle on Guppy where the enemy was returning fire, but the Japanese gunners were firing blindly, spraying across the channel. None of the bullets came close enough to cause any real concern.

The mortar crews worked with great relish after their first reward of smoke and flames. They had obviously hit some type of petroleum storage because oil was burning in large quantities. It was pure joy for the mortar men who watched the flames licking up from behind the trees. It is one thing to practice with a weapon—to use it successfully in battle for the first time is another. They watched each new column of smoke and stabbing flame rise above the tree line. There was also an ammunition dump on Guppy Island and random explosions with flaming debris made them think they had hit it, too. Soon giant pillars of smoke extended hundreds of feet into the sky. The mortar teams fired every last round they had—142 shells—and when they finished, Guppy Island was wreathed in the black smoke of burning oil.

They were out of mortar ammo and had completed their mission, so Major Bigger ordered his force back to the Warrior. After inflicting considerable logistical damage on the enemy, they would try to make a clean getaway. The mortar men packed up their equipment, pleasantly aware of how much lighter their loads were, and headed back. It was a brutally hot day and the sun beat down relentlessly.

Private Russell never saw anything until they moved out to leave. He had been deployed to cover the company during the mortar attack. With his big A-4 .30-caliber machine gun against his hip, he stepped out of the jungle onto the coastal trail. Ned could see large clouds of smoke rising up from the island. It was obvious they had set a lot of fuel on fire.

1400—Sergeant Wilson's Patrol

Pfc. George Adams, Private Hamilton, Pharmacist's Mate Walker, and Sergeant Wilson reached the headwaters of the river, but they were in no hurry to cross it. It was not quite accurate to say they were uneasy about the crossing—terrified was more like it. They had crossed it just the day before at this very spot, but that was before four enemy soldiers had captured Gallaher. Now they were sure it was certain death. Three times that afternoon they had found suitable places to cross the river, and three times they had decided against it, unable to shake the feeling that Japanese soldiers were shadowing them on the opposite side. But they were running out of time. They had to get across the river and they had to get help.

Once again, they decided to settle the question of who would go first by drawing straws. Hamilton was the unlucky man this time. They all watched nervously as he stepped down into the river with his rifle above his head. "At least he doesn't have to swim," thought Adams as he aimed his rifle at the opposite bank ready to shoot the first Japanese soldier to show his face. When Gallaher had been taken, it was completely unexpected, at a range of about a hundred yards. This was about fifty yards, so they planned to take a couple of the enemy this time, if it came to that.

With every step, Adams expected a rifle shot to kill his friend, but then Hamilton was out of the river and in the jungle on the opposite side. He did a quick recon of the area and waved for them to come across. One at a time they forded the river until all four were safely across.

With Sergeant Wilson in the lead, the four men began moving along the Warrior River again, only this time they moved south, back toward the ocean. They figured they had been away from the main force for more than two hours now, and had to hurry. Major Bigger had said they would arrive at the river at 1500, and that was roughly an hour away. They wanted to help the others but they did not want to die by moving carelessly. There was no question that there were Japanese in the area, but how many? Sergeant Wilson was in front, with Adams and the others behind him in single file. Adams had been a hunter before the war and he thought Wilson probably had been, too. He knew how to move without making noise. Each man put his feet forward and down carefully, and brought his body through. Wilson would often signal for them to hold up by raising his hand,

and he would disappear ahead of them. After a few minutes, he would return and signal them forward.

They had gone maybe half the distance back toward the coast when they heard the sound of swarming flies and came upon the body of a man tied to a tree. They could not tell who the man was because he had been too badly mutilated—carved up beyond recognition. But he had definitely been Caucasian. He had been stripped naked and used for bayonet practice. It was the most horrible sight Adams had ever seen. He knew then that he would never surrender to a Japanese soldier or allow them to take him alive. The dead man still wore his dog tags and Sergeant Wilson yanked them off. He had to wipe the blood away to read them: Gallaher, Robert. "It's Gallaher," said Wilson, looking down at the bloody tags.

The four Marines stood around their dead comrade in silent rage, each man quiet with his thoughts. Wilson put one of the metal tags into his pocket to take back to headquarters and went to put the other in the dead man's mouth. This was standard procedure so graves registration would be able to identify the body if and when they came back for it. Wilson reached out, but then stopped and turned back to the others. "I can't find his mouth," Wilson said solemnly.

At that moment, Adams felt a rage he had never experienced before. He had come to the Solomon Islands as a U.S. Marine, prepared to kill men in combat because that was what his country asked of him. Nothing could have prepared him for what he saw in front of him. He never imagined human beings were capable of such evil. The Japanese were waging a war of unimaginable brutality. Gallaher had been naked and unarmed when they took him. They had tortured, dismembered, and murdered a helpless man. This changed Adams inside. He now knew that this war was a fight to the death every time. No quarter was to be given or taken. For the first time in his life, Adams wanted to kill another human being. "I want ta' get the Jap sons-a-bitches that done it," said Adams in his thick Alabama accent to his three companions.

Colonel Krulak's CP

Lieutenant Duncan was called to Colonel Krulak's CP. The Brute told him to go get Major Bigger and the rest of G Company. Cpl. Mike Vinich was cooling off in the jungle stream that ran around the battalion bivouac when Duncan passed him going the other way. "Hey, Mike," said the lieutenant, "gear up and come with me. We're going to get the rest of the company."

Vinich put his socks and boots on and hurried to follow Duncan back down to the waiting LCPRs. Vinich was a battalion scout, so he assumed that Duncan wanted him to come in case they could not find the others. They arrived at the boats but did not leave immediately. They needed a radioman, and a Fox Company TBX operator was supposed to be on the way.

Lieutenant Justice's Patrol

The first platoon under Lieutenant Justice had been moving steadily all day in the unrelenting heat and humidity of the tropics.[3] They still had not made contact with any Japanese troops and many of them felt they were battling the heat more than the Japanese. Before they reached the Vagara River, most of the men had drained their canteens and some were showing signs of heat exhaustion.

Because the possibility of walking into a Japanese ambush was likely, the Marines moved more slowly than they would have liked. When they finally reached the Vagara River, they were behind schedule. The Japanese who had fought E Company the night before had obviously pulled back. Lieutenant Justice decided not to cross but to wait and observe the eastern shore in the direction of Sangigai because with the daylight they had left, they would never be able to make it down to Sangigai and back to Voza.

After an hour of surveillance, with just enough daylight to make it back to battalion, Justice ordered his patrol to return to Voza. Before they left, the lieutenant told his demolitions men to follow behind, setting trip wires attached to mines along likely avenues of approach and to continue leaving them at random intervals along the trail as they moved back. This was precisely why Private Ward, who was in the Hq Company's demolitions platoon, had accompanied the patrol. He set blocks of TNT with a trip wire battery along the trail. The blocks were about two inches by four inches and had devastating explosive power—equivalent to about five hand grenades—for their small size. They did not have shrapnel like a grenade, but that was easily remedied by tying them to a tree. The explosion would send wood shards flying in all directions. They did not set all the explosives in the form of a trip wire, either, because the Japanese would be alert after their first point man was blown to pieces. They would be wary, so Ward and his buddies set more ingenious booby traps: ones that exploded if a branch that hung across the trail moved or bombs that detonated if a log on the trail was stepped on.

They set twenty-five booby traps in the jungle northwest of the Vagara River on the return to the battalion hideout. Ward was glad to be rid of the weight of the demolitions.

Sergeant Wilson's Patrol

The small four-man party continued down the Warrior River in the direction of the ocean. Sergeant Wilson was at point again, about ten yards off the bank of the river. About fifteen minutes after they had left Gallaher's body, Wilson signaled them to halt. Everyone stopped and they all heard it instantly. It was laughter and conversation—but it was not in English. It was in Japanese.

Adams was about ten feet from Wilson, who signaled for them to stay put. He slowly crawled forward, disappearing into the brush. After about five minutes, he crawled back into sight. He signaled "assemble on me" and whispered, "There are five Nips sitting around a cooking fire. Another one is sitting guard up on the river. I think they're the ones who killed Gallaher. I wanna hit 'em. You guys okay with that?" Everyone nodded in agreement. "Okay," Wilson continued, "once we get into position, when I lower my hand, we open up. Okay?" Again, everyone nodded.

They crept slowly on their stomachs toward the sound of the laughing Japanese. Adams crawled into a position that gave him enfilading fire in a line with the others. They were on the military crest of a small rise when Adams got his first look at the enemy. There were the five Japanese soldiers.[4] They were sitting around a listening post with their rifles stacked in a neat teepee-shaped pile about ten feet from them. Just beyond, a lookout was sitting on a branch with his toes just touching the water of a small rivulet that extended out from the Warrior. The lookout seemed preoccupied with the water that lapped at his toes, and he was swinging his feet back and forth. He was the only man with a weapon in his hands.

Everyone was on line now, about five feet apart, with a relatively unobstructed view of the enemy troops who were lined up like ducks directly in front of them. Out of the corner of his eye, Adams saw Hamilton and Walker aimed and ready. Adams sighted in on the sentry. Adams did not know whom the others were aiming at, but he would quickly turn and fire to help kill the other five Japanese. From his peripheral vision, Adams saw Sergeant Wilson slowly lift his hand, wait with it extended for just a second, then plunge it downward.

BLAM, BLAM, BLAM, BLAM! All four Americans fired at once. "What in the hell," thought a frantic Adams (and probably his three companions, too).

When they had sighted in on targets, they had not picked their men ahead of time. They just chose a man and waited for Wilson. What they did not know was that all four men had sighted in on the same man, probably because he was the only one holding a weapon. One second the lookout was sitting on his perch splashing his toes, and the next he was hurled back off the log and into the water with four gunshot wounds to the chest. He was dead before he hit the water. As the other five Japanese soldiers scrambled for their rifles or fled for the jungle, the Marines corrected their mistake. They went bang happy, blasting away to make sure no fleeing enemy soldier escaped to the safety of the jungle. Purging his seething anger, Adams emptied his magazine at the panicking Japanese, and so did the others. Within seconds, all the enemy troops were lying dead on the ground. The Marines shot each man again, just to make sure. Adams figured each body probably took at least five or six bullets apiece. The jungle became deathly quiet again and the Marines quickly reloaded, listening for the sound of approaching enemy troops.

Tense minutes passed, but they only heard the sound of the flowing river. There were either no Japanese in the immediate area or the enemy was waiting for the Marines to move first.

As they waited nervously for something to happen, a scent came to their nostrils. It roused primal instincts and pushed aside fear. It was the overpowering aroma of cooking food. Then they noticed the large pot suspended above the fire. They did not know what was cooking in the bowl, but they were going to find out. Still fearful of enemy snipers, they were nevertheless so hungry that they decided to chance moving into the camp. They decided to go one at a time, run up to the big pot, scoop up whatever was in it with their helmet, and run to the opposite side of the lookout post. They all took their liners out of their helmets and put the tough plastic liners back on. They would use their steel helmets like big ladles. There would be no stopping. They would get their food on the run.

Sergeant Wilson went first while the others covered him. Running as fast as he could into the camp and up to the pot, he scooped his helmet in and was immediately off for the other side. "Okay," thought Adams, "there's food in there. Good." Hamilton and Walker went next; then it was Adams's turn. Wearing only his liner, Adams held his helmet in one hand and his rifle in the other, like a pistol. Faster than he had ever run in his life, he sprinted up to the pot. It was full of rice. Without stopping, he scooped up a helmet full and raced to join the others.

Once they were all safely on the other side, they resumed moving carefully down the river toward the ocean. If there were any Japanese around, they would have heard the shots. And the Marines were alarmed because that pot had held more rice than six enemy soldiers could eat. It was enough to feed a platoon, maybe two. The Marines wanted to get away from there as soon as possible.

As they pushed through the jungle, they greedily devoured their booty, shoveling the food into their starving mouths. It was black rice, and in whispers, each man commented on how fantastic it was. Adams was so hungry that at that moment the rice was the best-tasting food he had ever eaten.

Major Bigger's Force

As the northern task force moved back down the coast toward its rendezvous with the LCPRs, the men began to get dehydrated. The heat was intense and every man was bathed in sweat. They had drained their canteens the day before, so had to fill them with swamp water earlier that morning before continuing. There was no other water available. Now, hours later, their canteens were empty yet again and the sun was still beating down, sapping their strength. Smith was so thirsty he stuck his canteen in a black, muddy fen that ran along the side of the trail and filled it. At that point, he did not care if he got dysentery or malaria. He was more worried about heat stroke and death. He dropped a Halizone tablet in the canteen but could not wait the necessary time and drank almost immediately. The others did the same. Being able to continue today was more important than bowel problems tomorrow.

Lieutenant Castle's Patrol

Because of Lieutenant Duncan's and the Coastwatchers' reports of alarming numbers of Japanese troops and their increased activity, Colonel Krulak ordered that the land approaches to the battalion flanks be mined. At the northwest battalion listening post, about two platoons of Marines were now spread out along the east bank of the Baregosonga River. Aside from the platoon ordered to guard the river, Lieutenant Castle and twenty-seven Marines were deployed with weapons, ammunition, demolition kits, wires, and explosives. Castle's men swam the river stringing wire and laying six mine groups. The control mines were placed, numbered, and the wires run back across the river to the defense platoon's CP. A control mine was the best possible booby trap because an observer could detonate it for maximum effect. Simple trip-wire mines, on the other hand, might detonate if a crocodile or large animal tripped them. The men carefully camouflaged their explosives with branches and covered the wires on both sides of the river with sand.

Sergeant Wilson's Patrol

Adams and the rest of Sergeant Wilson's patrol reached the mouth of the east bank of the Warrior River, but they did not find anyone, Japanese or American.

"What the hell is going on?" whispered Adams to Hamilton. "Where's the TBX team? Where's Duncan?"

There were no Marines, no radio, and no boats. Without the boats, the only option the four men had was to keep moving to the southeast. They hoped that the boats would be waiting at Nukiki Village. Major Bigger had found Nukiki empty the day before so it was a likely rallying point. They turned left at the ocean and followed the coastal trail to the southeast, par-alleling the beach just inside the jungle. Seeing the cool ocean not twenty yards off was torture. It was unmercifully hot and the humidity was pun-ishing, but they did not dare expose themselves out in the open surf just to cool off. Nukiki was not far, maybe another mile or two. They might even be able to cool off there.

Lieutenant Justice's Patrol

As Lieutenant Justice's patrol continued through the hot day, many of the men were dangerously dehydrated, and some were suffering from heat exhaustion. For an island teeming with water and streams, Justice's patrol had not found any drinkable fresh water, and the men were forced to drink from muddy bogs. They had not been able to refill their empty canteens at the Vagara River because they had stayed hidden the entire time. It was more than likely that Japanese troops were doing the same thing on the other side. Backtracking toward Voza, the Marines finally came upon a decent-looking rivulet and everyone spread out to drink. Some of the men lay down in it, soaking up the cool, life-giving water to bring their body temperature back down.

Each man was filling his canteen and sating his thirst when Allman noticed Justice moving up the trail toward Voza. Carns looked up and saw Justice disappear, too. Surprised to see their lieutenant leave his platoon,

Carns and Allman looked around at the rest of the men. They were all still drinking and filling their canteens. "We gotta go," said Carns.

"Allman, bring up the rear. Make sure nobody gets left behind," ordered Sgt. Frank Banner.

"Let's go," said Allman to the others. "The lieutenant's moved out. We need to catch up." Stumbling after him, the rest of the platoon continued, but Justice was long gone up the trail, and they could not catch him.

1600—Northern Force

A day late and thirty-one men short, the northern task force arrived at the Warrior River. It was 1600 and they were more than an hour late for their new scheduled extraction time. Still in single file, the column began to deploy along the river, being careful not to surprise the friendly forces in the area. They knew that the rear guard would be expecting them, and hoped they would not be too jumpy. The raiding party expected to see the LCPRs; the rear guard squad under Sergeant Seifke, with TBX team attached; Lieutenant Duncan, with Sergeant Lipscomb's squad; and Sergeant Hamilton's patrol—or all four of the groups. What they saw was an open river and jungle. No boats and no Marines were anywhere to be seen.

The paratroopers were hot and dehydrated. Many of the men wanted to get in the river to cool off. With that in mind, Major Bigger ordered four men to swim across the Warrior to locate the TBX crews. The men stripped down, waded into the water, and were soon swimming for the opposite side. Private Blum heard men around him calling out for the rear guard and others joined in, but no one called back—they fired back. Bullets blazed across the river, ripping into the jungle around the surprised Marines.

Pfc. Willis "Rich" Fegley, a six-foot-tall blond Californian, was behind a tree two feet from the river when a bullet tore through his thigh. It knocked him back, and he lost his balance and fell. Charged with adrenaline, Fegley crawled behind cover where he examined the wound. He was more surprised than hurt. The bullet had entered the side of his upper thigh and went out the back without causing serious injury. It had only torn the skin and muscle; he was lucky it had not hit bone, vein, or artery. It did not really even hurt that much although it bled a lot. Fegley quickly put a compress on it and began returning fire on the opposite bank.

Pharmacist's Mate Salfrank was standing next to the battalion chaplain sharing a K-ration when the bullets started flying. Salfrank immediately hit the deck, diving behind a log. When the corpsman landed, he came down on an unseen protuberance that stabbed his genitals. Salfrank was out of the fight for the moment, almost as if he had been shot. Writhing in agony, he drew his .45 and tried to keep his attention on the area in front of him.

Bullets kicked up in the water around the four swimmers, who dove immediately and swam back to the northwest bank underwater. A full-blown firefight erupted across the river, but none of the Marines could see anyone to fire at. They saw only smoke and muzzle flashes from the jungle on the opposite bank. The four swimmers reached the Marine side of the Warrior and clawed their way to the protection of the jungle. Bullets slapped the dirt around them. All four made it safely to cover, but it did not seem like there was protection anywhere. All hell was breaking loose on the northwest bank of the Warrior, and the Marines appeared to be taking fire from all directions.

Cpl. Max May took a bullet in the hip and went down. Pharmacist's Mate Holland was the closest corpsman and May crawled over to him. Holland pulled up May's shirt and pushed down his dungarees to expose the wound. Holland saw right away it was superficial. While bullets ripped into the trees and branches around them, Holland dumped Sulfa liberally on May's wound and put a compress on.

Private Baxter was lying next to his JLMG man, Private Fagoni, as bullets snapped past them. Barney heard the sound of strange weapons and knew they were Japanese rifles and machine guns. The Marines were reacting quickly, too, and soon the jungle reverberated with gunfire from both sides of the river.

Crouching low, Private Russell moved forward to set up his A-4 .30-caliber machine gun. His ammunition bearers crawled up next to him to provide covering fire and to give ammunition when he needed it. Aiming at muzzle flashes across the river, Ned raked the opposite bank with short controlled bursts.

Salfrank was in so much pain it was all he could do to keep quiet. They were taking fire from all sides, and his main concern was of a Japanese attack from the jungle behind them, not the river. He was lying between the battalion chaplain and Cpl. Henry Selby when a flash of movement charged out of the jungle ahead of him. A Japanese soldier sprinted at them, his long bayonet sticking out menacingly. Selby knelt and fired as coolly as if it were a training exercise. The enemy soldier dropped and Selby calmly looked for another target. Salfrank noticed another flash of movement to his side and turned just in time to see Sgt. Edward Thomas of Baldwin Park, California, drop a charging enemy soldier with a burst from his Thompson submachine gun. "We are in it now," thought Salfrank.

It was a bad spot for G Company. Enemy troops fired at them from front, side, and back and nobody could see what was happening. The jungle was so thick they could not see farther than five yards away. Holland was moving down the line paralleling the river, looking for wounded. The firefight was so intense Holland knew they were taking casualties. Enemy fire made him duck down behind cover, and from behind a big log, he saw a Japanese soldier across the river run up a coconut tree as nimbly as a monkey. Before the man could reach his perch, however, a bullet blew him off the tree. The enemy soldier dropped ten to twelve feet to the jungle floor and stayed there. Almost simultaneously, another Japanese soldier about twenty yards to the side of the first scampered up a different tree. Holland had only a .45, and the river was a hundred yards across. He was powerless to do anything. Suddenly, that man, too, was shot out of his tree. Someone was a damn good shot. He turned and saw Sergeant Skotnicki squatting, exposed, in front of the same big log Holland was hiding behind. "Goddamn Skotnicki," warned Holland. "Get back behind this log. You're going to get your ass shot off."

"I can't see anything from back there."

"How the hell do you think I can see you?"

Skotnicki ignored him and continued to fire. Holland saw him shoot another Japanese soldier out of a tree. This time he knew exactly who had fired.

Private Bay knew they were in a huge firefight, but he could not see anything through the dense jungle except the bullets that ripped through the branches around him. Bay was not going to give away his position by firing blindly, and he kneeled behind cover. He would wait for someone to shoot at. The foliage was so thick he knew a Japanese soldier would practically have to walk on top of him before he would see him. Because of that, whoever remained motionless would probably live and whoever moved would likely die.

Barney was beside his JLMG man Fagoni lying down about five yards from the river. Major Bigger was crouched behind a root close by. With their backs to the water, Fagoni was spraying random burst at muzzle flashes in the jungle ahead. Charging movement rushing at them made Fagoni blast away. It seemed like total chaos to Barney because they were taking fire from the opposite bank of the river, the jungle directly in front of them, and their inland flank. How many Japanese were attacking them? As assistant, Barney's job was to watch out for his JLMG man, give him ammunition, and keep him healthy so that the automatic weapon could continue firing. Barney searched the trees for snipers when suddenly, not ten yards away, a Japanese soldier came rushing out of the jungle. Barney whirled to fire as the enemy soldier ran straight up the side of a tree. Just as he was about to shoot, Fagoni killed the Japanese soldier with a burst of automatic fire. Multiple shots ripped open the man's chest, hurling him backward out of sight.

"I got one!" shouted Fagoni over his shoulder to Major Bigger.

"Great, Fagoni," shouted Bigger, "keep it up!"

Barney went back to searching the trees ahead, but all he could see were swirling leaves, smoke, and shredded branches. He then became aware of the battalion chaplain moving along their line, roaring at the top of his lungs. Carrying a .45 in one hand and a Bible in the other, he was bellowing to God and Marines alike. "Conduct our case, O Lord, against our enemies. War against those who are warring against us. Take hold of buckler and large shield and do rise up in assistance, draw spear and double axe to meet those pursuing us." Barney had not even been aware that the battalion chaplain was with them; it was obvious that he was either uncommonly brave or crazy.

Pfc. Paul Peabody saw a number of helmeted heads rushing laterally to try to flank them. They disappeared in the jungle before he could take a shot.

Holland continued moving inland along the edge of the river. Every man he passed was blasting away, although few were firing in the same direction. Unbelievably, Holland had not come across any more wounded. The firefight was raging as bullets and tracers shot back and forth. The Marines were spread out in an extended triangle from the jungle trail near the ocean to about fifty yards inland along the river.

Holland stepped over a log and looked down just in time to see a young Japanese soldier aiming his rifle directly at him. The kid's eyes were wide in surprise and Holland froze, knowing he was a dead man, but the soldier never fired. He just stared with eyes agape in surprise up into the sky, and Holland realized he was dead. Blood stained his tunic a dark crimson. The rifle aimed upward because it was propped against the log he was under. That was enough for Holland. He would move no farther until someone called for a corpsman. If that man had been alive, Holland would be dead. From his new position, Holland watched the firefight ravage the jungle around him and across the river. The Marines were entirely defensive and the Japanese probed them continuously from the northwest side of the river while pouring suppressing fire from the east bank.

Lieutenant Morton was moving along the line shouting orders and encouraging his men.[5] In Holland's opinion, Morton was one of the best officers in the corps. He calmly moved under fire just as if he were conducting a field problem back on New Caledonia. As Morton got closer he saw Holland and took cover next to him. Because Holland was a corpsman, older, and also a married man, the two had become friends.

"What do you think our wives are going to say?" said Morton.

"What the hell do you mean?" asked Holland, confused.

"You don't think we're going to get out of this do you?" asked Morton.

"What do you mean?" Holland asked again, alarmed.

"No boats and too many Japs," Morton replied, shortly. He did not say anything else; he just fired his weapon repeatedly. Finally, he rose up and continued down the line, shouting orders and urging his paratroopers to keep firing.

Holland was worried. The thought that they were in a situation they would not get out of had never occurred to him, but now a Marine he had a great deal of respect for had stated the obvious. There were a lot more Japanese than American—that was obvious. Also, the boats that were to extract them were nowhere to be found.

The mortar section under Sergeant Jackson had been toward the rear of the column still in single file. They were on the jungle trail near the ocean. When the fight broke out, they could not see who was firing or from where. Jackson and O'Gieglo were close together, as were Jimmy and Bigby. O'Gieglo carried a sawed-off Browning automatic shotgun. He knew he was in the perfect combat environment for his weapon. His shotgun had no range, but that was okay. O'Gieglo could not see more than five yards anyway. If a Japanese soldier ran at him, he was going to get five bullets of 12-gauge buckshot in the face. O'Gieglo listened to the sounds of gunfire and waited for targets.

Private Russell was pounding away in short bursts at muzzle flashes across the river. Ned could not see if he was hitting anything because of the dense jungle, but he noticed a lot fewer muzzle flashes from the bushes and reeds he fired on. Ned tore up the opposite bank with his machine gun.

The firefight blasted back and forth for more than half an hour, but the Japanese stopped trying to rush the Marine line. Too many casualties must have convinced them of the foolishness of charging into automatic weapons. The Marine officers shouted to "conserve ammunition," and then they took stock of their casualties. They were surprised to find that only two Marines had been wounded. Unbelievably, no Americans had been killed, but the ground around their perimeter was ringed with Japanese dead. The paratroopers waited for a *banzai* but it never came. Either the enemy had withdrawn from the area or they were waiting patiently for reinforcements. In the jungle, with so much defensive cover, whoever revealed himself by moving died. The Marines waited tensely for something to happen. After so much noise, the silence of the jungle was almost more unnerving than the gunfire.

PT 59

Two navy PT boats sped toward the coast of Choiseul searching for a navy LCPR. The Higgins Boat would transfer Marines that would guide the PTs to the surrounded paratroopers. The men on the two 80-foot gunboats thought they had traveled too far east so turned to the northwest to start their search. The PTs were ideally suited for their present mission. Although they were called patrol torpedo boats, the 59 had had both her torpedoes removed and fitted with .50- and .30-caliber machine guns behind steel-plate shields. To add to their firepower, they had .40-mm antiaircraft guns fore and aft that could be lowered to fire on ground targets. For its small size, the 59 could put devastating fire on whatever it aimed at, but for all its firepower, it was useless unless they could get it to the surrounded Marines. The gas gauge on the 59 was dropping in a hurry. Skipper Kennedy and the crew worried it would run out of fuel before they reached the besieged leathernecks.

Sergeant Wilson's Patrol

Private Adams, Sergeant Wilson, Pharmacist's Mate Walker, and Pfc. Paul J. Hamilton were moving just inside the jungle in a southeast direction, hugging the shoreline. They had been moving steadily for half an hour and were maybe half a mile from Nukiki Village. They knew the rest of the company was probably at the Warrior River looking for them. The four men contemplated going back to let Major Bigger know there were enemy troops in the area, but if the LCPRs were at Nukiki, they would do more good for the company by reaching the boats. If they did go back to the Warrior, someone would just have to return to Nukiki anyway, over the same route they were now taking. If the boats were not at Nukiki, they did not know what they would do. It was twenty long miles on foot to Voza, and they knew they would never make it by nightfall. At least Nukiki was empty. They could stay in that village for the night if they had to.

Suddenly, they heard an engine. At first, they could not see it or even tell what direction it came from. They moved the few yards toward the beach and peered out from the jungle edge. Two specks were approaching from the southeast, shadowing the coast and moving toward them. At first, the men could not tell whether or not they were friendly, but as they got closer, the unmistakable shape of navy LCPRs came into sight.

Hamilton quickly took his shirt off, tied it to the end of his Johnson rifle, and stepped out onto the beach. The others stayed back. It was a gamble for Hamilton to expose himself. There might be Japanese in the area and the boats might fire on them before making visual recognition. Hamilton waved his shirt back and forth in big semicircles above his head. They were elated when one of the boats turned to come in for them. All four immediately moved into the surf and waded out. About 150 yards out the LCPR hove to, waiting for the Marines to come to them. Adams and the others moved out into the surf; almost immediately, the water became the water became chest deep. They feared they would have to swim, which was impossible with rifles and helmets. Why did the boat not come in for them? They hit the reef and it was shallow again. They were standing in water up to their knees 150 yards out—which was why the boats could not get in. Adams saw the LCPRs had big World War I machine guns on the front of them and he felt better knowing those guns were covering the tree line. Once on the LCPR, a soaking wet Adams breathed a huge sigh of relief. They were going to make it.

"The rest of G Company's waiting at the mouth of the Warrior," said Sergeant Wilson to the navy officer in command of the LCPR. "They've been there since 1500. You better hurry. We made contact with the enemy and killed six of them, but there have got to be more because their little camp had a big pot of rice that had enough food to feed at least a platoon."

Wasting no time, the LCPRs continued up the coast to the northwest. Adams looked around the almost empty Higgins Boat. Aside from the four of them and the coxswain, the gunner, and the naval officer, the craft was empty. It was kind of nice. Looking over at the other LCPR, he saw it too had only a few men. It looked like Lieutenant Duncan's head sticking up above the side, searching the shoreline ahead. Adams and his three companions also began watching the coast for any sign of movement, Marine or Japanese.

PT 59

The two PT boats continued northwest along the coast of Choiseul searching for the rendezvous boat, but they still had not seen it. In the distance, they saw the little island with the red cliffs they recognized as Moli Point. That meant they had gone too far to the northwest, and they needed to backtrack to the southeast. Frustrated and concerned about the 59's dwindling gas supply, the two gunboats turned back and moved in the opposite direction looking for the rendezvous LCPR.

Major Bigger's Force

The firing had died down, and the jungle returned to normal. It was so strangely peaceful after the violent firefight that it almost seemed safe. It was not. The officers were amazed that they had only two wounded. They had chewed up the Japanese and made them think twice about rushing into automatic weapons. The bodies of enemy soldiers surrounded the Marine perimeter. While the paratroopers nervously waited for the next attack, Captain Day and Major Bigger squatted together to discuss what to do. Holland was beside his buddy Sgt. Frank Muller when Major Bigger turned to them. "Sergeant, I want you to go across the river and get back to Voza. Report to Colonel Krulak and tell him what's going on here. We need those boats."

"Major, there are Japanese over there," said Muller in stunned disbelief, pointing to the opposite side of the river.

"I don't think so," said Bigger. "I think it's the TBX team. Those are our people over there. We took friendly fire."

They all knew that Sergeant Siefke's squad with the attached TBX team should be within one hundred yards of the spot they were looking at. Also, Lieutenant Duncan and Sergeant Lipscomb's squad should be waiting with them, too, keeping a beachhead open for the boats. To add to their numbers, Sergeant Wilson's TBX team should have arrived. That made a total of thirty-one Marines. Someone had to be over there.

Many of the men listened to the conversation. Yes, Marines were supposed to be on the other side of the river, but those weapons did not sound like friendly American ones. "Hell," said Lieutenant Johnston. "I got us into this mess, I'll swim across." Johnston started to strip down as Bigger began to brief them.

"Get back to Nukiki, or even Voza if you have to. Tell the Brute to come get us."

As Muller and Johnston prepared to go, a third man, Cpl. Paul Pare, volunteered. While Pare stripped down, Johnston entered the water. Muller stepped over to Holland and handed his friend his Johnson rifle and ammunition. "You might need it," said Muller.

"You'd better take it," Holland protested, knowing Muller would have to walk miles through enemy territory.

"Hell," said Muller, "I can't swim with that thing." He turned to go, but stopped and turned toward Holland once more. "You may as well take this too," he said, handing Holland his pistol and ammunition. "You're going to need it."

"Frank," said Holland, surprised, "you better have that with you. You better be armed." "No, John, I won't even make it over. There are Japs over there."

With that, Muller tied a floatation device around his chest and waded out into the river. Holland did not know what to think. Muller seemed resigned to his fate, but Holland knew his friend. If Muller really thought there were Japanese over there, he would have told Major Bigger to go to hell.

Pare followed the others out into the river. Lieutenant Johnston, a strong swimmer, was almost halfway across when Pare pushed off. There was a reef-like outcropping in the middle of the river, just at the surface level of the water. Johnston swam through a hole in it easily enough and continued swimming for the other side. Muller reached the middle of the stream and went to climb across the coral just as Johnston was reaching the far side. Pare was about fifteen feet behind Muller, almost to the coral.

Just as Johnston reached the far bank and climbed up the muddy side, three Japanese soldiers came out of the jungle. Two of them had bayoneted rifles pointing at the unarmed man. They grabbed Johnston and vanished into the jungle. It happened so fast nobody had time to react. From the American side there was stunned silence. Japanese machine-gun fire blasted out of the jungle, raking the two men in the water. It seemed to the watching Marines that the jungle along the entire southeast bank of the river exploded with muzzle flashes.

To his horror, Holland saw his buddy Muller get shot several times while climbing across the coral in the middle of the river. Muller's back exploded as the bullets went through him. He slumped dead in the water, but he did not sink because his flotation device prevented him from going under. The current took him downstream toward the ocean. The Japanese kept firing until bullets popped the floatation device and Muller went under, but the nightmare was not over yet. Holland saw a ripple in the water near where his friend went under. He immediately flashed back to the Lunga River on Guadalcanal, when crocodiles were in the water. He had watched them come ashore to gnaw on Japanese dead before pulling them into the river. These ripples looked like the same he had seen in the Lunga. Pare dove for protection. Underwater, he turned around and frantically swam back to the northwest bank.

Blum watched it happen but didn't shoot for fear of hitting Johnston. When he began returning fire, he spread his shots away from where the lieutenant had been taken. Russell immediately started blasting the jungle on the opposite bank to suppress the enemy gunners. Everywhere he saw muzzle flashes he sent a hail of bullets in answer. Private Smith was deeper in the jungle and could not see what was going on, but he saw movement in the water as Pare neared the bank. Pfc. Robert Winner stuck a log out for Pare to grab onto and pulled him out of the water. Pare scrambled out and Winner pulled him so hard, he hurled Pare into the protection of the jungle. Pharmacist's Mate Salfrank could not see the other side of the river through the jungle, but he listened to the others and found out what was happening.

"They shot Muller; he's dead. He couldn't get underwater."

"They got Johnston. He had his hands up when they grabbed him."

The firing was violent for a couple of minutes, but neither side could see more than flashes from behind greenery. The shooting abruptly died down until the Marines were again sitting anxiously along the river. For the second time after they had been fired on, they settled in to wait.

Ned was thinking about the predicament they were in and knew there was no way out across the Warrior. It was safe to say they had two men killed in action. Lieutenant Johnston was taken alive, but he was a dead man. The Marines now had fifty-four live men. Ned wondered how many wounded they had after two firefights. If they had to carry wounded, they would not be able to move fast. At that moment, Russell's thoughts were, "How are we going to get out of this?" Just then, he heard the sound of boat engines.

Hope. It is a dangerous emotion. Once hope rises in a man's heart, nothing can devastate morale like the loss of it. Were these engines the Higgins Boats? They had to be. The LCPRs were supposed to move into the mouth of the river to pick them up, but that was impossible now, not without getting shot to pieces. Major Bigger, worried that the boats would begin taking fire and leave without them, ordered his company down to the beach.

Some of the paratroopers worried that these engines were not LCPRs at all, but Japanese barges armed with heavy machine guns. They had already been fooled once, and two men were dead because of it. The Marines holding a corridor open for them had turned out to be Japanese. Why was everyone so sure these were navy boats?

Captain Day shouted for his men to move down to the beach and stay alert. The Marines hugged the jungle edge, not wanting to expose themselves in the open until they were sure the boats were friendly. They looked out and saw two American LCPRs about five hundred yards out. Captain Day took the battalion chaplain's American flag and moved onto the beach. Day signaled to the approaching LCPRs, waving the Stars and Stripes in big sweeps above his head. At first it appeared they were coming in, but when they got roughly two hundred yards from the beach, they stopped. For some reason, they made no move to come in to the beach.

"Out to the boats," shouted Captain Day. "Move out to the boats." Under orders from their company commander, the Marines waded into the surf. As they stepped into the water, though, they began to take fire from the opposite side of the river.

Lieutenant Duncan's LCPRs

Vinich was standing next to Lieutenant Duncan and Cpl. Roy Homerding, the F Company radioman, peering over the side of their LCPR. As they approached the mouth of the Warrior they could see Marines along the shore waving a flag. Immediately, Duncan, Vinich, and Homerding began shouting to the coxswain, pointing to the left of the river mouth. The coxswain moved in toward the beach, but at about two hundred yards from shore, the hull started scraping against coral in the shallow surf. Vinich remembered the day before when they had to wade in from almost two hundred yards out and knew the boat would not get in.

Suddenly, they started taking sporadic rifle and machine-gun fire. A number of shots ricocheted off the hull. It was too much for the navy officer. He was responsible for the protection of his boat, and he promptly ordered the coxswain to reverse engines. Vinich could not believe his ears. His buddies were taking fire on the beach and their only hope was to get on the LCPRs. Vinich went to say something, but Lieutenant Duncan beat him to it.

"What the hell are you doing?" shouted Duncan over the roaring engine.

"It's too shallow. We can't get in and we're taking fire."

"Get us in there! Those guys are desperate."

"It's too dangerous," the officer yelled to Duncan before turning back to the coxswain. "Coxswain, reverse engines."

"Hold what you got," roared Duncan at the coxswain while pulling out his pistol. Duncan stepped over to the naval officer and aimed his pistol directly at the lieutenant's face. "This boat is going in there," stated Duncan, "with or without your head."

PT 59

The PT boats had moved back along the coast of Choiseul to the southeast for about fifteen minutes. They approached Voza and tiny Zinoa Island, still looking for the LCPR they were supposed to rendezvous with. They were becoming increasingly agitated about their fuel supply; the skipper and crew of the 59 were understandably relieved when they saw the navy LCPR about three hundred yards off Voza.

On the LCPR waiting for the PTs, Colonel Krulak and Lt. (jg) Richard Keresey waved to the two large gunboats. Keresey himself was a PT skipper, attached to the Marine parachute battalion to search for a future PT boat base on Choiseul. Krulak had asked Keresey to assist because of his knowledge of these waters.

PT 59 pulled alongside and Krulak and Keresey transferred on board. "Dick," said Lieutenant Kennedy, "what are you doing here?"

"Never mind that now," answered Keresey. "We have to haul ass up the coast. There are a bunch of Marines trapped up there."

As it turned out, Keresey knew Kennedy well. They were friends and had been out on patrol together a number of times. One of the patrols was a few months back when a Japanese destroyer in Blackett Strait chopped Kennedy's *PT 109* in half. Keresey had been the skipper of *PT 105* on that dark, fateful night.

With Krulak and Keresey now on board, the PTs turned around, and for the second time in less than an hour, they headed northwest up the coast of Choiseul. The gas gauge on the 59 read almost empty and they had not even picked up the stranded Marines yet. Aside from their grave concerns about fuel, it was now past 1800. That meant they had less than thirty minutes of daylight to reach the surrounded paratroopers. If they could not find them before dark, the Marines would be stranded for the night.

Major Bigger's Force

Two Higgins Boats had finally arrived, and the surrounded Marines were wading out into the water to reach them. Bullets kicked up in the surf as the Japanese on the southeast riverbank began to concentrate their fire on the retreating Americans. A small rear guard at the edge of the jungle pumped suppressing fire at the Japanese side of the Warrior.

O'Gieglo, Jackson, and Jimmy were standing near the broad mouth of the Warrior where it meets the ocean. They could see two Higgins Boats and roughly half of their raiding party already wading out to board. They were taking sporadic rifle fire from the southeast bank of the Warrior, but the Marines left the jungle to move onto the beach as ordered. Jackson was in front, with Jimmy just behind him, and O'Gieglo brought up the rear. As Jimmy turned to say something to O'Gieglo, a bullet struck Jimmy in the chest. O'Gieglo watched the round slam into Jimmy just below and to the left of his St. Christopher medallion. Jimmy dropped instantly to the sand and lay still, moaning softly.

Jackson had been looking out to sea. He thought Jimmy fired his rifle beside him. Thinking the Japanese were rushing them from the jungle behind them, Jackson turned to defend himself but saw only Marines. Then he saw Jimmy lying on his back in the sand. It dawned on him that the noise had not been a rifle shot at all; it was a bullet striking Jimmy. "Corpsman!" shouted Jackson as he dropped to one knee beside Jimmy. The wound looked fatal and he figured Jimmy was already dead or very near to it. Bigby ran over to help, as did Pfc. Dale Carlton.

"Corpsman!" yelled O'Gieglo as well.

Pharmacist's Mate Holland heard the urgent cry and ran over. Much to O'Gieglo's relief, the corpsman dropped to his knees beside Jimmy and began attending their wounded buddy.

By now most of the Marines were in the water and a few were already boarding the closest boat. Back on the beach, Ned, Skotnicki, Howard "Barney" Baxter, Fagoni, Bigger, Morton, and a few other Marines made up the small rear guard that was providing covering fire from the edge of the jungle.

"We just might make it out of this," thought Barney, although for some reason, the LCPRs were not coming in for them. The fifty-six Marines had to wade out into the dangerous surf for two hundred yards in order to reach them.

Holland was still on the beach, squatting next to Jimmy. Holland could tell by the sound of Jimmy's breathing that he had a sucking chest wound, which was probably fatal. Jimmy had been shot through the lung and was bleeding internally. He needed more help than Holland could give him here at the jungle edge of the Warrior River. Holland dumped a liberal amount of Sulfa on the wound and covered it with a compress. He stuck Jimmy's arm to get an IV started because the way he was losing blood, Holland knew he would bleed out if he did not get plasma right away.

Smith was kneeling over his fallen friend when the corpsman instructed them to carry Jimmy out into the water. Smith, O'Gieglo, Jackson, Bigby, and Huffer carried their fallen buddy out into the surf while Holland fought to keep the plasma going. Jimmy went through one bag and Holland quickly put in a second.

Barney Baxter and Fagoni were providing covering fire on the opposite riverbank until Lieutenant Morton ordered them out to the boats. Barney thought it was crazy to leave the cover of the jungle to move onto the exposed beach, but if they stayed in the jungle, they would eventually be overwhelmed. The only safety lay in reaching the boats and getting out of there. Barney and the last of the rear guard were worried that they would be shot to pieces before they could reach the boats, but they left the jungle and moved into the surf.

Russell held his A-4 against his hip and moved into the ocean, ready to fire. He waded out to the boats beside his sergeant, Skotniki. He could hear the rage of his fellow Marines as they cursed the navy for not coming in to get them. About one hundred yards from shore, Holland was doing the best he could for the wounded Jimmy. Five Marines held Jimmy's head above water while Holland struggled to elevate the plasma with one hand, get a second one ready with the other, and keep his footing. The men were up to their chests in the surf while enemy rifle and machine-gun fire kicked up water around them. Out in the surf, the LCPRs' machine guns were spraying the southeast side of the river mouth to suppress enemy gunners. The covering fire was some comfort because the Japanese on the beach seemed to be organizing and firing with greater intensity.

Sergeant Wilson's LCPR

Adams and the rest of Sergeant Wilson's patrol were watching the surreal scene from the side of their LCPR. They were taking fire and bullets, ricocheted off their hull. Adams suddenly lost that feeling of being saved. They were not going to get out of this without a huge fight. Tracers from the big Lewis guns on the boat were tearing up the tree line along the shore where muzzle flashes spit back at them. The enemy fire began to pick up in intensity as bullets kicked up among the wading Marines, and the Japanese began to lob mortar rounds on them. As if that were not bad enough, a dark rainsquall came out of nowhere to give the scene a more sinister appearance, and sheets of rain fell heavily on them.

Surf

"Just keep his head out of the water," shouted Holland to the Marines holding Jimmy. Holland did not worry about saltwater getting in the wound. Jimmy would not drown by water; the lung was already full of blood. If anything, it would have a cleansing effect. They were taking machine-gun fire and things were about as bad as they could be when suddenly it began to pour down rain. They were about a hundred yards off the beach with that much distance still to go. Holland figured it could not get any worse when a mortar round exploded twenty yards in front of them. Now the enemy was using their deadly knee mortars. As Holland struggled to hold up the plasma bottle, maybe ten yards to his side, a geyser in the surf exploded right next to Fagoni. Holland felt the concussion from the blast, and the needlelike spray from the water stung him. Fagoni was blown sideways in the water, but the tough Marine got back up and kept going.

Farther out, men were piling into the closest LCPR; it looked like it was filling up fast. Too fast. It was over capacity. The navy crew now became alarmed that their overloaded boat would not make it out of the shallow water. They had been scraping the coral even before thirty-five Marines had climbed on board. "No more," shouted the coxswain. "She's overloaded. No more."

Russell was standing in the surf close to Major Bigger. "No more," shouted Bigger. "The rest of us to the other boat."

Private Peabody was ordered to get out and push, along with three other Marines. They pushed the LCPR off the coral and climbed back in.

Less than half an hour before, Adams and the rest of Sergeant Wilson's squad had enjoyed being on an empty LCPR. At this point, they were packed like sardines with thirty other men in the overloaded boat. The LCPR revved its engines and backed out, but its bottom scraped hard against coral, alarming everyone on board. They were worried that they had gashed a hole in the bottom; the boat backed out with its antiaircraft machine guns shooting an arc of tracers through the blinding rain back at Choiseul. The coxswain realized he had a bent rudder, and he tried unsuccessfully to steer his craft.

Back in the surf, taking sporadic fire from enemy small arms and mortars, the remaining Marines moved to the other LCPR under the cover of the rainsquall. Even though they were still spread out in the water, nobody was lagging. Men were climbing in as Barney neared the boat, but he decided he would wait near the ramp until everyone was on board. He had seen too many brave men fighting and they deserved to make it. Barney decided he would be the last to go.

The Marines carrying the wounded Jimmy were up to their chests in the surf. They were almost to the second landing craft, struggling to keep Jimmy's head above water, when they hit a coral ledge and were able to stand in water up to their thighs. In shallow water, they moved quicker and, once to the boat, they lifted Jimmy on board and climbed in. Holland instructed the Marines to put Jimmy on the motor box.

The last of the men were nearing the boat. They were still taking sporadic fire from the enemy, and Barney aimed to fire back at the shoreline. Because of the intensity of the rain, however, he could not even see the beach. Waiting for the last men to board, Barney heard a sergeant shout to him, "Get in. I'm goin' last."

Barney hauled himself up into the overloaded landing craft with the sergeant climbing in right behind him. With everyone on board, Major Bigger told the coxswain it was okay to go. One look at the coxswain's face, however, told the Marines he was not so sure that was possible. The landing craft was so overloaded that it was now lodged heavily on the coral. Putting the craft in reverse, the coxswain tried to back out but the engine only roared and spewed up bubbling water. The boat grated against the reef, barely moving. Mortar rounds landed randomly in their vicinity, kicking up explosions in the water, and gunfire ricocheted off them. Thankfully, they could not see the shore, which meant the Japanese could not see them either. The enemy was just guessing, firing out into the surf toward the sound of the American boats. They knew they had to get out of there before the rain lifted or a mortar round got lucky. The coxswain gunned the engine all the way. The boat made a terrible screeching noise as it grated on the coral, but it shuddered and started moving out to sea.

Corpsman Salfrank looked over and saw Holland attending Jimmy on the motor box of the LCPR. Paul wanted to help but he did not want to get in the way. As he watched, Holland put another IV in, Jimmy's third.

Just then, Salfrank felt water rising on his ankle and looked down. Their boat was taking on water.

They all noticed it. Their Higgins Boat had a bad leak. Water was pouring in around their feet and was already up to their calves. "Bail," yelled Major Bigger.

"Bail," shouted Sergeant Skotnicki. "Keep your weapons dry. If she sinks, we're going to have to go back in."

Ned was holding his A-4 against the side of the LCPR. It was aimed at the shore in case he saw any Japanese. Luckily, the rainsquall was so intense he could not even see the shore. As their landing craft filled with water, though, rising up to their knees, Russell realized they were going to have to go back in and fight it out. They had no other choice. It was obvious that their boat was sinking and that the other LCPR was already over-loaded. If they sank, they would have to swim to shore without weapons. Russell would rather go back in and fight it out while he had his machine gun and they had a chance. With one hand keeping his weapon above water, Ned used the other hand to bail with his helmet.

Everyone was bailing, but it did not seem to help. The water level inside the boat was rising so fast, Russell worried they would sink before they could even turn for shore. The way the sea was pouring in, the hole had to be big. The driving rain did not help, either. It was a losing battle. Nobody could even locate the gash because the water was rising too quickly and the boat was overcrowded. The water was now up to their waists inside the landing craft, and the engine stalled from the strain of so much weight. "This is it," thought Russell.

The navy lieutenant knew they had only a few minutes before they would sink, so he quickly signaled to the other landing craft for a towrope. They watched as the other LCPR worked its way to their foundering craft, moving erratically. They did not know that the coral had damaged the other boat, too. Its bent rudder made steering difficult.

The Higgins Boat with the bent rudder reached the sunken LCPR. They threw a towrope over but did not know what good they would be. The over-loaded boat was full of water; the only reason it did not sink was because it was lodged on the reef. Their own boat was overloaded and had a bent rud-der. If they tried to tow the sinking craft, their engine would likely stall, too. It was a mess. They hooked the towrope on anyway and signaled to the other boat that they were ready. At least they had to try. The LCPRs' engines roared and both boats shuddered from the strain. Suddenly the towrope broke and the boat with the bent rudder roared away to the left.

When the towrope broke, so did the last remaining hope that they would get away clean. They stood inside their boat in water up to their stomachs, bailing frantically; the parachutists watched as every swell pushed their foundering boat closer to shore. The Marines had their weapons propped against the side of the boat aimed at the shore but at least for now the rain still concealed them. The Japanese were still firing blindly at the sound of the boat engines. Sporadic shots pinged against the side of the hull and occasional mortar rounds exploded in the water nearby. It was not a good place to be.

The paratroopers knew they were going to have to fight it out and were painfully aware that they had already been in an extended firefight for almost two hours. Many of them had used up a lot of ammunition. The situation was chaotic. Marines from the Second, Third, and weapons platoons were in the two boats. In water up to their chests, Major Bigger and Lieutenants Duncan and Morton conferred in the small boat about what to do. They made three makeshift squads and Lieutenants Duncan and Morton explained to the NCOs what they wanted.

"If we have to go back on shore," said Duncan, "I want the first squad to face left up the beach, the second squad in the center facing the jungle, and the third squad on the right facing down the beach. Fight your way into the jungle." He added, "If there are any of us left, we'll try to find the trail and move back to Voza."

Vinich could not believe what was happening. He had escaped certain death earlier that morning at Nukiki Village when his squad was surrounded by more than two hundred Japanese troops. They had been fifty yards from them but got away clean. Until now he figured he had led a charmed life. Now, as he listened to Duncan's cheerful briefing, a mortar round exploded in the surf thirty yards away while machine-gun fire kicked a nearby trail in the surf, searching blindly for them through the squall. To make matters worse, he was standing in water up to his stomach inside a sinking boat during the most intense rainsquall he had ever seen.

As the Marines prepared for a last stand, Holland directed his attention to the critically wounded Jimmy. The gunshot Marine was now halfway through his third bottle of plasma. Holland knew their Higgins Boat was as good as sunk, but at least it seemed to be resting on a reef. Maybe that would keep them from having to swim in and at the same time prevent them from being pushed to shore by the surf. If the rain held up until dusk, they might be able to sit tight in the sunken LCPR and avoid being seen. It would be night soon and maybe in the cover of darkness they could wade parallel to the surf to reach land a few hundred yards off the Japanese flank. All they could do was wait.

Lookout Post

At the last light of day, Pfc. Herbert "Blacky" Bell was standing along the west side of the little stream south of Voza. It was the battalion's eastern flank listening post and Blacky's platoon was guarding it for the night. The big stream provided the best natural defense against any force that might approach from the Sangigai coastal trail. It gave a tactical advantage that might offset the defenders' lack of numbers.

He watched the stream and longed for the day when he could throw a line in and relax by the side of an Oklahoma river in peace. He had grown up hunting and fishing and loved to do both. He looked down at the water and wondered if there were any edible fish in the stream. One of the natives had been assigned to his squad and Blacky walked over to him. Cradling his Johnson rifle in one arm, he pointed at the water and began speaking in broken English, hoping the native might understand. "Stream—fish—eat," he said slowly and deliberately. He made gestures with his hands undulating back and forth to simulate swimming fish. The native looked puzzled, but Blacky continued with his version of pidgin English, all the while moving his hand from side to side like a swimming fish. "Fish—good eat—yum-yum," he said patting his stomach for effect. The man wrinkled his brow, trying to understand, but Blacky knew he had not gotten through to him yet. He continued, determined to communicate with this man when suddenly the native spoke. "Indeed yes," said the man with a sophisticated English accent, "there are quite a few edible fish in these waters." Blacky was astounded. He began to talk to the guy and found him fascinating. The native spoke four languages: English, French, Dutch, and his own dialect.

1830—Sunken LCPR, Warrior River

The Marines were in a bad way. One of the boats was sunk, resting on coral, with almost thirty Marines standing in water up to their stomachs while the surf pushed them toward shore. The other boat was operational, but it had a bent rudder. Despite the shielding rainsquall, Japanese mortar shells and machine-gun fire continued to seek the Marines, exploding and spraying the surf around their boats in a hundred-yard radius. More than one man wanted to kill the engine of the one functional LCPR because the Japanese were firing at sounds.

"I hear something," shouted someone. Everyone was instantly quiet, and then they all heard it. It was the sound of boat engines. Hope rose in the heart of every man on board. Everyone listened for another few seconds.

"That sure doesn't sound like a Higgins Boat," someone said matter-of-factly.

"Get ready," warned Major Bigger, "it could be a Jap barge." The sunken LCPR bristled with rifles and machine guns as the Marines hurriedly aimed all available weapons to the southeast side of the craft.

"Oh my God," thought Salfrank, figuring it was a Japanese machine gun barge. "We're already dead in the water."

"Ship," shouted one of the men pointing into the dark haze of rain and dusk.

Russell looked out and saw the silhouette of a baby aircraft carrier against the darkness and he realized it was a PT boat, a lot closer than he thought it was. Out of the dark rain came a second one.

"It's a PT boat," shouted a voice hysterical with joy. As the sound of the boat got nearer and nearer, O'Gieglo heard the crew cranking up their .50-caliber machine guns. "Now we're going to get shot by our own guys," he thought.

It was almost dusk, so even if the rain had not blocked their vision it was getting difficult to see. Holland was holding an almost empty third bottle of plasma over Jimmy and saw Lieutenant Morton signal with a flashlight in Morse code out toward the approaching boats. In the darkness, mortar man O'Gieglo heard the best four words he had ever heard in his life. "Tom, is that you?" It was Colonel Krulak. He was on the PT boat that pulled up alongside the sinking craft, putting itself between the Higgins Boats and the shore. *PT 59* was lettered on its hull. Private Russell was shocked at the size of the boat. He thought PTs were small, speedy boats, but these were not. A PT boat was either a small ship or a huge boat, and it was laden with machine guns. The LCPR with the bent rudder pulled in close and the 78-foot PT hove to, taking men from both LCPRs.

Private George Adams quickly transferred from the landing craft with the bent rudder. He saw Marines lifting a wounded man onto the deck of the PT boat from the sunken LCPR. Adams moved over to help haul the wounded Marine on board. "Where can we lay this man down?" asked corpsman Holland of the PT's skipper.

"Take him down below," said Lieutenant Kennedy. Holland, Adams, and Hamilton carried the wounded man inside the PT to Kennedy's bunk and stretched him out in the cramped confines.

Up on deck, Marines from both boats, along with the navy crew from the sunken LCPR, scrambled on board. The crew with the bent rudder stayed on their craft and took off for Voza. The rain whipped in sheets across the slippery deck.

Vinich climbed on board and saw Lieutenant Kennedy. He had gotten to know him well during his many visits to the PT base at Lambu Lambu to see Lt. Byron White. "Boy, are we glad to see you, lieutenant," Vinich said.

"Hi, Mike," replied Kennedy.

Colonel Krulak was there, too, conferring with Major Bigger. The last of the men climbed on board, and Kennedy looked down at the empty LCPRs. "Anyone left?" he asked. By way of reply, Colonel Krulak told Kennedy to get them out of there.[6]

Russell was sitting on the deck of the PT watching the skipper move among the Marines. He was a calm, skinny, light-haired guy with a New England accent. The skipper took his place at the helm and ordered the motorman to get them out of there. The PT, heavy and low in the water, pulled away from Choiseul in the dark, laden with more than sixty paratroopers.

More than one Marine suddenly felt religious due to their narrow escape. The harrowing rescue was the best feeling Corpsman Salfrank ever had in his life. Everyone had been convinced they were going to have to go back in and fight to the death. As the PT sped to the southeast, the exhausted, famished Marines lay spread out on the deck, the rain washing their stress away. As they made their getaway, the crew brought out some canned peaches. The Marines crowded around like starving wolves on a fresh kill, pushing their mess kits forward. They each took their food and found a spot on the deck in the pouring rain where they could devour it in peace.

Barney Baxter sat on the deck and stuffed peaches into his mouth. It was like the ambrosia of the gods, it was so good. The canned peaches were the first real food he had eaten in six days. After he finished his meal, he began idly talking to one of the crewmen of the PT boat. "We accidentally shot down a Corsair earlier today," the man said. "He strafed us and we fired back. We never meant to hit him; we were just pissed off. Hell, we always miss Japanese floatplanes when we're trying to hit them." Barney was not surprised. It had been that kind of day.

Private Adams and his buddy Private Hamilton were sitting on the deck of *PT 59* with their legs sticking over the sides. Adams was thinking of how many times he had tempted fate that day, November 2, 1943. As the bouncing craft sped through the surf, for the first and only time in his Marine Corps service, Adams got seasick.

1915—Mountain Camp

At 1915, an exhausted Allman, Carns, and the other men from the Vagara patrol arrived at the battalion hideout. They never did catch up with Lieutenant Justice. When they arrived at camp, they watched their platoon sergeant go over to the CP to report in. Apparently, Justice made it back safely, but they would hear later that the Brute was not happy. Both Allman and Carns wondered why the lieutenant had left them. He must have suffered from heat exhaustion. It had almost gotten all of them. They knew Justice was a great officer, and he obviously thought his men were behind him. The Marines stumbled into their hammocks to get badly needed rest. They had been marching in the heat since 0800 and the only food they had eaten had been a D-bar and a K-ration. Most were asleep within seconds of crawling into their hammocks—except for the unlucky few on guard duty.

Lookout Post

Dugan, Blacky, and the rest of the platoon were deployed in the jungle along the west bank of a stream in ambush positions. They were on the rivulet designated as the battalion's southeast flank listening post. They had been sent down to guard the stream earlier that day and would remain until another platoon relieved them the following morning. If the Japanese came at Voza from Sangigai by land, this would be where the attack would come. As the threat of a strong Japanese probe became increasingly likely after the Sangigai attack and subsequent firefights, Colonel Krulak ordered the security teams on the flanks beefed up to an entire platoon.

Dugan and the others spread out in a perimeter with most of their firepower facing the southeast in the direction of Sangigai. Dugan had been told to climb a tree along the riverbank and spend the night up there. He climbed up to a spot high in the tree that afforded him the best vision and tied himself in with the rope he had been given. He had never been a sniper before, but tonight it was time to start. From his perch, he not only had a commanding view of the Sangigai approach, but also of the mouth of the stream. It was a wide stream or a small river, about fifteen feet across and five feet deep. He had already crossed it once when they had marched down to Sangigai on October 30. Dugan was only five feet, six inches tall, and he had waded across water that was up to his neck. The current was so strong it swept him downstream a good five or ten feet. He had carried his weapon over his head and that helped ground him. Dugan figured it must have been murder on Colonel Krulak, who was even shorter than he was.

PT 59

The two PT boats raced back along the coast in the direction of Voza. The gas gauge on the 59 now read empty. The LCPR with the bent rudder struggled to keep up behind the PTs and fell back in the distance. Many of the Marines assumed they were being taken to Vella LaVella and could not wait for a real, hot meal. They found it very disconcerting to hear they were going back to Voza.

Holland was down below in Lieutenant Kennedy's bunk with Jimmy, who was lying on the PT skipper's bed with a fourth plasma bottle in his arm. Holland was trying to keep him alive long enough to get him to a field hospital on Vella LaVella. Holland would have worried about the wounded man going into shock, but Jimmy was warm and calm, albeit scared. Even with his dungarees soaking wet he was not cold. It had been a brutally hot day and it was still steamy down in the skipper's bunk.

They made good time getting back to Voza and began to transfer the Marines to a waiting LCPR. The Higgins Boat would carry them the short distance to shore. When everyone was off the 59 it turned and raced to Vella LaVella. The medical facilities there were Jimmy's only chance for survival. Down below, Holland sat beside the bleeding man.

"Am I going to be okay?" asked Jimmy weakly.

"Hell, you've got it made boy," said Holland. "You're headed for San Diego."

"Do you really think I'll be alright?" asked Jimmy.

"Sure. I'm working on you aren't I?" replied Holland. That seemed to put the wounded man at ease quite a bit. He lay quietly, breathing with difficulty as he continued to lose blood. Holland put in a fifth bottle of plasma, and Jimmy stayed conscious right up until he bled to death several minutes later.

The PT boat was not halfway across the channel to Vella LaVella when they ran out of gas. The other PT threw them a towrope and pulled them the rest of the way. Down below in Kennedy's bunk, Holland covered Jimmy with a blanket, and returned to deck to inform Kennedy. Kennedy just shook his head and did not say anything. Holland moved off to get some fresh air and saw that Fagoni was still on board the PT boat. Holland went over to him.

"Frank, what are you doing here?"

"I'm all sick inside. A mortar landed right next to me in the water."

"I know," said Holland, "I saw." Holland proceeded to check him out from head to toe but could not find any wounds.

"You look okay to me."

"It tore me up inside."

"Hell, it couldn't have."

"It did."

Lookout Post

Dugan waited with his rifle across his lap as he sat high in the air tied to a banyan tree branch. He scanned toward the southeast, but it was so dark he could not make out anything in the blackness. Then, a flicker of movement from the side caught his eye. "Japs!" he thought, his heart pounding.

At the mouth of the small river, moving toward him, a long white line moved in the water. Dugan aimed to fire but the more he watched, the more he realized it could not be a man. The line was moving against the current and it was moving fast.

"What the hell?" thought Dugan. He watched the stream all night and saw the white line continually reappear. It was movement in the water and it moved below him before disappearing.

Chapter 9

SURROUNDED: NOVEMBER 3

He was a hell of a good leader.
PM1 John Holland, G Company, of Lt. Col. Victor H. Krulak

0230—Mountain Camp

Early on the morning of November 3, Pfc. Robert Perdzock was awakened by a message coming in over the radio from IMAC. It was 0230, and as Perdzock wrote the message down, it made his eyebrows rise. "Sizable enemy force converging on Second Marine Parachute Battalion from both flanks. IMAC advises battalion to leave Choiseul November 3."

"Wait a minute," thought Perdzock, "today is November 3." The battalion was supposed to be on Choiseul for another week, but IMAC was advising them to leave that day? They had to be in a world of hurt to get a message like this. Not just a little concerned, Perdzock immediately woke up Lt. Col. Victor H. Krulak and handed him the message.

Krulak read the message and knew it was time to leave Choiseul. Although his battalion could keep up their patrols and continue to raise hell, the Bougainville invasion was already a success with the Third Marine Division on shore. There was little his battalion could do on Choiseul, especially because at that point the enemy knew the real invasion was elsewhere. The Brute knew his battalion was in an excellent defensive position and could still hold out for at least a week, but what was the purpose? Without a clear objective or a good reason to continue the fight, if even one more of his men died on Choiseul, it was too many. It was time to leave.

Lambu Lambu Cove, Vella LaVella

PT 59 was towed by her sister ship up to the docks at the PT base at Lambu Lambu on Vella LaVella just after dawn. It had taken all night to cross the seventy-mile-wide channel. PM1 John Holland helped carry Cpl. Edward "Jimmy" Schnell's body on shore where they placed the fallen Marine into a waiting jeep. Pfc. Frank Fagoni hobbled up and got in the passenger seat and a driver took them to the Regimental Hospital where Jimmy's body was turned over to grave's registration and Fagoni was admitted to the hospital.

Meanwhile, Holland returned to the 59 to make a request of her skipper, Lt. John F. Kennedy. He and his crew were already in the process of refueling their boat when Holland walked up. "Will you take me back to Choiseul? They're going to need every corpsman they have and I need to get back there. There are too many Japs coming in."

"I can't," said Kennedy. "I'm not authorized to do that."

"How the hell do I get authorized?" asked Holland.

"You need to see your commanding officer," replied Kennedy.

"He's on Choiseul," Holland replied.

"Then you need to see *his* commanding officer," Kennedy persisted.

"Can I borrow a jeep?" asked Holland.

Kennedy had a driver take Holland over to the headquarters of the First Marine Parachute Regiment, where he would see Col. Robert H. Williams, its commanding officer.

Battalion Outpost

At dawn, an exhausted Pfc. James P. Dugan was still tied to his tree, scanning the jungle for any sign of an enemy approach from the southeast. The Japanese had not come yet, thankfully. Now Dugan was spent and in dire need of sleep. All night long a strange white line moving back and forth up the river had spooked him and kept him awake. At dawn, that same flicker of movement caught his eye. In the light of day he examined it from his perch. It was a huge crocodile that was moving downstream toward the mouth of the river directly below him. "Oh my God," he said aloud.

Dugan had never seen anything so large in his life. It looked like a submarine. He figured it was at least fifteen feet long, maybe more. Dugan felt himself get cold with fear remembering that he had crossed this very stream just a few days before.

When it was time for him to be replaced, Dugan untied himself and climbed down as his relief went back up. Dugan immediately told his buddies about the crocodile. To most of them, it was nothing new. They had all seen crocodiles in the Lunga River on Guadalcanal and, because Choiseul was a neighboring island in the chain, it seemed reasonable that they were here, too.

Word passed to Dugan's squad that they were making a contact patrol a mile down to the southeast. Dugan would have to cross that stream two more times. He held his weapon above him when he crossed only minutes

later. He was terrified: he was up to his chest in water, and he held his rifle
with the barrel pointing down, the butt high in the air. It was an awkward
way to hold a rifle, but he was ready in case he needed to fire at a crocodile.

Regimental Headquarters

When Holland arrived at the First Marine Parachute Regiment's headquarters hoping to see Colonel Williams, he was surprised to be admitted so quickly.

"Sir, I'd like to get back to my unit," he said. "Can I hitch a ride to
Choiseul?" Holland knew the battalion was to remain on Choiseul for
another week and as the Japanese were closing on them from all sides, he
knew they would need all the corpsmen they could get.

"Don't worry," said Colonel Williams, "there's no need. They're pulling
them out tonight."

Mountain Camp

Pfc. Norman Wurzburger was sitting at his radio in Colonel Krulak's lean-
to command post. They had been on this hot, miserable, humid, mosquito-infested island for seven days, and he was hungry, exhausted, and
suffering from malarial shakes. Although it was almost 100 degrees, with
humidity close to 100 percent, Wurzburger could not get warm. He knew
about the message earlier that morning telling them of the "sizable enemy
force" descending on them from both flanks, and it did not help his frame
of mind. Greatly dispirited, he looked around at the men in the Hq
Company area and all he saw were potential casualties. The Brute himself
was covered in bandages.

"Colonel," said the tired New Yorker looking over from his radio, "when
are we gonna get out of here? I'm sick of this."

"In due time," replied Krulak. "Don't worry, we'll get out."

Wurzburger did not respond aloud, but he thought, "Don't worry? Hell,
I'm worried sick."

1200—Voza

When the battalion had landed seven days before they came ashore by
LCPR. They would be extracted, however, by landing craft, infantry
(LCI). Since an LCI was much larger and sat deeper in the water than a
Higgins Boat, the colonel needed to make sure the ships would clear any
coral reefs they might not know about. They did not want a repeat of the
Warrior River fiasco when the boats were chewed up in shallow water.

At around noon on November 3, Pfc. Joe Lennon and Pfc. James Ward were asked to swim out into the channel between Voza and Zinoa Island to make sure the water depth was sufficient for LCIs. Zinoa Island was about two thousand yards off Voza. The two men were told to swim out just about halfway to the island. As they swam, they were to submerge as far as they could from time to time and make a mental note of the depths.

The two men stripped down, waded into the surf, and started swimming. They were in deep water at less than twenty-five yards from the shore. They swam into the channel, staying about fifty feet apart, and dropped about every thirty feet or so to check the depth. Neither man had touched bottom yet.

Lambu Lambu Cove, Vella La Vella

Lt. Arthur H. Berndston and his intelligence officer, Lt. Byron White, received orders that would send their boats back to Choiseul that very night. The diversion was going to be cut short by a week and the Marines were going to be pulled out in fewer than eight hours. These were the same paratroopers that Kennedy's *PT 59* had saved from annihilation the day before on the Warrior River. Berndston's PT boats would cover their extraction again tonight. He immediately relayed the order to his PT skippers. This would be no small operation. All five of his boats were requisitioned. Kennedy's 59 and four sister boats were already loaded up with ammunition and fuel and soon all five boats would be headed out into The Slot to rendezvous with the three LCIs that were going in to withdraw the besieged leathernecks.

1450—Mountain Camp

The Second Marine Parachute Battalion broke camp in the mountains at 1450. Leaving nothing but a half-full slit trench, a few thousand discarded cellophane D-bar wrappers, the same number of K-rations cans, and dozens of deadly booby traps strewn around their former jungle bivouac, the Marines hurried to carry everything down to the coast. Pfc. Rudolph Engstrom and the other men in his platoon spent their day carrying cases of ammunition down to the beach. Once everything was at Voza, they were ordered to set up a defensive position with their backs to the ocean. Engstrom and his section dug foxholes in a semicircular perimeter in the jungle. After setting their position, they cut firing lanes in the jungle in front of their emplacement. When they had finished, they went out twenty or thirty yards to set up their trip wires. They knew the demolition men were farther out setting booby traps and mines for the approaching enemy troops, but each Marine also set up his own personal wires, mines, and traps. The wires Engstrom and his section set were tied to grenades with loosened pins or empty ration cans full of rocks and pebbles. If any Japanese soldiers tried to sneak up on them in the night, they would either be blown to pieces or the Marines would hear them approaching.

Surf

Although it had taken them almost two hours, Lennon and Ward finally reached their thousand-yard mark. They had found the depths were, in fact, sufficient for the LCIs; there was no danger of coral ripping up the bottom of the ships. In fact, as the intelligence reports indicated, this area was devoid of coral reef. By the time they had signaled to each other that they had gone far enough, Ward was as exhausted as he had ever been in his life. Now they just needed to get back to inform the colonel. They turned back, breathing heavily. As they labored back to Voza, Ward began to fall behind. After a while, he could not keep up and signaled Lennon to go on in without him.

Ward struggled on and watched Lennon get farther and farther away from him. He had been fighting a terrific current and began to wonder realistically if he could make it back alive. He turned to look at Zinoa Island, and wondered if it was closer. If so, he would swim there. Ward was more worried about drowning than about being left on the island. But Zinoa was just as far away. Ward soon realized he was just too tired to make it back. He had been subsisting on K-rations and D-bars for seven days while marching with the weight of weapons and ammunition all over that accursed, blisteringly hot island. It had sapped his strength.

"Jesus Christ," he said to himself, struggling just to keep his head up while treading water, "I'm not sure I can make it back." He was so far beyond exhaustion he did not panic. Actually, the thought of drowning did not frighten him. In fact, it would be a welcome relief to his misery. Just as he had decided that he could not go any farther, something bumped into his shoulder. It was a Japanese life preserver bobbing next to him in the water.

Ward was not a religious man, but he knew at that moment he should become one. That was the first time in his life that he knew something extraordinary had occurred, something that he could not attribute to just blind luck. Although it took him more than an hour, Ward was able to make it back to shore using the life preserver to keep him afloat. Like an exhausted shipwrecked sailor in a cartoon, he crawled up on the beach clinging to his life preserver, stumbled up the mountain, and reported to the Hq Company bivouac to inform the colonel about the channel. Lennon had already let them know, but Krulak thanked Ward anyway and dismissed him. Completely exhausted, Ward returned to his company bivouac, but instead of climbing into his hammock for badly needed rest, he had to take it down and help carry the last remaining stocks of supplies and munitions down to the beach.

1600—Voza

It was late afternoon and the Second Marine Parachute Battalion was deployed on Voza Beach, ready for the navy to come in and get them. Pfc. William O'Gieglo from the G Company weapons platoon was sitting with his buddies Pfc. Barney Bigby and Pfc. Leonard Laaksoner. Having already dug their mortar pit and set up their defensive positions, they began going over what happened to them the day before on the Warrior River. O'Gieglo said he had heard that on the day they had become lost, turning the one-day mission into two days, one of the men sent to tell the waiting boats had shouted out loud along the Warrior, "Be here tomorrow at 0515," instead of wading out to the boats to tell them. If that were true— and they all hoped it was just a rumor—it sure explained a lot. If the Japanese had a listening post in the jungle, they had heard it all because they were sure there at 0515 the next day.

Discussing their narrow escape along the Warrior River, they agreed on another point. They should have known they would have trouble with the reef when they were not able to get ashore on November 1. They had had to wade ashore, so why did they think it would be any different the following day? Thank God for the PT boats.

The men grew quiet and O'Gieglo reflected on the loss of his friend Jimmy. O'Gieglo and Jimmy had made a pact that if either one of them were killed, the other would go visit the dead man's family. O'Gieglo would honor his pact, but he did not look forward to it.

Pfc. Bynum Jacobsen was sitting in his hole along the F Company perimeter. As he waited, he thought of his buddy, Sgt. Frank Muller. Earlier that morning he had heard about Muller's death, crossing some river the day before. Jacobsen and Muller had gone through chute school together. Jacobsen remembered a near fiasco they had while trying to get twenty men out of a DC-3 in less than ten seconds. He had practically leaped out on top of Muller and gone through the middle of Muller's chute, which of course collapsed and wrapped around him. Jacobsen's own chute had deployed and held both their weights. Jacobsen struggled to hold onto Muller's chute.

"Don't let go," Muller had yelled up at him.

"Don't pull your reserve," Jacobsen yelled back at him. They landed hard, but they were alive and had laughed about it ever since.

Jacobsen also remembered how two days before they shipped overseas he had met a woman in a local bar. They hit it off and an hour later, in a drunken stupor, he had proposed to her. Equally intoxicated, she had tearfully said, "Yes." Jacobsen carried her out of the bar to his Harley and proceeded to drive off in search of a chaplain to marry them. As he swerved away from the bar, though, he could not get his bike out of first gear. After about ten minutes of roaring at five miles per hour, he and his drunken bride-to-be turned around and went back to the bar. As it turned out, Muller had pulled the pin on the Harley's gearshift so he could not get it out of low gear. He did not want to see his buddy do something he would regret. Muller had been a great friend.

Pfc. Ned Russell was sitting behind his A-4 machine gun with an excellent field of fire. He and his section had spent a good deal of time cutting fire lanes in the jungle in front of them. He felt he did not have any blind spots, and he would also set a few traps himself in front of their position using hand grenades and trip wires. They would mow down the Japanese when they came. He also knew the entire perimeter was fortified like his area because he had seen his buddy Pfc. Ralph Nield earlier and briefly spoken to him.

As he sat and waited, Russell listened to the men around him talking about Lt. Samuel Johnston's fate. Apparently, some of the natives working with Sub-Lt. Carden Seton had come across the lieutenant's body. Johnston had been staked to a tree and tortured. The Japanese had carved him up with knives while he was alive before they executed him. Russell thought right then that no matter what, he was not going to be taken prisoner— ever. He would rather die in his hole, fighting.

Pfc. Howard "Barney" Baxter was sitting next to his squad leader Sgt. Edward Thomas and Cpl. William R. Zuegel. They were talking about the fight on the Warrior River the day before. "Did you see the battalion chaplain?" asked Barney. "He was running up and down our line shouting quotes from Revelations, Psalms, or whatever it was."

"No," replied Thomas almost laughing. "What firefight were you at? The battalion chaplain wasn't even with us, was he? I never saw him."

Thomas popped a Benzedrine tablet in his mouth and washed it down with some medicinal brandy. When Barney saw him do that, he suddenly realized how tired he was, too. He also took out a tablet and put it on his tongue and washed it down with his own vial of medicinal brandy that Lt. Rae Duncan had given him. The clean-cut Barney was turning into a raggedy-assed gyrene.

1800—Listening Post

It would be dark in less than an hour and the navy boats still had not arrived. The paratroopers wondered about the proximity of the enemy with growing concern. In the last light of day, Colonel Krulak decided to send out patrols to get an idea of the whereabouts of the Japanese closing in on them. Krulak ordered Lt. William King to send one of his squads out to reconnoiter to the southeast. With one of their Choiseulian allies as a scout, Pfc. Norman Dibbens, Pfc. Reece Canady, Pfc. John Buckley, and the other members of the first squad, First Platoon, F Company, made a contact patrol to the southeast to find out how close the Japanese were to Voza. Colonel Krulak told them not to go far. He only wanted to know if the Japanese were on the Marine side of their former southeast listening post, the same outpost Dugan and Pfc. Herbert "Blacky" Bell had guarded the night before. It was abandoned because they were supposed to have been extracted from the island by now.

The eight-man squad moved out of the battalion perimeter behind a native guide.[1] The men moved carefully to the southeast through the jungle, avoiding the coastal trail. At almost five hundred yards from their perimeter, the paratroopers heard something that made them stop. It was an unnatural noise in the jungle, a sound that could only be made by man. Although they could not make out just what it was, they got low and waited for the sounds to get closer.

Dibbens kneeled behind a tree root and in the fading light of dusk suddenly noticed a bloody dressing on the ground at his feet. It was an odd-looking bandage he had never seen before. It had to be a Japanese field dressing. Dibbens whispered to the others and showed them the bloody bandage. The noise continued and they heard voices talking in Japanese. Their first clue that Japanese were nearby should have been the disappearance of their native guide. The natives just seemed to melt into the jungle when danger was near. Dibbens and the others looked around and their guide was nowhere to be found.

That was enough for the patrol. The Japanese had obviously crossed the stream at the former listening post and were nearing Voza. Dibbens's squad made it back to their lines and reported the contact to Lieutenant King. Dibbens and the others took their positions and waited for the Japanese attack. "Get ready," whispered Lieutenant King as he passed down his platoon line. "They're coming." King immediately sent his runner to tell the colonel.

1900—Voza

Reports of enemy movement began to filter into Colonel Krulak's temporary CP near the beach. Native scouts reported Japanese barge traffic moving in large numbers from Moli Point southeast toward Voza, and an F Company patrol had just reported contact less than a mile away to the southeast inside what had formerly been the battalion perimeter flank. Wurzburger was sitting in the temporary CP watching the colonel, and this information alarmed him. The situation was going to get terminal quickly if the boats did not get there soon. It was past 1900 and, as the Marines knew well, nightfall in the jungle brought blindness. The entire battalion was arrayed in a semicircular perimeter, dug in behind fixed positions.

Waiting in his hole with his Johnson rifle propped on the dirt lip, Pfc. Richard Zimont of Chicago's south side waited for the boats to come in or the enemy to attack, whichever came first. He watched and listened and was in as much discomfort as he had ever been since joining the Marines. No sleep, poor diet, and incredible stress had all combined to give him the worst migraine headache of his life. It was so bad that it erased any fear of a Japanese attack he should have felt. Zimont came ashore on Choiseul at 225 pounds seven days earlier; if they left the island right then, he might still make it off the island at 210 pounds—maybe. "Is there a corpsman nearby?" he whispered in his strong Polish accent to a neighboring hole. [2]

"Yeah," came a response out of the darkness, "whaddya need?"

"Do you have any aspirin?" asked Zimont. "My head's killing me."

"No," came the whispered reply, "but I do have brandy."

Farther down the line, Pfc. Albert Hyle was in his foxhole with his weapon aimed into the darkness. Albert was also in the First Platoon, in the second squad. They had nine men left in their squad after Pfc. Milton O'Neal died from his wounds. Lieutenant King ordered, "no movement" along their perimeter and Hyle liked that order. Now he did not have to worry about shooting a friendly because only a Japanese soldier or a complete fool would be moving in the darkness. They did not know when the boats were coming in and it was possible that they would not leave until the dawn of November 4, so they were rotating guards.

Hyle was sitting out his shift when he heard movement coming from the side. He instantly whirled to fire. "This is King," warned his lieutenant quickly. "I'm coming in." The lieutenant slid into Hyle's small hole, brushing up against Hyle and Pfc. Bernard Best in the confined space.

"Lieutenant," whispered a shaken Hyle, "I almost killed you." It was enough to convince King to stay put. He remained in the hole.

A tense hour passed, followed by a second and a third. The Marines waited nervously in the darkness for the Japanese to attack. The Marines had learned their lessons well at Guadalcanal. The enemy preferred to fight at night, and for the last year, the battalion had conducted countless field problems simulating night fighting. The Marines were ready. Even so, it was hard on the nerves to stay alert hour after hour, waiting for an attack. Many of the men were wired on Benzedrine and brandy.

At 2230, Perdzock received a message from the boats. They were out in the channel somewhere beyond Zinoa Island. Colonel Krulak and Lieutenant Seton immediately boarded a Higgins Boat to move out to find them. Using a signal flashlight, they would rendezvous with the LCIs that were to pick up the surrounded battalion. The navy was unfamiliar with these waters and landmarks, so Krulak and Seton would guide the big landing craft safely in.

2300—Listening Post

Pfc. Harold N. "Hal" Block was in an E Company outpost on the outer perimeter of the battalion. If the Japanese probed the E Company line, Hal and his squad would be the first to find out. It was so dark Hal could not see his hand in front of his face, just like every other night since he had been on Choiseul. Word passed to him more than three hours prior that the Japanese were in the area, and it was getting hard to stay alert. Everyone had expected an attack already, but it had not materialized. All afternoon and evening they had waited in the jungle just off the beach for the navy to come in and get them, but even hours later, at 2300, in the black of night, the navy had not arrived.

All of a sudden, Hal heard movement approaching in the jungle ahead and felt that familiar stab of adrenaline. He could plainly hear voices, and they were not speaking English. Hal waited behind his weapon and heard the sounds getting closer and the voices getting louder. They were so close there was little doubt they were anything but Japanese approaching in numbers. Suddenly, an explosion fifty yards in front of Hal lit the darkness for just an instant before it was just as quickly gone. The explosion was loud against the silence of the night and it echoed off the mountains before dying out. Some unlucky Japanese point man had just triggered one of their booby traps.

Chapter 10

EXTRACTION: NOVEMBER 4

They were two giant men! One in size, the other in heart.
Pfc. W. Garth Bonner, E Company, of Sub-Lt.
Carden Seton and Lt. Col. Victor H. Krulak

0130—Voza

A single explosion flared up in the darkness of the jungle just outside the Marine perimeter, alerting the entire six-hundred-plus battalion of Marine paratroopers. The blast signaled to everyone that the time had come to sit up in his dug-out hole and tense behind his weapon. A number of uneasy minutes passed in complete silence, until another explosion ripped into the night a few hundred yards laterally from where the first trip wire detonated. The Japanese were spread out and closing in on the Marine beachhead. The paratroopers waited nervously for their rush. If the boats did not get there soon, the battalion was going to be trapped with their backs to the ocean. They had a good defensive perimeter, but once the enemy sighted in on them with mortars it could get terminal. Also, this was still The Slot, and enemy destroyers ranged up and down just like they had at Guadalcanal ten months before. Caught on the beach, the Marines could fall prey to naval guns with devastating effects.

Wounded Pfc. John Erotas woke up for the first time since an explosion had knocked him unconscious four days earlier. He was in a great deal of pain, deaf in one ear, and barely able to hear anything out of the other. Erotas woke to find himself in darkness along the beach. He could feel the heavy bandages around his head and he drifted in and out of consciousness. His last memory was of an LCI running up on the beach.

At 0130, Colonel Krulak and Lt. Seton came back ashore guiding three big LCIs. Wasting no time, Krulak told his officers to start their pre-designed withdrawal. While corpsmen and stretcher bearers ran the wounded on board, others started carrying supplies onto the three waiting Higgins Boats or up the LCI stairs. Simultaneously, runners moved out from the beach to the company perimeters with orders to begin the withdrawal.

Soon the first squads of paratroopers came sprinting out of the trees toward the boats, running low with weapons ready.

E Company Outpost

Lieutenant Averill looked at his watch. He worried that the battalion had pulled out and left them. Suddenly, a soft whistle came over the headset. He picked up the phone and whispered, "Outpost. Ave."

Silence. Then a quiet, "This is Vic. Take a powder."

"Ave here. Will do."[1]

It was time to go. Averill hissed the order down the line for his men to pull back. With explosions erupting in the jungle ahead, the Marines silently formed up, hooking onto the belt of the man in front. After a quick roll call to make sure everyone was present, they moved off for the beach. As they neared Voza, Averill heard the bolt of a rifle move back and forward.

"Outpost!" he snapped quickly. Then, more softly, "Outpost coming in." He heard a laugh that could only be American followed by, "God, Ave, you looked just like a damned Jap coming into that clearing [like Krulak, Averill was very short]. I almost drilled you."

Averill and his men moved through and started helping load the five tons of equipment and munitions back onto the boats for extraction.

0145—Listening Post

Ned heard the squads positioned on both his flanks receive their orders to pull back, and although he could not see anyone, he heard them pick up their weapons and double-time it back to the beach. Ned sat in his hole with his A-4 trained on the jungle in front of them, waiting for his own orders to go. They could not all go at once, but it was his bad luck to be in the last squad in his area to pull back. He waited tensely for Sgt. Anthony J. Skotnicki or Lt. Douglas Morton to order their withdrawal. An explosion in the jungle lit up the night fifty yards in front of him and he knew the Japanese were closing in. Russell had been watching the explosions creep closer and closer for the last half hour. "What am I doing here?" he thought, gripping his machine gun tightly.

The tall, reclusive Apache knew they had been extremely lucky the day before and worried that their luck was running out. The Japanese could come any second, and now most of the weapons platoon was gone. The mortar guys had already taken off and the squads positioned on their flanks too. If the Japanese had come at them five minutes earlier, Russell was confident they would have had the firepower to handle a *banzai*. If the enemy came right now in a mad rush, they would probably be overwhelmed. The jungle and the night gave the Japanese room to fight.

0200—Voza

"Let's go," ordered Lieutenant Murphy to his experimental rocket platoon.

Pfc. Eugene Gibbons and the other eight men in the platoon picked up two rockets each from a pile stacked on the beach and headed for the nearest LCI. The LCIs were each about sixty yards apart. It was so dark they were like huge shadows against the backdrop of the ocean. Picking the closest one, the men struggled up the sides of the big landing craft. The cumbersome rockets weighed 45 pounds each. When they got to the top, a navy officer told the Marines where to stack the rockets, and then they turned to go back down for more.

In the faint moonlight, Gibbons could see the shadows of entire platoons running quickly back along the beach and streaming up the sides of the other LCIs. Explosions erupted very close behind them—seemingly just inside the jungle—and cast an eerie light that flashed on the inland mountains. Gibbons and the others pushed their way against the grain of boarding infantry and moved back down the stairs, bumping and jostling in the darkness against the men climbing up. The Marines muttered curses at them as Gibbons and the others struggled past. Once back on the beach they ran over to the pile of rockets and picked up another load. Grabbing two each, Gibbons turned to run back up the side stairs of the LCI.

Pfc. Bruce "Red" McClure and the rest of Sgt. Norman Law's squad were deployed along the F Company perimeter waiting to pull back. They could hear movement from their flanks and behind them on the beach, and in front of them multiple explosions lit up the night with increasing frequency to echo off the mountains. The Japanese were definitely closing in while the paratroopers were in the midst of a withdrawal. They might *banzai* any minute, but just then Marine trip-wire mines and C-2 traps exploding in the darkness held the enemy back. Things were getting tense for the waiting Marines. Most of their firepower had already left the line to move back to the beach.

"Okay, Law, pull your men back." Red, Pfc. Orrin Hall, Cpl. Benjamin F. "Cape" Caperton III, and the others picked up their weapons and moved as quickly as they could back through the jungle toward the beach. In the trees, it was pitch black and they could not see a thing, but on the beach they could just barely see three big LCIs spread out and waiting. The farthest ship was maybe a few hundred yards away and barely more than a shadow. The stairs of the LCIs were teaming with men as they climbed up both sides two and three steps at a time.[2] Others carried the last of the battalion's supplies onto three Higgins Boats.

Red took in this information on the run. He was double-timing it to the ships. An officer directed Law's squad to the closest LCI and they ran up the side. When Red reached the top, he moved to the front of the LCI and got down behind the steel-plated hull that stuck up a few feet from the deck. He aimed his M-1 back at the tree line and watched the surreal scene before him. Explosions in the jungle directly ahead indicated where the Japanese were closing in on the Marines' shrinking perimeter. Red saw squads of paratroopers pulling back and expected to see platoons of enemy troops racing onto the beach behind them, charging for the ships like the Trojans' attack on the Greeks. Red could see just off the shore several patrol torpedo boats interspersed between the three LCIs and the battalion's four overloaded Higgins Boats. Helmeted sailors manned machine guns on the PTs' sides, and the 40-mm guns fore and aft added firepower Red did not know the battalion had for their extraction. He had heard that the PTs had saved G Company the day before.

Cpl. William D. Cole received word and ordered his squad back to the ships. Pfcs. Thomas Preston, Ralph Bagwell, Earl F. Nevins, J. N. Clark, Mel Lavine, and the others picked up their weapons and double-timed it back to the beach. When they neared the boats, Clark saw the bow of a ship stuck in the sand on the beach. He exploded in anger. "Goddamn dumb navy. They beached a destroyer. What the hell good is it going to do us to board the damn thing? It can't get off the beach."

"For Christ's sake, Clark," said Cole, "shut the fuck up. It's an LCI."

Nevins ran up the stairs, and when he got to the top deck he ducked inside a portal where a sailor was standing, handing out cigarettes to the Marines as they boarded. Since they had been on Choiseul no one had had a smoke. Chain-smokers like Nevins had been going out of their minds after seven days. He grabbed a cigarette and went deep below into the darkness of the hold. Safely hidden from enemy eyes, he lit up and inhaled deeply.

0200—Listening Post

Hal peered intensely into the jungle in front of him expecting enemy troops to rush his squad at any moment. Just then an explosion detonated fifty yards in front of his outpost. Almost simultaneously, screams of pain echoed into the night. The Japanese were close. Hal knew the LCIs were here and wondered what the holdup was. They needed to head back to the beach, and quick.

"Let's go," ordered Capt. Robert R. "Chesty" Manchester. "Pull back." With weapons ready, the paratroopers made a quick withdrawal to the boats. By the time Hal reached the LCIs it did not look as if there was anyone else on the beach. The Marines had already boarded and were ready to go.

Some of the last paratroopers to leave the line manned the covering machine guns. Sergeant Skotnicki's machine-gun section with Pfc. Ned Russell's A-4 finally got word to pull back. "Time to go," said Skotnicki. Picking up their weapons and tripod, they double-timed it back to the LCIs. Two of the boats looked like they were getting ready to pull out. Ned and his section almost flew up the side stairs. Once he was on deck, Ned turned toward the front to set up his A-4 again. The front of the LCI bristled with Marines, their weapons aimed forward, and Russell had to push his way between two men to set up his machine gun. He knew that they were not out of this yet.

The LCIs were filling up and preparing to pull out. Private Gibbons had just finished stacking two more experimental rockets. He had already made three separate trips carrying the heavy bombs that were now stacked in a neat pile on the ship's deck. Gibbons looked back toward the beach and saw multiple explosions lighting up the jungle one hundred yards or so inland. When their LCI began to pull out and it looked like the Marines were going to get away clean, Sgt. Nolan Burnett suddenly ran over to Lt. Bob Murphy. Murphy was standing next to a naval officer when the agitated Burnett grabbed his arm. "We left some rockets on the beach," Burnett said with panic, his eyes wide. "We're missing seven."

"They're lost," said the naval officer.

"They can't be," said Murphy, also panicked. "They're experimental, highly secretive weapons. They're classified and can't fall into enemy hands."

Gibbons listened as Murphy convinced the officer to signal, "Stop engines." The rocket platoon guys were already rushing for the stairs as the naval officer yelled behind them, "We won't wait. If we take fire, we're leaving you."

Gibbons and the others raced down into the surf and waded to shore. They were surprised to see five of the rockets on the ground and two in the hands of a shaken Pfc. Charlie Jones. "I thought you left me," mumbled Jones, as white as a sheet. Gibbons did not have time to ask him what had happened. They grabbed the remaining rockets, waded back out, and climbed up the LCI's side stairs.

Once the rockets had been stacked out of the way on the craft, the men ran over to Jones to find out what had happened. Why had he been standing on the beach when their LCI was pulling back? Jones knew there were still seven rockets on the beach, and he had gone down for a fourth time to get two more. He thought everyone was right behind him. He was not alarmed when he heard the engines roaring. The three LCIs were just getting ready to leave; loud, revving engines seemed normal. Jones grabbed two rockets and turned back to the ship, but to his horror, it was moving away in the darkness. "I screamed as loud as I could, but nobody heard me," he explained, still visibly shaken. "My life flashed in front of my eyes." Gibbons and the others were in tears from laughing so hard. Jones would never hear the end of it, and he would be the brunt of a great many jokes to come.

PM3 Paul Salfrank watched the tree line for enemy troops. His LCI was pushing out to sea when a figure darted from the trees to sprint toward the closest ship. Something about the man's body language did not look right, and as he raced across the beach, Salfrank saw that he was a Marine. Salfrank and just about everyone else expected to see Japanese troops attacking out of the jungle, so it was a miracle that nobody accidentally shot this guy. He was shouting hysterically, "Wait for me!" Explosions lit the jungle behind him.

"There's always one," thought Salfrank angrily.

Hal Block heard someone roar, "Leave the dumb son of a bitch! Anyone who'd fall asleep deserves to be left."

One thing was certain: neither Hal nor Salfrank wanted the boat to go back in for him. The Japanese were close and everyone on board the ship would be in danger if the craft headed toward shore.

Instead of running down the beach to the remaining beached LCI, the panicking man sprinted for the closest one, which was already pulling out. He ran out into the surf, begging them to wait, and started swimming for it. They were far from the beach, but a sailor threw a lifesaver to him. Fear seemed to make this guy an Olympic swimmer, too, because he reached that donut faster than Hal and Salfrank thought possible. He was pulled to safety, and the LCI gunned its engine and turned out to sea.

Almost all of the last Marines to leave had boarded the last remaining ship. One of these squads included Pfc. James P. Dugan and his buddies, who were supporting a machine-gun section when they received their order to pull back. Dugan was almost to the remaining ship when he came upon Colonel Krulak, Lieutenant Seton, Peta Kiri, and Peta Nu. They were standing together in the darkness in front of the last LCI. Dugan slowed down to catch the end of their conversation.

"Seton," Colonel Krulak was saying, "why don't you come home with us tonight?"

"I'm already home," replied Seton. He stuck his hand out to Krulak and they shook hard. Seton turned and with his two friends disappeared into the jungle as more explosions erupted all around the Marines' former perimeter.

"Where would he go?" thought Dugan running for the stairs of the last LCI. "The Japanese are closing around the beach and the whole area is booby-trapped." As Dugan and the last of the Americans gained the stairs, Colonel Krulak turned and walked back to the LCI behind him.

Corporal Caperton watched the whole scene from the bow of the ship. He saw explosions light up the jungle around Voza, Seton and his two friends slip into the jungle, and Krulak walk back to their ship alone on an empty beach. The colonel gained the LCI's side stairs and moved quickly to the top. Within seconds, they were under way, heading out into The Slot.

The small flotilla of three LCIs and five PT boats slipped away into the darkness heading westward for Vella LaVella. Red had moved to the back of his LCI to watch the island disappear behind them. Explosions still lit up the night back on the beach. There was no telling how many enemy soldiers their traps were going to kill before the night was over. The Japanese probably had no idea that the Marines were even gone. Looking back, Red saw something that caused him concern, though. Their LCI was towing a Higgins Boat so overloaded with supplies and munitions that it was impossibly low in the water. It was slowly taking in water and it soon became obvious that the LCPR was sinking. Red worried it would slow them down or, worse, strain the LCI's engines to the point that they might break down. He was glad when one of the officers ordered the towrope cut because the last place he wanted to have trouble was The Slot where enemy destroyers and night fighters constantly patrolled the waters. Red watched the Higgins Boat disappear quickly beneath the black water as they pulled away in the night.

Down below in the hold the Marines smoked cigarettes and drank hot coffee, simple pleasures they had not enjoyed for what seemed an eternity. The paratroopers rushed to the galley to scrounge whatever food they could get their hands on. The meager provisions in the small ship's mess were like a Las Vegas buffet compared with what the Marines had had over the past week. Cans of Spam and peaches were a veritable feast for the starving paratroopers. Some smoked, others ate, but even more slept. Up on the deck, Dibbens—who had not slept for more than two hours at a time for the last eight days—was stretched out, dead to the world. The ship's crew had to step over dozens of unconscious Marines as they moved about the deck. Dibbens never woke up until someone shook him upon docking in Vella LaVella more than four hours later.

Chapter 11

THE LAST DAYS OF AN ELITE BREED

He was the last Marine to leave that island. I saw it myself.
Cpl. Benjamin F. "Cape" Caperton III, F Company,
on Lt. Col. Victor H. Krulak

The Choiseul invasion had sufficiently rattled the Japanese just long enough to keep them off balance and failing to commit their reserves in the early days of the Bougainville invasion. The first real ground threat to the U.S. Marine invasion force on Bougainville was on November 6–7, when a five-hundred-man Japanese landing force hit the beach behind the Marines and fought their way inland along the Koromokina River.[1] It took the U.S. Marines several days of violent fighting to kill the entire Japanese force. Still, those five hundred Japanese troops had little chance against the more than fifteen thousand Marines who were already on shore and dug in, having been supplied seven days after the invasion began. Col. Robert H. Williams, the commanding officer of the First Parachute Regiment, later stated that the Choiseul diversion proved to be "A brilliant little bit of work."[2]

Maj. Gen. Alexander A. Vandegrift, who would shortly become the commandant of the Marine Corps, would write in his commendatory letter to Lt. Col. Victor H. Krulak, "These highly commendable and aggressive actions on the part of the Second Marine Parachute Battalion (Reinforced) contributed greatly to the success of the current operations in the South Pacific Area and were carried out in conformity with the highest traditions of the Marine Corps." Adm. William F. Halsey would personally pin the Navy Cross on Colonel Krulak for his "extraordinary heroism displayed against an armed enemy."

Although the Japanese quickly recognized that the invasion of Choiseul was just a diversion, it had served its purpose. Because of the Treasury Island, Choiseul, and Bougainville attacks, the enemy was unsure as to just where the real threat was. The Second Marine Parachute Battalion did everything that was asked of them and more. Krulak's 650-man battalion had landed on Choiseul, disrupted the enemy on a twenty-mile front, and kept the Japanese high command guessing for one critical week. When the real landing at Bougainville came on November 1,

237

Gen. Haruyoshi Hyakutake withheld his orders to counterattack for seven days, trying to determine if the Bougainville attack was the real invasion or just another diversion.

Although the damage inflicted to the Japanese on Choiseul was relatively minor, there were 143 confirmed enemy soldiers killed by Krulak's paratroopers, several hundred tons of enemy fuel and supplies destroyed, and two landing barges sunk. Keeping the enemy high command from reacting to the Bougainville landing in the first critical hours was the real success of the diversion for it undoubtedly saved lives. The capture of the Sangigai documents was also one of the great fortunes of the attack. These maps alerted Admiral Halsey's landing force to the threat of enemy minefields in the sea-lanes approaching Bougainville. The Allied planners used the captured maps to navigate their task force safely through and to mine the routes that the maps indicated were used by the Japanese. This resulted in the loss of two Japanese ships.

The real successes of the Choiseul diversion were the Allied casualties that never occurred.

Bougainville and Choiseul would be the last days of the elite Marine units fighting in World War II. The jungles of the South Pacific had prevented the utilization of the paratroopers, and in the coming years the strategic planners no longer saw the need for quick-hitting, specialized "commando" type units. The Marine paratroopers and raiders would be disbanded to provide uniformity in the Marine Corps and to save the extra fifty dollars a month hazard and jump pay that every paratrooper received. The First Marine Parachute Regiment was shipped back to the United States on January 2, 1944, disbanded, and used to form the combat nucleus of the new Fifth Marine Division forming at Camp Pendleton, California.[3] As Marine paratroopers, the Second Marine Parachute Battalion was never to fight again. As Marines, most of them would go on to immortal fame in American military history for their roles on Iwo Jima.

Herbert "Blacky" Bell would survive thirty-four days on Iwo Jima without being wounded. All through the war Blacky felt that he was protected with some kind of divine intervention—the bullet between his liner and helmet being only one example. Another time was on Iwo Jima when a Japanese grenade landed in his foxhole but did not detonate. The last was during the occupation of Japan when Blacky and his buddies decided to take their leave to go to Nagasaki to witness firsthand the devastation of the atomic bomb. While they prepared to go, Blacky's sergeant gave him a last-minute guard detail, forcing him to remain behind. He was furious at missing the opportunity, and he could only listen to the awe in his buddy's voices as they described the devastation. Blacky could not know that the sergeant had probably saved his life. Blacky Bell is now eighty-four years old, the only survivor of his squad. The others have long since died of cancer because they had been exposed to high levels of radiation from their visit to Nagasaki.

Hugh Greely's machine-gun section would be hit hard on Iwo Jima. Greely would be wounded while Harold Frackelton, Burt Bueller, and Samuel C. Walker would be killed in action. Only Hardy Brown would live through the war untouched. He was standing in line on the docks at Pearl Harbor next to his buddies Brutinel and Cagle, waiting to ship out to Iwo Jima, when his appointment to West Point sent him to safety. Laughing and waving to his buddies as he walked away from the dock at Pearl, he could not know it would be the last time he would see many of them. Nobody knew how violent the fighting on Iwo Jima was going to be. Because Brown missed Iwo Jima to play football at West Point, his best friend, Billy Joe, said Brown suffered survivor's guilt for the rest of his life.[4]

Billy Joe Cagle would go to Iwo Jima and take shrapnel in the shoulder. Crawling to a corpsman under mortar fire, he would see the medic frantically trying to save the lives of a dozen wounded men lying in a huge shell crater stained with blood. Billy Joe's buddy Harvey Prinz was lying critically wounded and Billy Joe thought, "I'm not hurt bad enough to be here." He crawled back to the hole he had dug out where his buddy Ralph Bagwell put a compress on his shoulder until a corpsman could look at it. Not one hour later Cagle was shot in the buttocks. He was evacuated to a hospital ship but after only one week, he was sent back in because the situation on shore was so critical. They needed men.

Robert Brutinel would be shot in the face. The bullet would blow a channel in his nose and nick the side of his eye and ear. He was happy to receive his million-dollar wound until he learned that after his recovery he would be displaced to a composite battalion and sent to a new unit. Fearful that he would be reassigned and lose all his buddies, Brutinel went back to his unit and, his face in bandages, walked off the island after thirty-four days.

Louis Komnenich would be shot off a tank on March 8 trying to get support for his pinned-down squad.

Oscar Frith would be blown into the air by a Japanese Spigot mortar. He would wake up lying on the beach in the freezing rain with a piece of shrapnel in his lung and a leg blown off at the thigh.

Paul Chelf would rise up to throw a grenade at a Japanese soldier who was doing the exact same thing to him. They would both hit their mark. Chelf lived, however, taking multiple shrapnel wounds to the leg.

Earl "Ed" Cassaday would take shrapnel in the arm and foot, but he hobbled off the island after thirty-four days.

Robert Zimmerman would receive permission to go to a Catholic mass service at the base of Mount Suribachi. With a "See ya' later," he left his foxhole and the two men in it. When he returned, both men were dead— an 80-mm mortar had made a direct hit on dug-out hole. Within the hour, Zimmerman had been hit, too, when a round exploded near him, stitching his torso with shrapnel. In 2003, he still has steel lodged in his chest. Zimmerman says it makes passing airport security tough.

Norman Wurzburger would be blown into the air by a Japanese Spigot mortar and take multiple shrapnel to his shoulder. Unconscious, he would be buried alive under the dirt, only his hand and wrist visible. A corpsman (PM3 Greg Emory) would see his hand sticking out and pull him from the earth, saving his life.

By the end of March 1945, Sgt. Thomas Siefke, Cpl. Mike Vinich, Pfc. Raymond Pierce, Pfc. James Moe, and Pfc. Robert Riebling would each be wounded in action on Iwo Jima. Pfc. Robert Neff, Pfc. Leo Henslick, and Pfc. Clarence Cameron would be killed in action. Only Pfc. Robert Poe would make it through Iwo Jima untouched.

Siefke would almost lose his hand. He was aiming to fire his weapon when a bullet went through his wrist and stopped in the butt of his rifle. The force of the impact against his cheek and jaw almost knocked him unconscious. He had been moved to the battalion aid station and doctors were stitching up his arm when a direct hit from an enemy mortar reinjured him and killed many of the wounded.

Norman Dibbens would be shot twice in the stomach by a sniper. He would lose eighteen feet of his intestines and reach San Diego weighing 98 pounds, down from 170 pounds. Convinced he was going to die, Dibbens refused to let anyone bathe or shave him. When he arrived at the hospital, two nurses were tending a wounded man when the bearded scarecrow was carried into their ward. One of the nurses, Jeanie Cavannagh of New York, saw the wounded Marine and stood upright saying to the other nurse, "I'm going to marry that man."

"You're crazy," said her friend.

It is now 2006, and Norman and Jeanie Dibbens are still happily married.

Billy Dale Bowman would take grenade fragments in the buttocks but stay on the line all thirty-four days.

Ned Russell would be wounded in action on Iwo Jima. A mortar round landed in his foxhole and killed his best friend, Melvin Welch. (Ned is convinced Welch saved his life by taking the brunt of the blast.) Ned was badly injured when a steel fragment lodged in his skull. He went berserk and tried to rush the Japanese lines. Barney Baxter watched three Marines tackle him and drag the crazed Apache into a hole. The next twelve hours were a blur as Ned lay on the beach waiting for evacuation. His equilibrium was gone, and he could only lie helplessly watching as mortar rounds came down one after another, hour after hour, to land amid him and the other wounded lying in rows along the beach. The corpsmen were unable to take Ned's helmet off for fear of killing him because the steel was lodged in his skull through the helmet. For more than a week on a hospital ship, he remained in that state, until neurosurgeons on Saipan could safely remove both.

Howard "Barney" Baxter would see his squad leader and friend, the brave Cpl. William R. Zuegel, killed right beside him on Iwo Jima. Barney's buddy Sgt. Edward Thomas would be wounded in action on Iwo Jima but survive the war to be the best man at Barney's wedding. Of all the Marines in the Second Marine Parachute Battalion, few, if any, would see more combat than the gentle, soft-spoken artist. Barney would survive the Warrior River and go on to see thirty-four days of action on Iwo Jima, make the Inchon Landing in Korea, fight at Kimpo Airport and the recapture of Seoul, and make the frozen withdrawal from Chosin Reservoir. Through all these actions as a frontline infantryman, Barney would never receive a scratch.

Rudolph Engstrom would take shrapnel in the throat fighting for Airfield #1. A doctor would hold a mirror to his neck and say, "See that white thing? That's your jugular vein."

A mortar round would temporarily paralyze Reece Canady. He and Engstrom were sent to a supply ship because both hospital ships, already dangerously overcrowded with wounded, refused them.

James Ward would be wounded. A Japanese hand grenade would explode beside him and he would take shrapnel in the back of his thigh and knee. Ward is convinced that if he had not been wounded and evacuated he would have died on Iwo Jima.

George P. Adams and Paul J. Hamilton would go on to Iwo Jima where they would be wounded when a mortar round landed in their foxhole. Of the four men in that hole, two would die, and both Adams and Hamilton would lie in a hospital in Hawaii recovering from their wounds, each thinking the other had been killed. A month later, still covered in bandages, Adams would accidentally bump into another patient while hobbling down a hospital corridor—his friend Hamilton.

William O'Gieglo would honor his promise to his fallen friend Cpl. Edward "Jimmy" Schnell and return to Illinois to visit Jimmy's family's restaurant. He would sit down with Jimmy's father and tell him the circumstances surrounding his son's death. At Jimmy's father's request, O'Gieglo returned with him to Jimmy's home to talk to the entire Schnell family, who asked question after question about the death of their loved one. O'Gieglo vowed never again to promise a buddy he would visit his home. No amount of combat could prepare a man for the tears of his buddy's sobbing mother and sister. It would be the hardest experience of O'Gieglo's life—harder than his thirty-four days on Iwo Jima.

Eugene Gibbons would go on to Bougainville and participate in the heavy fighting for Hill 1000. He never would fire their experimental rockets there because the thick canopy of trees prevented their use. His friend Charlie Jones, who had been accidentally left on the beach on Choiseul, would be ribbed about the incident for the rest of his life. At their last reunion, more than forty years later, when a bus driver told the group he would wait for them, Jones turned to Gibbons, Bob Murphy, and the others and said, "I've heard that before."

J. N. Clark would take a bullet through his thigh on Iwo Jima while trying to direct a tank to wipe out enemy snipers that had pinned down the shattered remnants of his company. The other members of his paratroop squad would also take their fair share of wounds.

William Cole, Raymond L. Hoskins, Ralph Bagwell, and Mel Lavine would all be wounded in action on Iwo Jima. Gilbert DeVault and Earl Nevins would not receive a scratch.

Thomas Preston would join the Fifth Marine Division but suffer a broken back when a cable broke during training at Camp Pendleton, California. Preston would be partially paralyzed in one leg for the rest of his life.

Bruce McClure and Carl Kuehne would become best friends and go on to Iwo Jima together to be Browning automatic rifle (BAR) man and assistant. Amazingly, both would survive thirty-four days as infantrymen without being hit. One man in their squad who was not so lucky was young Stanley H. Keller; he would be killed in action on Iwo Jima.

Eugene Gesch would survive the war and marry his wife wearing his fallen friend Samuel Johnston's immaculate and highly prized green Marine paratroop uniform.

Carl Desanto would be struck in the back by a mortar fragment within five minutes of hitting the beach on D-Day. The piece of steel would go through three rounds of 37-mm shells in his pack before lodging in his back.

Larry Smith would be in charge of a 60-mm mortar crew on Iwo Jima. He would be hit when a mortar round landed in his foxhole; he bears the steel fragments to this day.

Don Carpenter would make it thirty-four days on Iwo Jima without being physically wounded. Like so many others, however, he would suffer emotionally from seeing so many of his buddies killed and wounded around him.

Benjamin F. "Cape" Caperton III would walk off Iwo Jima after thirty-four days of combat.

John Erotas took shrapnel in the head on Choiseul and was unconscious when they carried him onto an LCI. He did not wake up again until he was in a field hospital on Guadalcanal a week later. Steel fragments had severed the nerve in his inner left ear, causing permanent hearing loss.

Harold N. "Hal" Block was crawling up the military crest of a hill to provide machine-gun support for an attack when an enemy soldier put a bullet through his shoulder.

Robert Winner would be in a huge shell crater with seven other Marines when a mortar round landed in the middle of them. Winner would take multiple shrapnel wounds and still carries shrapnel in his leg after more than sixty years.

Donald "Hink" Hinkle would go on to Iwo Jima where he would survive weeks of combat only to take a sniper's bullet through the thigh while standing guard at the Fifth Division cemetery on D+15. A Japanese soldier who had covered himself with a Marine's poncho would pop up from a grave to shoot unsuspecting Marines far behind the lines. The Marines had been unable to locate him until one of his bullets brought down Hink and killed a lieutenant at the same time. As a corpsman tended his wound, Hink's buddies came over. "Did you get the sniper?" asked Hink.

"You're the last Marine he'll ever shoot," replied one of his buddies.

John Holland honored his promise to Sgt. Frank Muller and returned to tell Muller's sister about his death. She asked questions about how her brother lived his life outside of the war, in everyday life. Only in the end did she ask how her brother had died.

Holland would go back to sea on an attack transport. Because he was a navy corpsman attached to Marine units, he did not follow the others to Iwo Jima. Instead, he would make two more landings in the Philippines and Okinawa. For Holland, the worst part of the war was Okinawa because of the kamikazes. Gunshot wounds were bad enough, but treating men in agonizing pain with horrific burns was unimaginable.

Paul Salfrank would go from the elite paratroops into the U.S. Navy's underwater demolitions teams. With them he went on to Okinawa.

Chester Finnegan would go on to be a medic with the air rescue service and have more than one thousand jumps as a paratrooper throughout his military career. He would take part in the Saipan, Guam, and Philippine invasions. He would earn his purple heart at Tanapeg harbor when a kamikaze slammed into the area where he was treating wounded waiting for evacuation. Finnegan would also serve in Korea, helping form the fledgling helicopter rescue.

Charles Allman was assaulting a cave on Iwo Jima when machine-gun fire from a hidden position wounded him. A bullet grazed his right temple and another slammed into his shoulder. He also took shrapnel in his back from bullets hitting his entrenching tool. He lay there with blood in his eyes convinced he was dying until a corpsman was able to get him evacuated to the beach.

Mike Vinich would be shot through both legs by machine-gun fire. He would lose six inches of his tibia and spend eleven months in traction. After the war, unwilling to leave Wyoming, Vinich would turn down a position in Washington, D.C., working for President John F. Kennedy. He did, however, accept a position back in his home state to work for the Democratic Party.

Brute Krulak would be promoted to lieutenant general and be instrumental in saving the Marine Corps from being disbanded by President Harry S Truman and Gen. Douglas MacArthur. He would have something far greater than that rank, however—the fatherly respect of his battalion.

Semper Fi.

APPENDIX

Awards and Decorations

Of the men interviewed for this book:

Pfc. George P. Adams—Purple Heart—Iwo Jima

Pfc. Charles Allman—Purple Heart—Iwo Jima

Pfc. Judson "Gene" Bay—Purple Heart—Iwo Jima

Pfc. Harold N. "Hal" Block—Purple Heart—Iwo Jima

Pfc. Billy Dale Bowman—Silver Star—Iwo Jima

Pfc. Robert Brutinel—Purple Heart—Iwo Jima;
Silver Star—Iwo Jima

Pfc. Billy Joe Cagle—Purple Heart—Iwo Jima;
Bronze Star—Iwo Jima

Pfc. Reece Canady—Purple Heart—Iwo Jima;
Silver Star—Iwo Jima

Pfc. Don Carpenter—Bronze Star—Iwo Jima

Pfc. Earl "Ed" Cassaday—Purple Heart—Iwo Jima

Pfc. Paul Chelf—Purple Heart—Iwo Jima

Pfc. J. N. Clark—Purple Heart—Iwo Jima

Pfc. Norman Dibbens—Purple Heart—Iwo Jima

Pfc. James P. Dugan—Purple Heart—Iwo Jima

Pfc. Rudolph Engstrom—Purple Heart—Iwo Jima

Pfc. John Erotas—Purple Heart—Choiseul

Pfc. Willis "Rich" Fegley—Purple Heart—Choiseul

PM2 Chester Finnegan—Purple Heart—Saipan

Sgt. Oscar Frith—Purple Heart—Iwo Jima

Pfc. Kurt Garbuschewski—Purple Heart—Choiseul

Pfc. Hugh Greely—Bronze Star—Iwo Jima

Pfc. Orrin Hall—Bronze Star—Iwo Jima

Pfc. Albert Hyle—Purple Heart—Iwo Jima

Pfc. Louis Komnenich—Purple Heart—Iwo Jima

Lt. Col. Victor H. Krulak—Purple Heart—Choiseul;
Navy Cross—Choiseul

Pfc. Mel Lavine—Purple Heart—Iwo Jima;
Silver Star—Iwo Jima

Sgt. Joseph Martin—Purple Heart—Iwo Jima

245

Pfc. Bruce "Red" McClure—Bronze Star—Iwo Jima
Pfc. Robert Perdzock—Purple Heart—Bougainville
Pfc. Ned Russell—Purple Heart—Iwo Jima
Sgt. Thomas Siefke—Purple Heart—Iwo Jima;
    Bronze Star—Iwo Jima
Pfc. Larry Smith—Purple Heart—Iwo Jima
Pfc. James Ward—Purple Heart—Iwo Jima;
    Bronze Star—Iwo Jima
Pfc. Robert Winner—Purple Heart—Iwo Jima
Pfc. Robert Zimmerman—Purple Heart—Iwo Jima

If I have unknowingly left out some of the veterans or not listed his medal, I apologize. Not one of the men told me of his awards; I only stumbled on them if one of their friends mentioned it or I read of them in the *History of the 5th Marine Division*. Only then would the veterans talk humbly about their medal, downplaying their role in earning it.

For instance, three hours into the interview with her husband, Mrs. Robert Brutinel came home. "Did you see this?" she asked, showing me Brutinel's Silver Star and a picture of Col. Thomas Warnam pinning it on Brutinel in 1945. Brutinel never would tell me how he got it other than saying, "They were just handing them out and I happened to be in line," or "I don't know. I was asleep when they pinned it on me."

Or consider the case of Hugh Greely, who joked that he received his Bronze Star for making formation on two consecutive occasions. Greely refused his Purple Heart for shrapnel in his leg—too many of his buddies had received one for losing theirs.

NOTES

Chapter 1

1. In 1947 Holland was at home with his wife when the phone rang. His wife said, "Just a moment," and handed Holland the phone. "Do you know who this is?" asked the voice at the other end. "You're damned right I do and I'm going to buy you a drink." Holland recognized the man's voice instantly: It was the man who had saved his life. "Do you remember my name?" asked the Marine? "I'm sorry," said Holland, "I don't." "Well, you think about it," said the man. "I'll call you back sometime and when you remember, we'll go have that drink." He hung up. The man never called back, and Holland has felt guilty for more than sixty years for not remembering that man's name.
2. Clark did not know at the time that he was looking at the bullet-ridden plane of future hero Greg "Pappy" Boyington, Marine fighter ace five times over.
3. Krulak suffered lifelong sciatic nerve damage from that jump.
4. Every man interviewed spoke with great regard for the big Australian. Only Krulak and Manchester drew more praise.
5. The USS *Ward* is the destroyer that fired the first shot by the United States in World War II. That shot sank a Japanese midget sub outside the submarine gate at Pearl Harbor.
6. Siefke was quoting from Shakespeare's *Julius Caesar*.

Chapter 2

1. *Barney Baxter* was a popular comic strip character from 1935–1942. More than sixty years later when the author called Baxter's house, Mrs. Baxter called him to the phone by saying, "Barney, telephone."
2. The squad was Pfc. Milton O'Neal, Sgt. John Baker, Platoon Sgt. Mehrl Hotchkiss, Pfc. Ed Mach, Pfc. Bernard Best, Pfc. Melvin Eaton, Cpl. Frederick Akerson, and Pfc. Albert Hyle.
3. The Glen was a submarine-based Yokosuka bomber. Its nickname, Washing Machine Charlie, came from the fact that its two engines were not synchronized and it made an undulating noise.
4. Pfc. Robert Brutinel, Pfc. Don Carpenter, Pfc. Rudolph Engstrom, and Pfc. R. Adams say they landed and were extracted by Landing Craft

Infantry (LCIs), of which there is no record. All four distinctly remember going down the side stairs onto the beach. Interestingly, the original plan was for the battalion to be inserted by submarine just like the Makin Island raid by Carlson's Second Raider Battalion. The reason they were not used was because there were not any submarines available. The Allies were spread so thinly that the Marines went ashore on transports that had taken New Zealander troops in on a similar attack the day before on the nearby Treasury Islands.

5.   The natives did receive the rice, several days later.

6.   If the U.S. military or government had ever done anything right, it was these hammocks. To a man, every Marine was amazed at how practical, useful, and comfortable they were. They had a camouflaged canopy to keep the rain out and the Marine hidden, and they were surrounded in mosquito netting. That alone in this part of the world made them every trooper's necessity but above all, they were comfortable. In short, they were a camper's dream and the Waldorf Astoria of hammocks. The hammocks were new and had never before been used by any of the armed forces. The First Marine Parachute Regiment was entirely equipped with them and the Second Marine Parachute Battalion would be the hammocks' field test. The men strung them up between trees in the dark and climbed in to go to sleep. If the U.S. military or government had ever done anything right, it was these hammocks. To a man, every Marine was amazed at how practical, useful, and comfortable they were. They had a camouflaged canopy to keep the rain out and the Marine hidden, and they were surrounded in mosquito netting. That alone in this part of the world made them every trooper's necessity but above all, they were comfortable. In short, they were a camper's dream and the Waldorf Astoria of hammocks.

7.   Atabrine was a synthetic quinine developed before the war. It was bitter, gave a yellow appearance to the skin, and had multiple unpleasant side effects, including headaches, nausea, and vomiting. It was effective for preventing malaria, if taken faithfully, but the correct dosage was still being worked out in the early 1940s, so some men got malaria anyway.

8.   On Vella LaVella the day after their landing, Vinich had been walking along the edge of the jungle with Pfc. Joe Ingram when Ingram noticed something in the brush at his feet. He bent down and picked

up a new parachute boot. Holding the boot aloft, he could see that part of a leg and foot was still inside. The ebony white bones of the tibia and fibula stuck out from the torn flesh of the foot still in the boot below the ankle. The boot had been hurled more than a hundred yards from the LST. That had happened twenty-seven days before.

9. Siefke gave the souvenir to his grandson in 2003.

10. Lt. Donald Cobb said he was in charge of the battalion's Navajo code talkers but because he was not with the battalion at the time of the Choiseul raid, his interview is not used in this book. Ned Russell said he often went over to talk to the code talkers (He spoke Navajo.), but he does not remember them being on Choiseul. Colonel Krulak says the battalion never had Navajo code talkers, although the regiment did.

11. "We almost did [get engaged]," said Colonel Krulak during his interview. "But we didn't."

12. All of the men talked about the incessant patrols made while on Choiseul, some at dawn the morning of the first day. The only patrols written in this book are the ones documented by the *War Diary* typed by Third Battalion, Pfc. Eugene "Gene" Gesch, but undoubtedly numerous smaller patrols were sent out all around the battalion hideout.

Chapter 3

1. Gerald P. Averill, *Mustang: A Combat Marine* (San Francisco: Presidio Press, 1987).

2. The *War Diary* said Krulak left with a seventeen-man patrol on October 29. General Krulak wrote in "Mission: To Raise Hell" that it was a nineteen-man patrol.

3. Gyrene is a slang term for Marine. It probably comes from "GI" and (Ma)rine.

4. A *banzai* is a suicide attack. The Japanese word *banzai* means, "May you live ten thousand years," referring to the emperor, and was used as a war cry.

Chapter 4

1. These spiders were Golden Orb Web Spiders. They are not the world's largest spiders—although the females are about eight inches wide—but

they make the world's largest webs. Their webs are about six and a half feet by twenty feet, and are so strong they can catch small birds.

2. Averill, *Mustang,* ibid.

3. For passwords, the Americans often used words that contained the letter "L" because it isn't a sound in the Japanese language, and they have difficulty mimicking the "L" sound. Even the best Japanese linguists, unless they'd grown up in the United States or an English speaking country, would mistakenly pronounce an R for an L. Thus, "Rorri-pop" or "Ruru's Rady" told the Marines the person speaking was probably Japanese.

4. The man that misfired his weapon laughed when he read the rough draft. He had simply tripped on a root in the darkness of the jungle. Mortified, he'd never told anyone. He was one of the seventy men interviewed for the book, but he wants to remain anonymous.

5. Both Engstrom and Carpenter still have the souvenirs more than sixty years later.

6. Every Marine interviewed held these natives with high regard and praised their strength and endurance.

7. Averill, *Mustang,* ibid.

8. A toggle rope is a 5-foot rope that every paratrooper carried. One side of the rope has a loop while the other an attachment. When a squad combines their ten toggles, they can make a 50-foot rope. Likewise, when a platoon combines theirs they have a 150–foot rope. It is a useful piece of equipment.

9. Dugan and the others called Pratt "five by five." They liked Pratt, but their captain had a bad habit of putting them in the brig for five days in a five-foot by five-foot cell on nothing but bread and water. It didn't matter that they always did something wrong to deserve it and had been caught. It happened so often it became a joke. "Five by five gave me five days bread and water," someone would say. "Did you call him and raise him? You can still get fifteen."

Chapter 5

1. All of the men that made the raid against Sangigai talked about the large size of the Japanese soldiers. Because of racial stereotypes, they had expected to see short, cross-eyed men wearing glasses. They were shocked by the sheer size of these soldiers. These same men would go on to Iwo Jima and comment on how much smaller the Japanese troops were than the Imperial Marines that they fought on Choiseul.

But when asked about their Japanese enemies, short or tall, the most common response was, "They were brave."

2. They had three rocket stands set up and each stand had four adjustable legs. The front legs were higher than the rear legs and provided the elevation for firing. After the rockets were laid in the racks, a battery was hooked up to the rockets, the way a bazooka was primed for firing. Anyone who stood too close behind one of them was in for a rough time, because once it had fired, the rockets had a terrific backlash. They were 4.5 inches and had huge payload, although their accuracy was often unpredictable.

3. The rockets were attempts to fool the Japanese into thinking the Marines were using heavy artillery. A battalion didn't have artillery— a division did. They hoped that the rockets would be mistaken for 155-mm artillery, helping with the ruse that a division had landed.

4. In an interview many years later, Adams said that the rumor that Gruidl stepped in front of his own machine gun is false. Adams says that the exit wounds were in the back of Gruidl's thighs. Private Cassaday saw Gruidl get hit and the machine gun that shot him, and Gruidl was facing the Japanese.

5. Lt. Richard "Dick" Cook kept a diary, maps, an aerial photograph, and a list of Japanese phrases the Marines were to learn. Here are some of those phrases, as they were written, that the Marines used while on Choiseul: *Tomare*, Halt; *Kotchi-coy*, Come here; *Suware*, Sit down; *Maware*, Turn around; *Damare*, shut up; *Ten-no hay ka baka*, The emperor is a fool; *Da to Kogun*, Down with the imperial army; *Uchika-ta*, Cease firing; *Bukio Shtani oke*, put down your weapon.

6. He still has the flag more than sixty years later.

7. *Totsugeki* is a Japanese war cry.

8. In 1943, before the advent of penicillin, men that took stomach wounds usually died a very slow, agonizing death by peritonitis. Ironically, Dibbens would be shot twice in the stomach on Iwo Jima and live because of the medical advances available two years later, in 1945.

9. At that time, a typical Marine rifle squad consisted of eight men with six M1903 rifles, one Browning automatic rifle (BAR), and one submachine gun. A modern U.S. Army squad consisted of twelve men, eleven semiautomatic M-1 Garands, and one BAR—after 1944 occasionally another BAR was added. A German squad consisted of twelve men with eleven M1898 bolt-action rifles and one MG 42. In 1943 a squad

of U.S. Marine paratroopers consisted of ten men with seven M1941 Johnson semiautomatic rifles and three JLMGs. Per man, the Marine paratroops in 1943 had more firepower than any army in the world.

10. Lieutenant Cook said that the reason the natives (at least the natives assigned to F Company by Seton) only pointed and never fired their weapons was because they had been under the tutelage of Seventh Day Adventist missionaries for a number of years. There were all kinds of missionaries in the different Solomon Islands. These natives were taught by Seventh Day Adventists that it was a sin to kill unless in self-defense. Very interesting when you consider most of the Marines were told they were headhunters and cannibals.

11. As far back as New Caledonia the Marines had practiced using football terms. A "left end run" meant a flanking attack to the left. It was believed that in battle, communications would break down. When that happened, the Marines needed a mode of verbal communication the Japanese wouldn't likely know. Last names with American Football terms were used.

12. Krulak thought it was Holland but Holland said he was not there yet. When the author interviewed now-General Krulak in 2004, he was surprised at the size and number of scars on the general's face. It was luck or grace of God that saved his eyes, and his life. General Krulak still has steel fragments below his left eye.

13. There were discrepancies about the TNT. Some of the men believed the TNT was used to cremate the fallen men. Others stated the TNT was used to unearth soil to bury the fallen, saving valuable time. When asked about the rumored cremation General Krulak said, "I had no such plan and never considered it." Corporal Caperton says the fallen troops were carried out, but he was the only F Company Marine to say that.

14. All the corpsmen carried an apron-like pouch designed by Dr. Richard Lawrence, the Second Battalion surgeon. The pack unrolled for easy access and each corpsman knew its contents like the back of his hand. Each pouch contained everything a front-line medic would use to stop bleeding and contain a wound: scalpel, morphine, clamps, forceps, hemostats, bandages, Sulfa, gauze, roll bandages, tape, but most important, plasma. A corpsman's primary job was to set up a temporary aid station and stop the immediate bleeding so that a wounded man could live long enough to be sent back to a field hospital for proper treatment. Yet more often than not a corpsman didn't have

time to set up an aid station. He had to administer to the wounded by kneeling over the fallen man, often under fire.

15. On Vella LaVella, Holland went to a Catholic priest and gave Slivkoff's confession.

16. In Colonel Cook's diary, written in 1943, he scribbled, "When Gruidl passed on, Doc picked him up in his arms and carried him. Said he thought we could get to beach soon. Wanted to bury him at Vagara. Left him along trail."

Chapter 6

1. The party comprised Cpl. Max May, Pfc. Richard Stanley, and Pvt. Harrell Sellers.

2. When the small plane approached from the ocean they could hear it coming from a great distance, and they had time to take cover. When it came at them from the opposite side of the mountains, though, they had very little time to hide. The Japanese knew there were U.S. Marines on Choiseul, so they didn't know where. The bombers were trying to pinpoint their exact location.

3. Major Bigger's patrol had not reconnoitered the Warrior, however.

Chapter 7

1. The Japanese sometimes wear footwear, called *tabi*, that have split-toes, thus the unusual footprints.

2. In his interview with Robert Donovan in *PT 109* Major Bigger said that they didn't land on the west side because of the noise made by the Higgins Boats. Bigger feared that enemy lookouts had been alerted and he did not want to give away their intentions or move into an ambush.

3. Halizone was a tablet given to the military to kill any infection that might be in the water they drank, since they couldn't always be choosy about where their water came from.

Chapter 8

1. Adams said his five-man patrol was sent back on the evening of November 1. The reason the author did not write the story that way was because the *War Diary* said it was the morning of November 2. It is known that Lieutenant Duncan went back on the afternoon of November 1. If Adams's patrol went back, too, that would send two

separate patrols in the same direction at the same time. Also, Pfc. Howard "Barney" Baxter and Pharmacist's Mate Holland said when they got to the coast in the late morning of November 2, a small party split from the main group although they did not remember who was in that party.

2. Eighty-year-old Brutinel still has his prayer book, the only souvenir he kept from the war.

3. Each of the men interviewed spoke of the suffocating, almost unbearable heat on the islands.

4. The *War Diary* said there were four Japanese at the lookout post. Adams insists there were no fewer than six.

5. He was a great Marine, and a great boxer, too. He was the Heavy Weight Champion of the South Pacific. In an exhibition match with Max Bear his men watched Morton give the former Heavy Weight World Champion "all he wanted and more."

6. In his interviews with Robert Donovan years later, President John F. Kennedy said that when he first saw the Marine paratroopers on Vella LaVella he thought they were the fittest looking troops he had ever seen. Kennedy was to comment that the Marine paratroopers he took off Choiseul were quite different from the ones he had seen on Vella LaVella a week before. Seven days on an enemy island with only one D-bar and one K-ration to sustain them per day (while hiking and hacking their way through miles of dense jungle in intense heat under the strain of combat) had understandably made its indelible mark on the paratroopers. The men lost an average of fifteen pounds each during their seven days on the island.

Chapter 9

1. Chicago had the largest population of Poles outside of Warsaw than anywhere in the world and Zimont spoke fluent Polish. In fact, he spoke it better than he spoke English.

2. Originally a ten-man squad, Buckley and Pfc. William Alexander were wounded at Sangigai and back on the beach waiting for extraction.

Chapter 10

1. The *War Diary* says they were LSIs (landing ship infantry) but every man interviewed said they were LCIs.

2. Averill, Mustang, ibid.

Chapter 11

1. There was an air attack and later a surface attack by sea on the night of November 1.

2. It is interesting to note that Lieutenant Seton reported Japanese casualties and men killed in action (KIAs) for days after the Marine withdrawal because of the ubiquitous booby traps left by the paratroopers. Also, from the many firefights there was an undeterminable number of enemy wounded and little to no medical equipment and supplies in the Sangigai area to treat them. The Marines destroyed it all.

3. Stories of the "three-day drunk" on Guadalcanal related by the Marines interviewed is enough for a separate book in itself. Before the battalion shipped back to the states from Guadalcanal they were given hundreds and hundreds of cases of beer to drink. "And if you drink it all," Cape remembers Krulak saying, "you'll get more." They drank it all. Pfc. Robert Brutinel (who didn't drink and simply got caught up in the frenzy) remembers when they began to run out and a supply ship came by to give them more. The supply ship loaded a barge with cases of beer and the barge headed for shore. About two hundred yards out, a wave tipped the barge and the beer slid into the ocean. It was too deep for the Marines to reach, but a landing ship tank (LST) with equipment and divers brought up case after case of beer. The LST then turned to sea, taking the coveted cargo with it. The Marines were furious!

4. It is arguable that no paratrooper was ever more athletic than Brown. Brown would go on to be an All-Pro linebacker for the San Francisco 49ers and be mentioned in Steve Sabol highlight reels with such famous athletes as Dick Butkus and Lawrence Taylor.

BIBLIOGRAPHY

The primary sources for this book came from the seventy-one men interviewed and the *Official Marine War Diary* typed by Pfc. Eugene Gesch more than sixty years ago while on Choiseul. This allowed me to form a template for the story and plug in the many different memories accurately.

Other important sources included Pfc. Norman Dibbens's personal notes from 1943, which gave me an accurate insight into F Company, and Gen. Victor H. Krulak's article, "Mission: To Raise Hell."

Another document that I found invaluable as a reference to locate the full names of every paratrooper mentioned was "The Association of Survivors: Master Roster of Marine Paratroopers." Most of the time the veterans interviewed would remember last names but not the first name of a man they served with on Choiseul. The Master Roster helped me organize the book with accuracy I would not otherwise have been able to achieve. *The History of the 5th Marine Division* was an extremely useful reference because, almost to a man, the paratroopers went and formed the Fifth Marine Division. The *Parachute Training School Yearbook* from early 1943 was also helpful.

Secondary sources included the Association of Survivors' *The Opening Shock* magazine; Gerald P. Averill's *Mustang: A Combat Marine*; Col. Joseph Alexander's *The Battle History of the U.S. Marines*, Garth Bonner's *Just Like Clockwork*; Robert Donovan's *PT 109*; Lt. (jg) Richard Keresey's *Gunga Dick and the Marine Paratroopers*; the Marine Corps' *Silk Chutes and Hard Fighting*; and Charles L. Updegraph Jr.'s *Special Marine Corps Units of World War II.*

ABOUT THE AUTHOR

James Christ has travelled extensively throughout Europe, Africa, and Asia, and has visited battle sights in such varying locales as Normandy, Italy, Egypt, Zululand, Jerusalem, and Pearl Harbor. He has interviewed over 200 veterans and is currently writing another book about Marines in the Second World War, in addition to a book about present-day soldiers in Afghanistan. James Christ lives in Phoenix Arizona and raises his two beloved sons, Nolan and Trace.